D1595849

"Dan Pontefract's *Work-Life Bloom* recognizes how my 'Working Together' leadership, management system, and its connected culture of love by design contributes to one's integrated life and life's work of service, which is one's love made visible. Great job, Dan!"

ALAN MULALLY, former CEO of Boeing Commercial Airplanes and the Ford Motor Company

"We all need help in our lives to realize our true potential. This amazing book is the help you have been looking for! It will guide you to a life that blooms and blossoms in all the right ways. Don't miss the chance to understand what it really means to flourish!"

CHESTER ELTON, best-selling author of *The Carrot Principle* and *Leading with Gratitude*

"Work-life balance? We've been labouring to achieve it for the last two decades. Clearly, we need a new approach and a new metaphor. So, we should all be grateful to Dan Pontefract for providing it with *Work-Life Bloom*. Dan offers not just sound principles but actions we can take to bloom together—testing our soil, remembering to water. Helpful, inspiring, and fresh."

SALLY HELGESEN, author of *Rising Together, How Women Rise*, and *The Female Advantage*

"When people bloom at work and in life, they flourish, and your organization does too. This book offers both soil and seeds—frameworks and tactics—that you can use to help unlock the greatness of your people and teams."

MICHAEL BUNGAY STANIER, author of *The Coaching Habit* and *How to Work with (Almost) Anyone*

"The best leaders not only enable people to do great work; they help people live a great life. This book will give you the tools to both grow your talent and help everyone on your team

LIZ WISEMAN, *New York Times* best-selling author of *Multipliers* and *Impact Players*

Dear Randi,
All the very best.

Dan.

Work-Life

B L C

How to Nurture a Team That Flourishes

**DAN
PONTEFRACT**

O M

Figure.1
Vancouver / Toronto / Berkeley

23 24 25 26 27   5 4 3 2 1

Cataloguing data is available from Library and Archives Canada
ISBN 978-1-77327-222-1 (hbk.)
ISBN 978-1-77327-223-8 (ebook)
ISBN 978-1-77327-224-5 (pdf)
ISBN 978-1-77327-225-2 (audio)

Design by Naomi MacDougall
Author photograph by Tory Robinson

Editing by Steve Cameron
Copy editing by Lesley Cameron
Proofreading by Marnie Lamb
Indexing by Stephen Ullstrom
Front jacket photo collage: iStock.com/cherezoff and shutterstock.com/Roman Samborskyi

Printed and bound in Canada by Friesens

Figure 1 Publishing Inc.
Vancouver BC Canada
www.figure1publishing.com

Figure 1 Publishing works in the traditional, unceded territory of the xʷməθkʷəy̓əm (Musqueam), Sḵwx̱wú7mesh (Squamish), and səlilwətaɬ (Tsleil-Waututh) peoples.

For Nicole and Adam, my bloom-box siblings.

In Bloom

At the patch of query, where paths gently wind,
A gardener ponders the choices that bind,
With petals of sweat, a soft, lilting song,
A green thumb strums, "Where does life belong?"
But by light and at night, it feels misaligned.

Two seeds meet through verdant embrace,
A quest to cultivate, a wilting race,
In the rhythm of time, decisions hold sway,
Through valleys and shadows, a journey each day,
Where work and life court, a subtle about-face.

The gardener muses, "In this ebb and flow,
No perfect balance we'll ever know,"
To *be our best*, a revelation dawns,
In the depths of soil, true growth spawns,
'Tis the wisdom and the path we now must sow.

After the sun and storm, the gardener imparts,
"Embrace the challenge, the pulse of your heart,
Don't balance, but *bloom*, it's the vision we seek,
In labour and life, nurturing and unique,"
When factors align, the flourishing will start.

DAN PONTEFRACT, June 2023

CONTENTS

"The flowers you see blooming in the sunshine were once hidden seeds waiting patiently for the rain."[1]

CHRISTY ANN MARTINE

CHAPTER I

Garden Box

ANGIE KIM WAS 10 years into a promising and award-winning career at Loblaw Companies Limited, one of Canada's most prolific and respected organizations, when, all of a sudden, she wasn't.

Loblaw—as it is often referred to—employs 190,000 people in full- and part-time positions across the country and posts revenues well in excess of Can\$53 billion annually. The company has proudly operated various grocery, pharmacy, banking, and apparel establishments since 1919 and is frequently ranked in the upper echelons of "great place to work" surveys by various external firms.

Born in South Korea, Kim, the daughter of a diplomat, lived in multiple countries before immigrating to Canada in 2001. After she graduated from the University of Toronto, Kim worked in various entry-level marketing and consulting roles. In 2011 she landed a job at Loblaw in the company's business development unit and was soon promoted to a buyer role. She felt she could start providing better for her family too. Work and life were humming.

Two more career hops at the company to strengthen her growing skill sets led to another juicy opportunity: running a store. This required a move in 2016 to Saskatoon from Toronto, but Kim didn't care. In fact, she would have sprinted to Saskatchewan if flying wasn't an option. She was all in, knowing that the experience of being a store manager would provide her with the real-world and frontline expertise she needed to continue moving up the ranks at the company.

1

After she had been in the Canadian Prairies for two years, the company saw a blooming talent and was eager to progress her career ascension. Kim was offered a director role on the merchandising team and subsequently moved back to Loblaw's headquarters in Toronto. She didn't stay in that role for long. In 2019, she was promoted to senior director of Finance. Just one year later, in November 2020, she accepted the position of vice-president of National Wholesale Operations.

In less than 10 years, and over eight different roles and five promotions—including a two-year relocation—Kim had catapulted herself from an individual contributor role performing business development duties to vice-president of a national team that conducted wholesale operations. Her leadership prowess attracted attention outside the company as well: Kim received the 2020 Star Women in Grocery award and 2020 Women of Inspiration award. In 2021, she was a nominee for Canada's Top 40 Under 40 and Canada's Most Powerful Women Top 100.

Then, in August 2021—less than a year into her vice-president role—Kim resigned from Loblaw.

Kim was leading a frontline team in the thick of the pandemic. For obvious reasons, every federal government (or the national equivalent) around the globe deemed grocery stores and pharmacies as essential services when lockdowns were the norm and the virus raged like a brush fire. Grocery and pharmacy chains—Loblaw included—were working tirelessly to ensure the safety of their frontline team members. Despite all their efforts, though, Kim knew she could not keep her entire team safe. That had a gnawing effect on her psyche.

"As a leader," Kim said, recalling her decision to leave the company, "the well-being of your team is everything . . . [I felt] so helpless, and so I asked myself, 'Angie Kim, what do you stand for?' If I'm talking about the importance of culture and well-being during my leadership and mentorship chats, yet I can't prevent my team from physical and emotional harm, what am I doing?"

Kim's calculation of her entire work-life situation had plummeted. In sum, she was no longer flourishing.

"My will to go on stopped. I burned out. I couldn't even get out of bed. I finally decided that I had to leave the company I loved."

Kim knew she still had much more to give to work and life, though. "It took me a lot of counselling and treatment to sort it all out," she confided.

"I was bedridden for about six months and sought medical help and counselling. Thankfully I had a very supportive family, great friends to talk to, and my husband, Matt, has been so patient with me."

In late 2021 and extending into 2022, Kim and her husband started discussing their next steps. They both realized that their work *and* life were in need of renewal. Stopping was simply not an option.

Kim's story is nowhere near complete. We'll pick up the trail of her incredible journey at the end of the book. You'll just have to be patient. Spoiler alert: there is a blissful ending with a gigantic bouquet of flowers. But her insights raise an important question for leaders to consider as we kick off this book: How do we define ourselves?

This is perhaps one of life's most existential questions. It is also a rather important one. A very reasonable answer to the question of what defines you is "my work." It's what you do, perhaps even what you're known for in your circle of friends and beyond. The organization that employs you is also proximal and thus an accomplice to that answer. You have a role and you perform it for a firm that pays you. In this way, you, as a leader, and your employer are like two peas in a pod. It can therefore be tempting to say that work *is* life.

But what *else* defines you?

All of us are more than simply our work, more than our jobs, of course. As the author Alain de Botton writes in his 2008 book, *Essays in Love,* "A 'good job' can be both practically attractive while still not good enough to devote your entire life to."[2]

Thus, for the purposes of this book, and despite your potential objection that work is a part of life, I posit that we demarcate work from life. Let's think of *life* as anything not directly tied to your place of employment. Life in this sense is equivalent to your identity: your *you.* It's the factors and influences that make you tick regardless of your surroundings, regardless of your job or career. Life is your character.

To illustrate my point, try this on for size: Imagine a typical weekend. You tend to all sorts of tasks. You clean your home. You cut the grass or shovel snow. You shop for groceries, then maybe bake some bread. Perhaps you have children and attend a sporting tourney or arts function. You visit a relative in long-term care. You go for a walk with a friend. Then, obviously, there is the laundry. So much laundry! Throughout the weekend, you hustle, bustle, exercise, eat, and rest. Ideally, there are some laughs too.

After all, it's your life: ups, downs, and everything in between.

It's now Monday. You're back at work, wherever that may be. You're the leader of a team. You have myriad responsibilities as "the boss," not the least of which is ensuring that goals are met and the team is motivated to perform. Whether your weekend was full of congenial or unpleasant life experiences—or both—are you able to forget everything that occurred over the previous 48 hours? It's unlikely, but work beckons, so you perform in your leadership role to the best of your abilities. Goals need to be met and tasks are to be completed. Rather obviously, your work is how you get paid. To afford the basics and niceties of life, you must work.

Fast-forward to Friday. The workweek is over. You've spent 40-plus hours doing your job. Throughout it all, you were part of several meetings. A few face-to-face ones flanked by Microsoft Teams and Zoom appointments. You agreed with some decisions, and felt conflicted by others. Innumerable emails, texts, DMs, and Slack messages had to be answered. During the week, there were some laughs but also several tense situations. Not everyone seems to be on the same page, but that's normal when you're a leader.

After all, it's work: ups, downs, and everything in between.

Since Monday, you have expended a significant degree of *emotional labour*, a term coined by the sociologist Arlie Hochschild in her 1983 book, *The Managed Heart.*[3] Emotional labour is the effort required to evoke and suppress feelings on the job. Work can become exhausting through the exertion and containment of all these feelings, but it's time to switch gears again and slip into the weekend jeans called *life*. Time to check those work feelings at the door.

You're exhausted. Whether the workweek elicited amiable or uncomfortable feelings—and let's be honest, you probably experienced both—were you able to forget everything that occurred at work this week? It's doubtful, but life beckons, so you perform your role as a weekend warrior to the best of your abilities. You attend a dinner party on Saturday night. For 32 minutes, you're immersed in a conversation with five other people, specifically about your job. You've forgotten it's Saturday night. That work text you answered about an hour ago en route to the bathroom got you riled up.

It's now Monday, the start of another workweek. During your commute to the office, you wondered about the term *work-life balance*. "Where did I go so wrong?" you ask yourself. Now you're in an intense meeting, but you keep thinking about that rather profound moment you had with your mother on Sunday morning. Cortisol begins to shoot through your body like a lightning strike. Why is that conversation with her bugging you so much? Your mom only asked if you were *happy* in your leadership role. Are you?

Mid-meeting, your mind wanders and you're now thinking about the team you're leading. Are they engaged? Are they happy? What even is happy? Why do they seem so burned out? And who the hell has been peddling this term *work-life balance*? Is there any such thing?

Work-Life Garden Box

This work and life scene-setting—albeit illuminating—paints a small portion of the work-life portrait I am about to reveal to you in this book. Angie Kim's story was 12 years in the making. Throughout the span of your career and that of the people you are privileged to lead, one fact, often overlooked yet hidden in plain sight, will forever be omnipresent.

Work and life are complementary and contradictory forces.

In broader terms, several factors influence the ability or inability of people to have the chance to flourish at work. The same is true for their lives. Thus, the relationship between work and life is critical. Yet, far too often, we kid ourselves and claim, "Work is a part of my life; it's not a separate thing. I just need better balance."

We must stop deluding ourselves. Work and life are not the same. That belief is obstacle number one to overcome, especially if you are leading a team. In parallel, leaders cannot create situations where team members believe they must put on a daily mask and park their life at the door when at work. For example, how does it feel for team members who fear wearing a short-sleeve shirt because of an archaic policy that tattoos are forbidden at work? This is just one example of a systemic culture that causes stress and disengagement in our organizations.

The flip side is also true. As Dr. Maja Korica, professor in Strategic Management at IÉSEG School of Management in Paris, pointed out to me, "We should have workplaces embrace the whole spectrum of human experience that workers come with. And individuals can still choose not to share some of that humanity with their employers, lest it be used against them or simply because they don't want to." Korica reminds us that better workplaces are those where humanity is recognized and individual choice is respected. "Without this," she suggested, "corporate caring risks devolving into yet another mechanism for employee control."[4]

I'd like you to imagine every one of your team members being the gardener of their own personal garden box. It's a metaphor worthy of your consideration. Several aspects of work and life will affect your team members. It's a given. In some cases, these elements—which I refer to as *work-life factors*—will affect an entire team simultaneously, but each member of the team will interpret the situation differently and react in varying ways. It stands to reason that certain work-life factors will determine if a team member's garden grows or not, whether they're feeling great or not-so-great. Likewise, work-life factors can help to explain why certain people are effortlessly growing great crops (hint: blooming) while others seem to be operating at levels that might feel a bit inhibited.

People not only will view these work-life factors through the unique lens of their personal garden box but will be individually affected by them too. For example, someone just joining your organization may be influenced differently than somebody who has been with you for five years and just returning from parental leave. One person may be going through a lengthy divorce or be in the midst of a part-time MBA with three kids under the age of seven at home. Those are vastly different situations, but they all have an impact. Thus, not only are there systemic work-life factors that affect a team member's garden box and, by extension, themselves, but there are discrete events that can affect those factors too.

For the purposes of my introductory argument, let me frame these discrete moments as weather events. Metaphorically speaking, sunlight, rain showers, a hurricane, drought, or frost can affect a team member's circumstances and that of the garden box they tend to. In literal terms, these could be events such as an acquisition, promotion, death, cancer, or a new baby. Everything in life and at work can affect how well a team member is gardening (aka performing).

Thus, all team members are in a constant cycle of work-life transformation. The four seasons are a complementary metaphor to the garden box. Winter, spring, summer, and fall are inescapable. Every year, they appear and then disappear. And they bring varying weather events that gardeners must tend to if they want their garden box to bloom.

During my research for this book, I discovered there are 12 unique yet surprisingly simple work-life factors that help to explain how people show up at work and in life. As a leader, I argue that you must become aware of these 12 factors, because they affect every team member. We will therefore spend significant time discussing them. For now, without getting into the weeds on the specific factors, I'm listing them here for you as a reference to be picked up on later.

Work-Factors
✿ Trust
✿ Belonging
✿ Valued
✿ Purpose
✿ Strategy
✿ Norms

Life-Factors
✿ Relationships
✿ Skills
✿ Well-being
✿ Meaning
✿ Agency
✿ Respect

However, I've also discovered something else. Because of differences in how people interpret the 12 work-life factors and are affected by them, they wind up adopting different work-life personas as their circumstances warrant. Not everyone will be blooming, and that is perfectly fine. But, as a leader, you must come to grips with four key points:

· The individuals in your team will likely never all be performing at the same level.

· Team members will be at different stages depending on how they are personally affected by the 12 work-life factors.

· It's perfectly fine for team members to be at different stages of performance; work and life are cyclical, and people are continuously changing.

· Discrete weather events will inevitably affect the performance of your team members, for better or worse.

Every gardener is continuously transforming, tending to their personal garden box. That's normal. Team members can and will adopt different stages or personas of growth throughout their lives. This too is perfectly normal. Systemic circumstances—like the work-life factors—and discrete situations—like one-time weather events—contribute to shaping any team member's circumstance.

I've also learned that no one garden box can continuously produce flowers, fruit, or vegetables without assistance. This is where you—as a leader of people—come in. Your goal is to help team members become better gardeners of their personal garden box. Ultimately, this is your chance to become a better leader. You can't do it for them, but you can help create the conditions for the possibility of growth.

As the Canadian poet Brittin Oakman aptly points out, "Every season is one of becoming, but not always one of blooming. Be gracious with your ever-evolving self."[5]

Work-Life Balance and Best Self? Balderdash.

I have to be straight-up with you. I've already alluded to it, but there is a term that you need to renounce, if not repudiate, from your leadership lexicon forthwith: Work-life balance.

It's my position that the concept is as ludicrous a term as "rightsizing" or "thinking outside the box." The term is flawed. Actually, it's worse than that. It's a downright lie. And the inherent promise that it offers is also delusory at best.

The phrase "work-life balance" first appeared in the 1980s. It was a key concept of the women's liberation movement,[6] which advocated for, among other things, a woman's right to maternity leave and flexible work schedules. While more should be done on this particular file in many global jurisdictions, those issues are not the topic of this book.

Work-life balance should not be the goal for your team members. I posit that work-life balance as a concept is ineffective because it entirely misses the point and has for decades. Yet, too many leaders continue to apply work-life balance as a prosthesis for a team member's happiness. It is not nearly enough to be balanced between work and life. If someone keeps all the plates spinning—as the idiom goes—they can be considered a balanced human being. Is that enough? Is that a way to live? To work? I suggest that striving for work-life balance is neither a fun nor a rewarding way to live or work. The sheer prevalence of workplace burnout points to the inanity of work-life balance as a goal. Even the World Health Organization decided to officially classify burnout as a syndrome related to "chronic workplace stress that has not been successfully managed."[7]

The goal is not to balance. I recommend something else entirely. In the following pages, I will provide evidence, stories, and helpful techniques for an exciting new leadership archetype. As a leader, you can provide the framework and the tools to help people *be their best* in work and life. You can also use them to help yourself achieve this.

LIKE "WORK-LIFE BALANCE," there is another phrase freely used by many leaders that requires examination: We want you to bring your best self to work.

Sometimes leaders refer to it as "whole selves" or "authentic selves" instead of "best self." The problem?

First off, the term is a catchphrase gone sideways. It's terrible H.R.-speak, as useful as "workforce optimization," "cost-efficiency programs," "soft skills," and "core competencies." We already have enough ineffectual buzzword bingo phrases to last a lifetime in the workplace. Bringing our best or authentic selves to work—much like work-life balance—cannot be the goal. To attempt to do so is also woefully useless.

The way many workers make a living is fundamentally changing, either by choice or out of necessity. And to make a living is to accept that there is an inherent bond between work and life, between what we do and our definition of self. Remember, every team member is a gardener, tending to their own garden box.

Subsequently, we must consider how work and life fit in with one another and how they are aligned. We bring our work to life every day. However, our life gets entangled in our work. There is no way around it.

Work is what we do *and* the place we do it. It's both a noun and a verb. In part, it's also how we are known to other people.

Conversely, life is our existence—the forming forces and principles of our being. It's who we are, how we act, and what we stand for throughout our time on Earth. You bring those forces and principles into work. It's unavoidable. Think about it: Your life is how people will eulogize you when you pass on. Life equals the *self. Your* self.

While work is distinct from life, it is still incorporated into life, not balanced with it. Team members do not need to bring their best selves to work; they simply require support to *be their best*. As their leader, you need to provide them with empathy and space when they are *less than their best* while working their garden box through the storms of life. You ought to know what garden tools you might encourage your team members to use, when, and why.

Work and life, therefore, ought to become allies. Indeed, they must. They both belong in the garden box. They're both alive.

When discussing the partial destruction of the House of Commons as a result of bombing raids by the Luftwaffe, Winston Churchill remarked in 1943 to his parliamentary colleagues: "On the night of 10th May, 1941, with one of the last bombs of the last serious raid, our House of Commons was destroyed by the violence of the enemy, and we have now to consider whether we should build it up again, and how, and when. We shape our buildings and afterwards our buildings shape us."[8]

I will pay homage to Sir Winston and put forward a new work-life allyship:

Our lives shape our work; nevertheless, our work shapes us.

This newly devised adage hints at something. You must rethink the very nature of your leadership role. There is an irrefutable coalition between work and life. The pandemic may have exacerbated this newfound state; however, it's been building for years. Leaders can no longer stuff their heads in the soil and pretend this dynamic does not exist. Few people check their life at the work door anymore. And I don't know anyone who doesn't bring work home with them. (Thank you, cell phones and tablets.) In this book, I will make the case that leaders possess a fiduciary obligation to

- Create workplace conditions in which team members can excel.

- Recognize that all team members are constantly in a state of transformation, never in a fixed state.

• Nurture the qualities in team members that will help them thrive in their lives and support their self-development, which in turn will aid their performance at work.

Before we go any farther, there is a question that I encourage you to take a few moments to reflect on: What permits people to *be their best*?

IT'S GOTTA BE THE SHOES

I have a soft spot for shoes.

My non-athletic shoes come from a single source: John Fluevog Shoes, headquartered in Vancouver. The shoes are funky and astonishingly unique, and I've become a Fluevoger, someone who passionately supports the company. I'm a Fluevoger because of the way I get pampered. Every single one of my interactions makes me feel as though I am somebody special. It's like I'm greeted online or in-person by an army of people who are amped to work there.

As CEO, Adrian Fluevog knows that the company bearing his family name is more than just a shoe retailer. John Fluevog Shoes is a culture company built on the belief that everyone should be treated like a human being. Life meets work, and work meets life. This philosophy has been the driving force behind the company's success for over 50 years. It has allowed John Fluevog Shoes to thrive, even during challenging times like the pandemic.

"We've been in business for 52 years," said Fluevog, "and we want to be here for another 52 years. I'm not worried about the day sales or the quarterly sales. It's about the overall ethos of the brand, of the people who work here."

When nearly 250 global employees adore the company, revenues are continually increasing, and the likes of Lady Gaga, Jack White, Scarlett Johansson, Kit Harrington, and Madonna rep your footwear, something is clearly going right. A clue can be found in the company's motto: "Unique Soles for Unique Souls." Maybe Fluevog team members ought to be called *Fluevog Souldiers*.

As a culture company that believes in the humanity of its team members, John Fluevog Shoes focuses on providing customers with an exceptional and enjoyable experience. The company's staff are trained to treat customers like people and to make them feel good about themselves and their purchases. This approach has helped to build strong relationships with customers, but it's also a driving force behind the Fluevog corporate culture. Adrian Fluevog believes that if you're not taking care of the employee, they will be unable to take care of the customer.

"We definitely empower our managers and employees," offered Fluevog. "And we don't have a lot of corporate guidelines. But I can tell you when sales might be slipping at a store. Quite often, it's when somebody is not happy in that store. If you don't have an engaged manager or the team dynamics aren't gelling, that's when sales get impacted. When people have negative things going on in their life or something external is getting in the way of their attitude, that's when sales go down."

According to Adrian Fluevog, the key to the company's success has been its focus on authenticity and honesty. Fluevog has always been a company that advocates for being real, delivering an experience customers and employees alike have come to appreciate. As a result, the company's culture exudes a positive and infectious atmosphere. Just stroll into any of their stores around the world and you will witness it first-hand. When you walk through the door and are greeted by one of the world's 200-plus Fluevogologists, you can almost see a bouquet of flowers shoot out of their neck as they offer to help you.

Ultimately, Adrian Fluevog believes that his company's success results from its commitment to treating everyone with respect and kindness. Feeling valued is an essential part of the operating style. Its community-giving is legendary, and employees experience a sense of meaning in what they do. Every team member is behind the company, and its brand, while honing their relationships with customers.

"Our marketing is really about word-of-mouth," said Fluevog. "Our advertising budget is nothing compared to other national and international footwear brands'. Everything is grassroots-based." If the company's culture wasn't one where team members are consistently excelling and marketing budgets remain low, you wouldn't have customers creating their own Facebook community groups like Fluevog Fridays!, Fluezies, Fluevog shoes B/S/T, Fluevogs Downunder, and For the Love of Fluevogs!, where thousands of people share stories about their Fluevog shoes and experiences with the company. And you would not have hundreds of people showing up for the annual three-day Flummunity Fest, a face-to-face event that gathers Fluevogers from around the world in support of the company, its products, and its team members. The agenda for this event is packed with guest speakers, designer chats, and special celebrations.

"Honestly, it's an incredible group of like-minded people getting together," explained Fluevog. "The love inside the room is almost overwhelming. But you know you're nailing it when an event like this happens. When you lead with the people side first, your employee engagement, customer engagement, and sales improve. If you lead with the heart, ensuring you have engaged people, everything else falls into place."

By building a culture of honesty and authenticity, John Fluevog Shoes has created a unique and enduring brand that customers and employees are proud to be a part of. And as the company continues to grow and evolve, this focus on a human-centred culture will remain at the heart of everything it does. It is a magnificent example of how thriving team members can ultimately create a prosperous company.

But how do they do it? How are employees permitted to *be their best* with the company reaping the benefits of that mantra?

Work-Life Framework

Numerous elements influence everyone's life and work. Through my research, interviews, and analysis, I have narrowed these elements down to six key work-factors and six key life-factors. Together, these 12 work-life factors allow team members to *be their best*.

You can think of the life-factors interchangeably as one's "self-factors," the attributes and traits that help people operate as individuals—as human beings—as is the case at John Fluevog Shoes. The work-factors are fundamental tenets that facilitate an employee's level of buy-in to the organization's ambitions.

The work-life factors will change over people's careers and lifespan. They will rise, fall, and rise again. The cycle is endless. They will positively or negatively affect people. Or both. It will be different for you and anyone you lead. In navigating this undulation, you, as a leader, need to be vigilant. The entire organization might not be fully engaged or high-performing at the same time. This is precisely why firms like Gallup are unhelpful. They continue to point out that employee engagement scores have not materially improved in nearly three decades. Well, of course the scores have not improved: we have been looking at the entire work and life scenarios wrongly for years.

Let's imagine one of your fully engaged and high-performing team members has decided to start a family. They've become nervous about the pending new addition. They're going through several changes with some of their life-factors. Are you able to help them through the transition? When they return to work after their parental leave, do they need to be high-performing again, even engaged? Maybe it's okay for them to be average for a few years. These are the questions you must ask yourself as a leader to help you become fully prepared to assess and respond to changing life-factors as required. Recall that various work-life factors and weather events constantly affect every team member's disposition. No one will ever remain highly engaged over their entire career. It's impossible.

What will you as a leader do to help your team members tend to their personal garden boxes? Are you prepared to handle the ups and downs of your team members over a given period? Have you thought about an individual's life-factors and what they may need to develop further should you genuinely want them to *be their best*? Do you understand how an employee's experience may affect their performance on the job? Are you paying attention to a team member's concealed long-term signals versus the in-your-face and in-the-moment detrimental weather events?

In sum, the 12 work-life factors I have identified create an impact on people's performance. Work and life *do* affect one another, whether simultaneously or independently, positively or negatively. There might be a short-term issue or a slow-building, long-term one. All of it will impact your leadership abilities, let alone your team's success. As Arianna Huffington points out in her 2014 book, *Thrive*, "It's not 'What do I want to do?', it's 'What kind of life do I want to have?'"[9] Put differently, what kind of leader do you want to be?

Let's imagine you're a vice-president of communications. Consider the hypothetical story of Sakura, someone who has been on your team for the past three years and fully subscribes to the organization's culture and its operating norms. Sakura is in her late 30s and has an extensive network that she has built up over her 10 years at the company. She is an effective director of communications and has mentioned several times to you this year that she's really clicking when it comes to operating with a sense of meaning. She feels valued and talks about how much trust there is across the team. Sakura certainly acts and performs like someone who is prospering at work and in life, an individual who is high-performing and confidently tending to her garden box. She might as well be working at John Fluevog Shoes. Heck, Sakura might as well be thought of as a master gardener.

Let's consider someone else from your hypothetical team, Arjun. Arjun has been a manager on the team for five years and doesn't believe the company operates with any higher purpose. He has told you repeatedly in your one-on-one meetings that he is also unclear about the organization's strategy. Worse, he recently doesn't feel like he fits in with the team. Arjun's trust levels are declining, his confidence is waning, his well-being is in question, and he's feeling rather lonely, both at work and outside of it. Arjun's work-life factors are almost the solar opposite of Sakura's. He has an entirely different garden box. Not much seems to be growing.

How does Arjun's frame of mind affect his performance? How does Sakura's? What issues could both situations cause for the rest of the team? How do both situations potentially shape you as a leader?

Sakura's and Arjun's work-life situations are unlikely to remain in these permutations forever. Work and life both ebb and flow. Sometimes the changes are as easy to predict as an earthquake; at other times they are as fickle as the daily weather. As leaders, we must always prepare for a potential pressure change. Seasonal weather events are inevitable. The above situations could easily shift depending on how work or life affects either team member. These two examples illustrate the need for you to

- Pay attention to the work- and life-factors that affect team members regardless of their job title.

- Be mindful of weather events that can positively or negatively affect a team member.

- Be fully equipped with a few garden tools to help them do something about the negative effect of work- and life-factors.

If we are to consign the terms "work-life balance" and "best self" to the compost heap while pioneering a new bond between work and life, we must advocate for team members to be given the opportunity and support to *be their best*. Therefore, we need to introduce a new philosophy that might better position you to assist your team members. It is time to appeal for a new, if not more benevolent, work-life philosophy.

What might that new philosophy be?

Hello, Bloom

May I take this opportunity to introduce you warmly and formally to a better word?

Bloom.

No, not the algal type. Don't be cheeky. "Bloom" is both a noun and a verb. If we focus on the word as a verb, to bloom is to mature into realizing one's potential.

At the intersection of work and life, you should begin aspiring to reach a state of blooming. As a leader, you should begin applying the same thinking while leading your team members.

If people are to realize their full potential and generate high levels of achievement, we need to study both work- and life-factors. Work ought to become a place of development, an enriching place of possibility that also helps team members in life, forging a growing repertoire of talents. You as a leader have a responsibility to help nourish your team members' life-factors, which will then benefit both the individual and the organization. Win-win.

However, that is only half the equation. As any garden box could tell you, a sunrise always follows a sunset. After the auburn colours of fall come the harsh whites of winter. Thus, you are also responsible for creating the circumstances at work in which team members can conduct themselves positively, regardless of potentially competing forces. You need to build an employee experience that not only allows people the chance to bloom but also draws on techniques to help people *be their best*.

If you are to create a high-performing organization that achieves its goals, progressive operating norms need to be defined. They then have to be upheld. Finally, irrefutable humanistic behaviours, systems, and methods must be adopted and practised if people are to bloom, to *be their best.*

However, the author Haruki Murakami reminds us in his 2007 book, *After Dark*, that work and life are not a binary combination. There is something in between the two that we also must pay attention to.

> It's not as if our lives are divided simply into light and dark. There's shadowy middle ground. Recognizing and understanding the shadows is what a healthy intelligence does. And to acquire a healthy intelligence takes a certain amount of time and effort.[10]

Leaders, take the time to become aware of the shadowy middle ground between a team member's work and life. It may be a given that leaders have the responsibility to create a "great place to work," but they should be equally willing to help team members develop a "great life to live." You're not in charge of a team member's garden box, but you have great tools in the garden shed to help make it thrive. The benefits accrue when you begin appreciating and acting on both work- and life-factors. Performance outcomes are more easily achieved, and the team member's life is improved. What's not to love?

You must embrace the *shadows* between work and life for the blooming to happen.

Thus, I am thrilled to welcome you to *Work-Life Bloom.* I believe it to be my life's work. (See what I did there?) It is an evolutionary work-life philosophy for leaders and team members alike, and it is written for you, a leader of people aiming to help your team (whatever the size) *bloom* in work and life.

Liftoff to *Work-Life Bloom*

The pandemic jarred us. (Well, most of us.) Tens of millions of people contracted COVID-19. I was one of them. Millions died. Mercifully, I wasn't one of them. It forced us to change in ways unthinkable prior to 2020. Masks, health tests, quarantines, sanitizers, and distancing became commonplace. Working from home, Plexiglas barriers, curbside pickups, and webcams became staples of the workplace environment. It all happened in the blink of an eye. Most of humanity had to rethink their lives. Many had second thoughts about work too.

Some people realized during the pandemic that corner office trappings were not what they once seemed. An office with windows, walls, and a closed door is not a lofty life goal. The jerk boss who doesn't care about you, your family, or your personal passions is as helpful as an annual performance review. The foosball table, all-you-can-eat fruit, free bus trips, and booze cart Fridays are nice, but they're not what's truly important. Time and time again, Gen Z and Millennials demonstrated that they were willing to walk away from employers if their holistic needs were not met.

Ups and downs are an unavoidable part of life. Your team members will undoubtedly encounter them at various stages of their life, and the feelings and experiences they provoke will be brought into work. You're no different, and you know it. The pandemic was a life setback we all had to face. Metaphorically, it was the most significant weather event that the communal garden box faced in our lifetime. It was like a seemingly unending plague of locusts was devouring crops everywhere.

The workplace is forever full of sunny peaks and bone-dry troughs. These extremes affect people in their personal lives too. Leaders who focus on several key aspects of the workplace that encourage a positive employee experience—which in turn fuels a positive customer experience—ultimately help team members to reach a blooming state.

Many team members need assistance in developing skills that inevitably get used at work. And when pertinent work-factors also get addressed, you increase the odds that more people will bloom. Despite the ups and downs that occur—the changes in the seasons and the weather events that cause havoc—each of us can bloom, but we must recognize that blooming is not a perpetual state.

But what does it mean to bloom?

I've spent 25 years thinking about and researching the concepts of work and life. I've interviewed more than 1,000 people from around the globe since 2012, some of whom you will meet in this book, like Angie Kim and Adrian Fluevog. Additional insights come from nearly 10 years of conducting organization-wide surveys, focus groups, and executive one-on-one discussions held through consultancies running culture assessments.

For the purposes of this book, I also conducted the Global Work-Life Assessment Survey in 2022, specifically targeting my Work-Life Bloom hypothesis. I asked people in the USA, Canada, the U.K., Sweden, Germany, France, Spain, the Netherlands, Australia, India, and South Korea, among other countries, pertinent work-life questions. The respondents were either leaders or individual contributors (aka non-leaders) across a multitude of industries, ethnographies, and roles. In total, I analyzed 8,243 sets of responses. (Full details of the survey questions can be found at www.worklifebloom.com/extras.)

The survey produced a trove of data that forms the arguments and the groundbreaking model I present in these pages. A leadership gardening handbook, if you will, that shines a few sunny rays on those aforementioned work-life shadows and pesky weather events.

Before we dig into the model, let's analyze one of the key findings from the Global Work-Life Assessment Survey. The response to the final question in the survey provides an insight into the shadows we must tend to as we help people to mind their garden boxes (and also as we mind our own). The question was relatively simple: "What best describes your current work-life situation?" Examine the results below.

"What best describes your current work-life situation?"

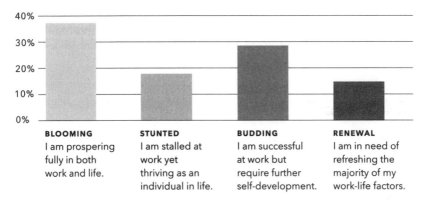

| BLOOMING | STUNTED | BUDDING | RENEWAL |
| I am prospering fully in both work and life. | I am stalled at work yet thriving as an individual in life. | I am successful at work but require further self-development. | I am in need of refreshing the majority of my work-life factors. |

No logic was applied. There are no fancy calculations. (Those come later.) Instead, it's a straight-up feelings-based, qualitative question.

Less than 40 percent of people who participated in the survey self-reported that they are blooming in work and life. There is clearly some gardening to do. But again, as leaders, we must come to grips with the fact that not all employees will be blooming at the same time. And not all team members will want to bloom. And that just might be okay.

If you—as a leader—know how to identify a non-blooming situation while aiming to take corrective action, you can help team members regardless of their work-life situation. The goal, of course, is for people to reach and remain in *bloom*. That's where your leadership is critical. But remember, a team member's interpretation of the work-life factors can rise and fall depending on specific dynamics, and their timeline to blooming may be different. There will always be weather events. There will always be version control issues. The soil in people's garden boxes might be different.

In terms of how this book flows, Chapter II further outlines the problem with our current work-life mindset, and also sets out the framework for the Work-Life Bloom model (defined by the 12 work-life factors and the four personas your team members inhabit).

Chapter III delves into the six work-factors. I provide identification methods and supporting change techniques for each one. There's also a section highlighting key findings from the Global Work-Life Assessment Survey that I call the "Farmer's Almanac."

Chapter IV outlines the six specific life-factors that affect a team member's performance. Think of them as those attributes that help to develop the character of a team member. It also includes each factor's identification method and supporting change techniques. More results from the Global Work-Life Assessment Survey are highlighted in the Farmer's Almanac section in this chapter as well.

Chapter V is a short chapter that ties everything together. It provides two self-reflection assessments—the Soil Test and the Water Test—to outline what you need to be on the lookout for with respect to applying the Work-Life Bloom model as a leader.

The book concludes with a coda. I get very personal in the coda, detailing a bit of my own journey. It demonstrates that no one—not even yours truly—is going to be fully blooming their entire careers or lives. It's impossible.

My aim in writing this book was to help you rethink your leadership responsibilities. I am not advocating for you to be an integral member of your team members' homes, assisting with family finances, debating whether to hold a garage sale, or advocating for the potential purchase of a dog. *Chicken Soup for the Soul*, this is not. It's a leadership book advocating for a new leadership style. But it is also written specifically for you, as an individual. There's no getting around the fact that you might need to make some changes in your own personal work-life garden box.

Nor am I suggesting that team members be willing to fully share their personal lives at work, divulging spats with a neighbour about a late-night balcony party or pending nuptials. Leaders must not obligate employees to disclose their personal lives for fear of reprisal, per the earlier and salient point made by Dr. Korica. Remember, this book is not an exercise to get team members to bring their most authentic selves to work. It is purely a book to help people to *be their best*. This premise includes you.

However, the 12 work-life factors are key. They represent the circumstances and conditions that can help to produce a blooming human being and, thus, the potential for a high-performing workforce like at John Fluevog Shoes. Once you begin to see how important the factors are to people and to your overall organizational culture, you will become far more self-aware as a leader. There is much to uncover, much to, ahem, *unearth.*

Before we move on to Chapter 11, let's hear from four Global Work-Life Assessment respondents about their current work-life plight:

✿ ✿

My manager is ruthlessly manipulative and deceitful. As a result, the company misses out on all I can be.

VICE-PRESIDENT, HIGH-TECH, CANADA, 45-54 YEARS

Even during the most challenging days and complex projects, it goes a long way to know that people at work (most importantly my supervisor) care about me as a person. This makes the entire experience more human, and I don't feel like I have to be an emotionless, perfect corporate robot that can never fail or be decommissioned.

DIRECTOR, HEALTHCARE/MEDICAL, USA, 35-44 YEARS

Employers aren't really helping, and all employees are struggling. The boss doesn't give advice or anything like that, but it's about being friendly and helping each other out.

PROFESSIONAL, MANUFACTURING, SOUTH KOREA, 35-44 YEARS

Give me a redundancy. In all seriousness, get some leadership 101 training or a coach that can help them structure a vision for the company that gives purpose to the team—not constantly talk about them acquiring another company (yet again), getting more profit, and selling off the business so that the investors can get their shares. Seriously, this is not exciting to hear ad nauseam.

CONSULTANT, PROFESSIONAL SERVICES, AUSTRALIA, 45-54 YEARS

✿ ✿

"Leadership is an art like other arts. It involves bringing an idea to life,
giving it shape, inviting others to gather around it.
Like any other art, leadership can be controversial and consequential.
It can be niche or pop, good or bad, but it is necessary—
for the same reason that all art is necessary. Because there is uncertainty,
suffering, fragmentation, and we are going to die—
even if we don't like to think about it. But we are here for now,
we have this gift called life, and we are looking for meaning,
direction, and connection to live it well."[1]

GIANPIERO PETRIGLIERI

CHAPTER II

Bloom or Bust

NICOLE FORWARD HAD the most challenging year of her life in 2017. After trying for over 10 years to conceive with her husband, she lost a child for the second time. Shortly afterward, one of her siblings attempted suicide. To top it all off, that same year, her husband, Terrence Woodson, inched toward a mental breakdown courtesy of the rampant racism, microaggressions, and incivility he experienced at work. With Forward's full blessing, he took a two-month break from his job and moved away to recover from the trauma.

At the time, Forward was a senior leader in a very large corporation known throughout North America. The personal pain she was experiencing was not related to her work but to her life. She questioned her life-factors such as well-being, meaning, skills, and relationships.

Then her workplace began to cause her problems. Forward encountered what some refer to as "mean girl" behaviours. Among other things, she was told that she was far too emotional. Some of her colleagues became untrustworthy. Others told her to "move on." As I pointed out in Chapter I, work and life can be both complementary and contradictory forces to one another.

"I learned quickly," Forward revealed to me, "that bringing my whole self to work was not permissible and that I had to take some extreme measures to show up as more stoic and emotionless at work."

She continued, "Survival, to me, is not living. I want to go beyond surviving to thriving. But finding leaders who know how to truly encourage, mentor, and be compassionate to folks through difficult times are few and far between. I find that leaders don't lead with curiosity as much as they should, and they are too quick to judge."

Forward believes that the future of work will require far more emotional intelligence from people. "I respect the leaders I've had who are willing to show me their human side," she explained, "much more than those that are detached from their emotions." Those are the sorts of leaders who embody the Work-Life Bloom mantra: we are humans in life and work. Endorse that fact. Embrace it. Then do something about it.

The irony of the type of behaviour that Forward and her husband experienced is that when their colleagues inevitably suffer from life's traumas, they will undoubtedly seek comfort, compassion, and assistance from others. Only then, when it's too late, will they realize they wasted years acting like a classless excuse for a leader. We need love and magnanimity, not clueless behaviour from sociopaths who cannot empathize with the realities of life or work's ups and downs.

Forward and Woodson were betrayed by the leaders at their respective places of work. The culture and purpose of their organizations did not encourage a positive employee experience. The two of them felt as good about their respective situations as a gazelle might in the tiger cage of a zoo.

Think about life for Forward and Woodson throughout 2017 and after. Imagine what they had to go through. How might their sense of meaning have changed? How were their relationships affected, both at work and outside of it? And what about their well-being and sense of belonging? These factors were undoubtedly impacted by the trauma they faced in their lives and at work. Yet, when it came to supporting them through their difficulties, their leaders were nowhere to be found, conspicuous by their absence. Perhaps that is symbolic of the moral turpitude too many organizations operate in.

Forward and Woodson were outstanding performers and incredibly high-achieving senior leaders. However, as time passed and the circumstances at their respective places of work failed to change, they made a decision. They left their firms. They had gone from blooming to needing renewal. They owned their change in circumstances and took action. Eventually, they moved across the USA to start anew and work their way back up to blooming.

It didn't have to end this way. Their leaders could not have prevented the various life traumas that Forward and her husband endured—those are weather events. But they most certainly could have done far more to help them in work and life. And now, Forward's and Woodson's former organizations have lost the benefits they previously enjoyed thanks to the couple's incredible talents.

Many people worldwide have similar stories about work and life. Forward and Woodson's story didn't have to end the way it did—and it doesn't have to end that way for others either. This is the point of both the Work-Life Bloom model and, of course, this book. Sadly, there are far too many stories like Forward and Woodson's. Leaders therefore have a new remit: to help people reach a state of blooming.

Are We Blooming at Work? Kinda.

My definition of "blooming" is not directly tied to happiness. Twelve unique factors can help make up a blooming state and you do not need to be blooming in all 12 to be in bloom. But it is evident that blooming and happiness are connected in some ways.

For example—and as we will discover in more detail in this book—well-being, which social scientists often call "subjective well-being," is one of the factors that can help someone bloom. It's also something regularly aligned with various happiness traits in academic research. Suffice to say, happiness and well-being are at times used interchangeably in external studies and findings. Blooming in the context of my model may not necessarily equal happiness, but it's not solely related to well-being either.

In its 2022 *State of the Global Workforce Report*, Gallup reported that 60 percent of people are emotionally detached at work, and another 19 percent are miserable.[2] Employee engagement numbers haven't materially changed since Gallup began its global research in 2000.

Case in point: In 2010, the researchers Alex Bryson and George Mac-Kerron conducted an experiment with tens of thousands of individuals across the U.K.[3] They developed an app that they cheekily called "Mappiness." Individuals used the app with their mobile phones and were asked to record their well-being status when prompted during the day. The process was simple, and the results provide insights for us that support the arguments I present in this book.

Participants received randomly timed notifications on their phones that asked them to complete a short survey to rate themselves on three dimensions of well-being. Specifically, they were asked to rate how happy, relaxed, and awake they felt at that moment in time. Mappiness even transmitted the exact satellite positioning location of each participant using GPS and the precise time the survey was completed. Both features allowed the researchers to ascertain whether people were at home, work, or elsewhere when they took the survey. (As an aside, I think it's the best word mash-up ever: map + app + happiness = mappiness.)

The millions of entries that the researchers logged help paint an important picture. The most pleasurable experience for individuals is intimacy and lovemaking. Individuals who participated in this category had a happiness of rating of roughly 14 percentage points more than individuals who didn't. I didn't think 14 percent seemed like a lot, but then again, I didn't partake in the research. (If my wife is reading this book, honey, those activities raise my happiness by at least 50 percent.)

Next on the list are leisure activities such as attending theatre events, dance recitals, concerts, and museums or participating in sports and gardening activities. These endeavours resulted in a happiness increase of between 8 and nearly 10 percentage points. Not bad. I do love attending live concerts. And gardening is right in line with this book's main metaphor.

Maybe you can see where this is heading. Bryson and MacKerron concluded that paid work is the second-worst activity for happiness, coming right before being sick in bed, which was by far the most harmful to one's level of life joy. According to their study, work does not increase people's happiness in life. In fact, on average, people believe their work results in a 5.4 percent decrease in overall happiness.

What may be worse is that individuals who work in the company of their boss are less happy than individuals who work alone. Individuals who work with their peers are more satisfied than their colleagues who work with their boss (but still net-negative). So, I suppose working with your peers can be considered the "best of the not very good" when it comes to happiness at work.

George Ward of the MIT Sloan School of Management was similarly interested in well-being at work and partnered with the jobs firm Indeed to conduct a survey to assess how employees in the USA, Canada, and the U.K. felt about their jobs and work. Over a 10-month period beginning in October 2019, people who visited the Indeed website were presented with a series of statements—for example, "I feel happy at work most of the time," "My work has a clear sense of purpose," "I feel a sense of belonging in my company," and "I can trust people in my company"—and asked to rate them from "strongly disagree" to "strongly agree."[4]

Ward collected answers from millions of people across thousands of organizations. His conclusions were rather sobering. He writes:

> Employee happiness is increasingly discussed by companies as a priority, a development that has only been accelerated by the COVID-19 pandemic in which large-scale workplace change was a key feature for most people. Workplace happiness is currently low in the U.S., with many people employed in relatively miserable workplaces across the country. . . . improving the happiness of these workers is not only in their [leader's] own interests but may also be in the broader interests of their employers.

It's no wonder that 80 percent of working adults get anxious on Sunday nights about the upcoming workweek, as outlined in a 2018 survey commissioned by LinkedIn.[5]

When Ward asked how employees define their version of workplace happiness, the top five criteria in order of importance were

- Work-life balance
- Experiencing positive emotions while working
- Team atmosphere/relationships with colleagues
- Purpose/meaning of their work, and
- The actual work that people do daily

As you can see, that hackneyed old idea of work-life balance sits at the top of the list. That needs to change.

It is also obvious, though, that work is quite central to people's lives. As part of a global survey of 18,850 adults across 17 advanced economies published in 2022, Pew Research asked an open-ended question about what makes life meaningful and fulfilling. Work was the second-highest-ranking reason, bested only by family.[6] Bear in mind, though, that the workplace organizational service firm Humu discovered that 95 percent of employees believe bad leaders end up making everything worse and 58 percent that a bad manager is the number one contributor to burnout.[7]

Part of your goal as a leader is to reframe what work-life balance means, something I will outline later. You can probably begin to understand, however, how Forward and Woodson had lost their state of blooming and why they fled their respective employers.

Would an employee be willing to take a pay cut to achieve more positivity at work? Ward's research answered that question as well. His data indicated that workers value life happiness as a workplace amenity and would be willing to cut their salaries by, on average, 10.6 percent in exchange for more life happiness. Imagine that: people are willing to give away money to bloom.

What we learn from these research studies is telling. Many people are not blooming at work. They're certainly not happy. Not even close. This angst is not a new phenomenon, though. It has been building for years. As the author of 2019's *The Joy of Work*, Bruce Daisley, told me in an interview, "There is an anti-work ethos developing."[8] Daisley believes that work gets in the way of people achieving what they want in life. Interestingly, employees have a pretty good idea of what helps them to bloom and are willing to take a drop in salary to reach that state.

Of course, work is only one half of the garden box. Are we blooming in life?

Are We Blooming in Life? Kinda.

Although often misattributed, the following passage from the June 23, 1848, edition of *The Daily Crescent* helps us begin our examination of the life-factors: "A butterfly, which when pursued, seems always just beyond your grasp; but if you sit down quietly, may alight upon you."[9]

Let us now sit quietly to examine life and—as Socrates said at his trial for impiety and corruption—equally agree that "the unexamined life is not worth living."[10]

One of the mandates of the Organisation for Economic Co-operation and Development (OECD) is to measure global levels of life satisfaction. The OECD contends that satisfaction is a valid measurement as it forces people to "evaluate their life as a whole rather than their current feelings."[11] In its most recent Life Satisfaction survey in 2022, people were asked to rate their general satisfaction with life on a scale from 0 to 10. The average global score was 6.7. That's basically a C on a teenager's report card.

There is a vast range, however, to ponder. People in Colombia, Türkiye, Greece, South Korea, and Portugal all reported a lower level of overall life satisfaction (an average score of 6 or below—if we're using the report card metaphor, let's call it a "D"), whereas people in Denmark, Finland, Iceland, the Netherlands, and Switzerland ranked their life satisfaction as 7.5 or higher. We'll be kind and give those countries a B+ on the report card. A few other countries to note: Canada rated life satisfaction at 7.0, Australia 7.1, France 6.7, Japan 6.1, the U.K. 6.8, and the USA 7.0.

The Sustainable Development Solutions Network also tracks global levels of well-being. It uses data primarily sourced from the Gallup World Poll and presents its findings in its annual *World Happiness Report.*[12] The 2022 report indicated that well-being and overall happiness were trending in the wrong direction. And they weren't in a good place to start with. According to researchers, the world is now a "slightly sadder, more worried and more stressed-out place"[13] than ever before. The pandemic certainly has had an impact.

Indeed, Gallup's Negative Experience Index—cited in both the *World Happiness Report* and the Gallup World Poll—rose to a new high in 2021, and now sits at 33. This index is based on participants' responses to questions about five negative experiences and whether they encountered them the day before the survey was conducted. The negative marker was only 23 in 2007, equating to a 44 percent increase in perceived life negativity in just over a decade.

In 2022, the software giant Oracle surveyed over 12,000 individuals, including more than 3,000 business leaders from 14 countries. The result was the *Oracle Happiness Report*, co-authored by Gretchen Rubin, the best-selling author of *The Happiness Project*. The data shone a light not only on the detrimental impact of COVID-19 but also on life satisfaction itself.[14] Key insights included the following:

- 45 percent of people have not felt happy since early 2020

- 25 percent of people don't know or have forgotten what it means to feel happy

- 78 percent of people are willing to pay a premium for happiness

However, the longest-running body of research on subjective well-being is the Harvard Study on Adult Development, better known as the Grant and Glueck study. It might be considered the precursor of all life satisfaction studies.

For over 80 years, researchers have tracked various criteria among two cohorts of men: 456 low-income people based in Boston (Glueck) and 268

Harvard male graduates (Grant). Both cohorts have been observed since the beginning of 1939. The researchers' original goal was simple: "Help ease the disharmony of the world at large."[15]

If you're wondering why the Harvard cohort was composed only of men, women weren't originally invited, because the school was male only at the time. I know, it's terrible, but it was a different age. The good news is that a different set of researchers at Harvard are studying the children of the original participants—the Harvard Second Generation Study[16]—which includes both men and women. We'll have to wait a few years for the results of that study.

Researchers have meticulously performed brain scans and surveyed, assessed, or taken the men's blood samples across several generations. In addition, numerous meetings and private interviews provide rich insights into what helps people bloom in life.

What have the researchers learned? After their analyzing 80-odd years of the participants' lives, one factor kept resurfacing: relationships. Happiness was found to occur when there was a strong correlation between the men and the quality of their relationships with their family, friends, colleagues, and community. Another point of interest: men considered to be flourishing in their relationships at the age of 50 were not only the happiest but also the healthiest at age 80. Having a great rapport with other people gives you a better physical quality of life.

So, what made some of the men miserable? As you might expect, it's the opposite of enjoying good relationships. When you keep to yourself, you wind up experiencing loneliness, and that becomes toxic to your well-being.

"People who are more isolated than they want to be from others find that they are less happy, their health declines earlier in midlife, their brain functioning declines sooner, and they live shorter lives than people who are not lonely," remarked Dr. Robert Waldinger, the current director of the survey, in a 2018 interview.[17]

I am privileged to be a member of Marshall Goldsmith's 100 Coaches, a hand-picked group of thinkers, authors, and strategists trying to do good in the world. Dr. Waldinger attended one of our sessions in January 2023, and noted the following when we were discussing the Harvard Study: "The people in the study who had the warmest relationships—the best connections with other people—not only were more engaged in their life, but they were healthier, and they lived longer."[18] In a wildly popular

TED Talk eight years prior, Waldinger said, "The clearest message that we get from this 80-year study is this: good relationships keep us happier and healthier. Period."[19]

The author Annie Dillard writes in her 2013 book, *The Writing Life*, "How we spend our days is, of course, how we spend our lives."[20] There is much still to come in this book as we unpack the relationship between work and life, but Dillard's point is where I would like you to focus next.

The 2021 *Indeed Workplace Happiness Report* indicated that 92 percent of people said how they feel at work impacts how they feel at home.[21] In addition, Gallup released results from a global survey in 2022 that revealed that 65 percent of employees had been rethinking the place that work had in their lives.[22] I therefore posit that Dillard's adage is entirely accurate with an emphasized twist for your leadership acumen:

How we spend our days is most definitely how we spend our lives.

My independent research offers additional clarity about the work-life relationship and is discussed later in this chapter. To contradict and play off Socrates, it's why the examined life is actually *worth* living.

Reflections

During the pandemic, people were quitting, or thinking about quitting, their jobs wherever you looked. It was branded the "Great Resignation" by the Texas A&M management professor Anthony Klotz. For all the media attention it attracted, the term actually buried the lede. The meat of the story can be found when we dig a little deeper. For example, a 2022 survey by The Harris Poll showed that roughly 20 percent of workers regretted quitting their place of employment just a few months after leaving.[23] Joblist, an artificial intelligence job-search platform company, put that figure at 42 percent in a separate 2022 survey.[24] So, was the "Great Resignation" actually the "Great Regret"?

Despite the tragedy of the pandemic, those incredibly strange times initiated society's most expansive self-reflection exercise. While death is the endgame for all of us—even the sun only has 8 billion years left[25]— the pandemic unremittingly reminded us of our mortality. People began questioning their disrespectful and uncaring employers and bosses, terrible work conditions, and low wages. Many of the globe's working adults entered a cocoon of contemplation. Your team members might have gone through this process. They might still be going through it. Whether or not people quit their job (or later returned to it) is missing the point, though. Many people kept musing and asking themselves a simple question:

Am I blooming?

While the word "blooming" might not have been explicitly used, the overarching concept of blooming contained several interrogative criteria that I discuss below. In late 2020, I began reviewing my notes from multiple organizational culture assessments I had conducted prior to the pandemic. A lightbulb suddenly went on in my head.

The enterprise-wide assessments that I carried out between 2014 and 2020 involved thousands of employees. The assessments consisted of one-on-one interviews, focus groups, and surveys, data points that produced various insights into both organizational and human behavioural needs. In addition, questions and discussions about culture, purpose, trust, well-being, operations, and other measures pushed me in the direction of the Work-Life Bloom thesis. The firms involved in my assessments were located all across North America, and comprised a wide range of industries such as insurance, public sector, financial services, academia, and high-tech.

Combining and contrasting the data points I collected from those enterprise-wide assessments I conducted with my own meta-analysis of external research in the field, I realized that the issues at stake were not solely a result of the pandemic. Instead, they had been brewing for a while. People had been ruminating on the question "Am I blooming?" for quite some time without necessarily defining or understanding what it meant to be blooming. Instead, they were seeking work-life balance and failing miserably.

Borrowing from a conversation that I had with author Eric Termuende in late 2022, I suggest the so-called Great Resignation was more akin to the "Great Reconfiguration" or perhaps the "Great Contemplation."

Dr. Ranjay Gulati, a professor of Business Administration at Harvard Business School, calls it the "Great Rethink."[26] In a conversation we shared in mid-2022, Gulati said that employees were thinking "about something meaningful to themselves and also consequential to the world beyond them."[27] People awoke. They envisaged. They reflected. Resignations became an outcome of a new form of rethinking. Job hopping also became the norm in several jurisdictions. Some countries, like Canada and Australia, didn't experience mass resignations; instead, plenty of employee reshuffling—shifts from one role to another in the same firm—happened, a hat tip to Termuende's point.

One important factor that is often misunderstood in all the discussions and analysis about the Great Resignation is the nature of the labour pool. In Canada, for example, the overall labour force participation rate among people 15 years and older has been gently declining over the years. In 2003, the labour force participation rate stood at 67.6 percent. In 2019, it was 66.1 percent. And in 2022, it was 65.6 percent, which strongly suggests that it has been falling not because of the pandemic but because of demographic issues.

The BMO economists Robert Kavcic and Douglas Porter write in a 2022 report: "It is critical to note that this ongoing slow decline is almost entirely a function of underlying demographics—that is, a rapidly rising share of the population in retirement age groups—and less to do with people exiting the labour force for other reasons."[28] Some retirees began to ponder whether they wanted to get back into the workforce and work part-time—or not. Again, the Great Reconfiguration.

Some people regretted leaving their roles, which generated the "Great Boomerang."[29] According to research findings presented by UKG involving workers in the USA, the U.K., Mexico, the Netherlands, Germany, and France in 2022, nearly 20 percent of people who quit during the pandemic boomeranged back to their original job.[30] The garden box may not have been lusher on the other side. Returning to a lesser form of misery seems cruel, but one out of every five people did just that.

Employed and retired individuals have been opening their eyes fully for years, deliberating what *might* be and perhaps what *should* be in their work *and* life. Perhaps everything since the Great Recession of 2007–2009 should be called the "Great Liminality." After all, recall that each of us is *in transformation*. We are liminal.

Two examples can help outline my claims about the contemplative if not reconfigurative nature that enveloped society before, during, and after the pandemic.

Let's take Monika, a middle-aged frontline worker. Every day during the pandemic she was battling both a highly contagious virus and idiotic people. At any moment of downtime that she could spare, Monika wondered aloud why she had to put up with the hordes of anti-maskers at the front door of her workplace. That would have sucked the life out of many of us. Monika also wondered not only about her inferior wage level while overtime mandates piled up but also, and perhaps worse, why her boss treated the entire team so inhumanely. She realized that her boss had always been like that. The result? Monika was nowhere near a bloom persona in her garden box. She was somewhere else.

For the first few months of the pandemic, at 7:00 PM sharp, people clanged their pots and pans on their balconies and at their front doors in a symphony of empathy and gratitude for frontline employees working in healthcare, food supply, and other essential services. But Monika's workplace hardship was not because of the pandemic. It was because of systemic issues in various leadership, personal, and workplace factors and it had been building for years.

For those not working in hospitals, long-term care homes, restaurants, dentist offices, grocery stores, or other frontline situations, the pandemic triggered the greatest work-from-home experiment in history. Millions of knowledge workers spent hours staring into a computer screen, multitasking in a Bubble Wrap of work-life scrutiny while trying to keep their pandemic puppy from barking during a video call. There might have been boredom, but there was also deep reflection. The result was emergent thinking, whereby people pondered what mattered most to them in work and life. Arguably, it was long overdue. It was garden box rumination at its finest.

You do not have to look far for other contemplation, rethinking, or reconfiguration examples, connected or not to the pandemic. The Reddit subreddit group titled r/antiwork, for example, is intended for those "who want to end work, are curious about ending work, want to get the most out of a work-free life, want more information on anti-work ideas and want personal help with their own jobs/work-related struggles."[31] Although it contains many childish memes and fair wage entries, people found it a safe place to vent, and so it also contains thousands of enlightening work-life posts, discussions, and comments.

For instance, a mid-level manager at a large I.T. company took the time to document a rather significant issue at their firm.[32] After the company's senior leaders had abolished its work-from-home program—forcing people back into the office by mid-2022—this manager watched 45 percent of their team resign. According to the post, the manager was pulled into a meeting with their director, who wondered aloud why people were quitting in droves. The director further suggested that the former employees were ungrateful and disloyal to the company.

The manager then pointed out to the director that employees were quitting for $300 more per month in wages and, as an extra bonus, they could work from home permanently. Finally, the manager pointed out the obvious to the director: "Extra time and money, would you blame them for leaving?" Thousands of views and comments ensued after the post was published. Most of them supported the need to demand self-worth and agency in one's life and work.

Whether it be through Reddit or other platforms such as Blind, YikYak, Koo, or Roomvine, people continue to gain steam by anonymously contemplating (and posting) their work-life issues from around the globe.

About Those Bosses

What about the leaders? For example, a 2022 survey of 1,000 senior executives across 12 countries and 10 industries conducted by consulting firm KellyOCG suggested leaders were not immune to the work-life reconfiguration issue.[33] The firm's research suggested only 42 percent of executives were happy in their current roles, and 72 percent planned to leave their employer within the next two years.

Furthermore, according to a 2022 study by Humu,[34] leaders had been struggling for quite some time. Leaders at all levels were twice as likely as individual contributors to be looking for new jobs because of those struggles.

A 2021 survey of 1,158 global senior leaders by LifeWorks (acquired by TELUS in 2022) and Deloitte indicated that 51 percent of senior leaders were contemplating leaving their roles at the time of the research.[35] Thirty-eight percent suggested it was due to workplace stress, while 22 percent felt underappreciated at work. Only 8 percent were thinking of leaving because of a better career opportunity. What may be worse is that 82 percent of all the senior leaders surveyed were experiencing exhaustion in their lives.

The Global Work-Life Assessment Survey I conducted in 2022 provided all sorts of data points that offer supplementary insights to the above. In addition, several responses from leaders delivered sobering opinions about the work-life struggle we are unpacking in this section. I have included a few choice examples below:

✿ ✿

I had to hide a medical illness at my previous work or risk demotion. In the end, they learned of my ailment and let me go because I could not be available beyond 60 hours a week.
SENIOR VICE-PRESIDENT, TELECOMMUNICATIONS, U.K., 55–64 YEARS

I'm not sure many organizations understand what people of colour go through, especially when they are looking to promote. I'm female, and EDI is a joke. It's all smoke and mirrors until they are caught showing microaggressions. I do support women, but at the moment, it's really white women who still want to maintain the white male status quo.
MANAGER, COMMUNICATIONS, CANADA, 45–54 YEARS

As a woman and a mother, I have often been asked to work long hours at the expense of missing family activities. This has prevented me from being able to be my whole self at work as the expectation was for me to brush off my family to accomplish work goals.
DIRECTOR, PHARMACEUTICAL, USA, 55–64 YEARS

My supervisor often takes credit for my work and that of others and is protected from repercussions for mismanagement by upper-level leaders. This makes me guarded about sharing ideas, taking extra initiative, or bringing forward concerns.
MANAGER, EDUCATION, CANADA, 25–34 YEARS

I am not supported in any way by my employer, rather the opposite.

MANAGER, PROFESSIONAL SERVICES, GERMANY, 25-34 YEARS

Unfortunately, I think I've been inhibited from bringing my whole self to work in the past as, working in a male-dominated environment, there's been a huge expectation to 'play tough' - often in ways I feel are toxic as these expected behaviours don't align with my personal values. Women are often fearful of doing so in case it harms their career progression.

DIRECTOR, PROFESSIONAL SERVICES, U.K., 45-54 YEARS

I experienced burnout last year. I now think about the role work has in my life very differently. Although my organization is very vocal about supporting employee well-being, their actions do not match their words, and I feel very alone in my views. I think if I continue to voice concerns, I'll eventually be released or at least negatively impacted in my career here.

DIRECTOR, TRANSPORTATION, CANADA, 35-44 YEARS

Being told that I couldn't have any input in a situation where I had personal experience as it didn't follow company policy, resulting in issues that I know I could have prevented.

MANAGER, BUSINESS/CONSULTING, AUSTRALIA, 25-34 YEARS

✿ ✿ ✿ ✿ ✿ ✿ ✿ ✿ ✿ ✿ ✿ ✿ ✿ ✿ ✿ ✿ ✿ ✿ ✿ ✿

For some, the pandemic was the catalyst that led them to scrutinize their work-life plight. Others, however, had been asking questions about their work-life state for much longer. The pandemic was brutal on multiple levels, but the issues many people faced, whether they were leaders or individual contributors, had been going on for years. The reflections I have presented thus far merely skim the surface of the amount of work-life contemplation and reconfiguration that was, and still is, happening.

It's time for a respite. I'm not trying to make you feel nauseous about the state of our organizations and the people who work in them. Next, I'll outline the basics of the Work-Life Bloom model—a potential antidote to the problem—to provide a bud of hope for a more promising work-life future and blooming garden boxes.

Basics of the Work-Life Bloom Model

The Work-Life Bloom model is based on the interpretive analysis of my research and first-hand practice from over 20 years as a leader, organizational strategist, and external consultant. As you now know, there are two key pillars: work and life. As I pointed out earlier, my research and findings identified 12 work-life factors that provide an affiliation between a team member's workplace, leader, team, and definition of self.

The work-life factors centre on organizational and team measures as well as conditions targeting the self what makes people tick as human beings while operating between work and life.

WORK-LIFE FACTORS

Work	Life
✿ Trust	✿ Relationships
✿ Belonging	✿ Skills
✿ Valued	✿ Well-being
✿ Purpose	✿ Meaning
✿ Strategy	✿ Agency
✿ Norms	✿ Respect

With the assistance of assessment analysts, we created a rubric to determine a Work-Life Bloom methodology that rated each participant. (To learn more about the methodology visit www.worklifebloom.com/extras.)

It quickly became evident that "not blooming" was insufficient as a descriptor for people currently "not blooming." After some initial beta-testing, four Work-Life Bloom categories surfaced. The personas and descriptors are in the table below.

WORK-LIFE PERSONAS

WORK-LIFE PERSONA	DEFINITION
Renewal	I am in need of refreshing the majority of my work-life factors.
Budding	I am succeeding at work but require further self-development.
Stunted	I am stalled at work yet thriving as an individual in life.
Blooming	I am prospering fully in both work and life.

We then established a Work-Life Bloom model as follows.

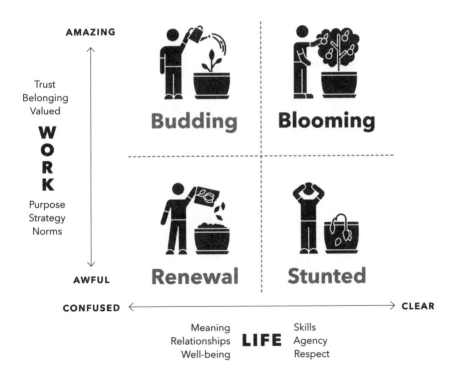

Each of the 12 work-life factors also revealed several independent insights when filtered via several parameters such as role, seniority, country, gender, and age. I will reveal highlights of these throughout the book, particularly in Chapters III and IV.

Before you go any further in this book, feel free to take the Global Work-Life Assessment Survey yourself. First, write down what persona you believe best represents you today, based on the definitions above (blooming, budding, stunted, or renewal):

Then, access the free assessment by visiting **www.worklifebloom.com/ assessment**. Once you have completed the survey, write down what the model categorized you as:

Survey Says . . .

What Work-Life Bloom persona did you self-assess yourself as, and what did the model suggest you were? Whatever you thought it was and whatever it is, don't forget, you are a work in progress. You are *in transformation*. And so is your team. And so am I. Your work-life persona will change again and again.

You will recall from the previous chapter that I asked the Global Work-Life Assessment Survey respondents to self-assess the persona that best matched their current state. In the table below, column two shows how participants assessed themselves, and column three shows what the Work-Life Bloom model assessed.

EMPLOYEES' PERSONA SELF-ASSESSMENTS
AND WLB MODEL ASSESSMENTS

ALL EMPLOYEES		
PERSONA	SELF-ASSESSMENT	WORK-LIFE BLOOM MODEL ASSESSMENT
Blooming	36.1%	41.3%
Budding	28.9%	11.9%
Stunted	18.7%	8.6%
Renewal	16.3%	38.2%

Thirty-six percent of global respondents assessed themselves as bloom-ing, and the model indicates strong agreement, at 41 percent. A difference of five percentage points between the two is enough to call it a draw in my books.

While that may seem a positive point, feast your eyes on the number of people with a renewal persona. More than 38 percent of global employ-ees are at the renewal stage. That figure identifies—in part, at least—why this book is necessary. Factor in the 21 percent of individuals who need assistance with their work- or life-factors (because they are currently in the stunted or budding stages) and opportunity abounds for leaders to help these two categories of team members as well. In sum, roughly 60 percent of all employees need some form of assistance to help them reach the bloom persona.

When the data is bifurcated between non-leaders and leaders as well as female versus male respondents, the picture takes on a sinister tone. Review the following data splits:

PERSONA ASSESSMENTS: NON-LEADERS VS. LEADERS

PERSONA	SELF-ASSESSMENT		WORK-LIFE BLOOM MODEL ASSESSMENT	
	NON-LEADER	LEADER	NON-LEADER	LEADER
Blooming	26.3%	40.1%	26.6%	47.7%
Budding	32.4%	27.5%	12.7%	11.6%
Stunted	21.3%	17.6%	9.7%	8.0%
Renewal	20.0%	14.8%	51.0%	32.7%

PERSONA ASSESSMENTS: BY GENDER

PERSONA	GENDER			
	SELF-ASSESSMENT		WORK-LIFE BLOOM MODEL ASSESSMENT	
	FEMALE	MALE	FEMALE	MALE
Blooming	33.6%	42.6%	31.6%	49.7%
Budding	30.5%	27.5%	11.9%	11.9%
Stunted	19.1%	16.7%	10.0%	7.3%
Renewal	16.8%	13.2%	46.5%	31.1%

Notice anything? The leader versus non-leader breakdown highlights an enormous chasm. The Work-Life Bloom output predicts 48 percent of leaders are in a blooming state compared with only 27 percent of non-leaders. The self-assessment scoring outlines a difference: forty percent (leaders) vs. 26 percent (non-leaders). While the Work-Life Bloom model scores both leaders and non-leaders relatively the same when it comes to their budding and stunted personas, a shocking 51 percent of non-leaders and almost 33 percent of leaders are in the renewal stage.

When broken down by gender, both the self-assessment and Work-Life Bloom model output portray large and concerning gaps between male and female participants. In the self-assessment, significantly more female than male participants believe they are in the renewal stage versus the blooming stage. Perhaps worse, the model produces a whopping 18-percentage point difference between female and male participants who are blooming. Furthermore, almost half of all female participants are in the renewal stage versus less than one-third of male participants.

What can we make of these initial results and how does our interpretation of them set things up for the rest of the book? Suffice to say, leaders need to pay careful attention to the state of their employees' work-life status. If we want more than 48 percent of leaders, 27 percent of non-leaders, 50 percent of men, and 32 percent of women to bloom in our organizations—and in their lives in general—we had better make a few changes to our leadership garden tools. Moreover, you need to be prepared to help your team members in ways that you might not have contemplated before.

The Global Work-Life Assessment Survey results reminded me of the wise words that American writer and activist James Baldwin once wrote:

"Not everything that is faced can be changed; but nothing can be changed until it is faced."[36]

You can't change everything, and not everything needs to be changed. Nevertheless, I believe it is time that you face the reality of this work-life predicament. While team members will always be *in transformation,* how you help them move toward a blooming persona is arguably one of your most important duties as a leader.

Maybe We Do Live to Survive Our Paradoxes

Centuries ago, Giovanni Pico della Mirandola, an Italian scholar and philosopher of the Renaissance, wrote about the potential of human achievement in *The Oration on the Dignity of Man.* A particular passage points out a paradox to note:

> [F]or it is not the bark that makes the tree, but its insensitive and unresponsive nature; nor the hide which makes the beast of burden, but its brute and sensual soul; nor the orbicular form which makes the heavens, but their harmonious order. Finally, it is not freedom from a body, but its spiritual intelligence, which makes the angel.[37]

The evidence is clear: We are in need of a different leadership lens. We need to peel back the bark of what we think it means to be a leader and devise a new "harmonious order" and "spiritual intelligence" for team members. Perhaps a better paradox is required—if we continue with Mirandola's line of thinking, it is not the position of authority that makes the leader, but the ability of the leader to nurture their people so they can *be their best.* Team members are constantly exploring, studying, and redefining their work-life relationship, and it is leaders (ahem, you!) who need to amend how leadership is characterized forthwith.

Let's examine two situations to shed some light on your need to rethink how you are conducting yourself in light of several of the work-life factors we continue to unpack. The first story comes from Netflix, and the other from a company called Zipline.

On the morning of October 20, 2021, several Netflix workers walked off the job in protest. It mattered not whether the team members worked in an office or from home. They were protesting against their own company because of a situation that gives us insight into a few of our work-life factors.

Netflix had released *The Closer*, a stand-up comedy special written and performed by the American comedian Dave Chappelle, earlier that same month. In the show, Chappelle delivered jokes about discrimination differences between the African American and LGBTQ communities. The show generated intense controversy, and was heavily criticized for what many believed to be transphobic and racist comments by Chappelle. Days before the walkout, Netflix had suspended Terra Field, a trans employee at the company, for posting comments on Twitter questioning the company's decision to release *The Closer*. Many Netflix employees felt this suspension was unfair, and others believed the special did not reflect Netflix's purpose, culture, or strategy, let alone its stance on belonging, inclusion, and diversity.[38]

A second reason for the walkout concerned the Netflix co-CEO Ted Sarandos. Shortly after Field was suspended and *The Closer* had been released to the public, Sarandos issued a memo to employees. In the memo—and partially as a response to Field's actions and the growing volatility emanating from the Netflix trans employee resource group—he wrote that "[w]e don't allow titles on Netflix that are designed to incite hate or violence, and we don't believe *The Closer* crosses that line"[39] and that "while some employees disagree, we have a strong belief that content on screen doesn't directly translate to real-world harm."[40] The lack of empathy and his emotionless tone toward the trans community at Netflix left many employees of all identities fuming and ultimately motivated to stage the walkout.

Let's be clear. Organizations are not run by consensus. It's not as though Field and her colleagues should have been asked for their input on whether *The Closer* ought to have been released. That's not how large publicly traded organizations operate. The issue was that Netflix's trans employees were not feeling valued. Their well-being and sense of meaning were being challenged by their employer, an employer that seemed late to the respect party. For many of these Netflix employees, life was spilling into work, and work was spilling into life as far as this particular issue was concerned.

Later that month, Sarandos admitted in an interview with *Variety* that he should have been more concerned about the feelings of the disaffected team members. In gardening terms, he forgot to water the work-life garden. He said, "I should have led with a lot more humanity. Meaning, I had a group of employees who were definitely feeling pain and hurt from a decision we made. And I think that needs to be acknowledged up front before you get into the nuts and bolts of anything. I didn't do that."[41] Kudos to Sarandos for recognizing his mistake, but what is my point?

You may be thinking that this is nothing more than the story of an isolated event at Netflix. That is actually the entire point. You are a leader of others. Consequently, there are many different permutations of an employee's perspective that you need to consider when you make decisions. When one isolated incident becomes another—or worse, the norm—you will eventually have an operational crisis on your hands. That crisis might wind up being a potential retention or hiring issue, customer satisfaction concern, revenue or profitability problem, or, of course, an employee experience that gets talked about negatively on Glassdoor, Blind, Reddit, and other social sharing sites.

The walkout at Netflix is not the canary in the coal mine—or perhaps beetle in the garden box—but it does demonstrate a changing course. Several other examples of preventable employee tumult and related activism occurred pre-, mid-, and post-pandemic at firms like Google,[42] Apple,[43] Activision,[44] Disney,[45] and Amazon.[46] Even publishers like Simon & Schuster were not immune to employee activism.[47] There are sure to be thousands more from organizations across the globe that do not attract the attention of the press. I posit that people are yearning for leaders and organizations who not only understand the *Work-Life Bloom* factors but also create an environment where those factors are consistently and supportively enacted.

The following comment via the Global Work-Life Assessment Survey supports my opinion:

✿ ✿

What I appreciate most is being able to share ideas in a safe space. Not all my ideas are good ones but knowing I can share my thoughts without fear is invaluable to me. I feel I can bring my best self and do my part to contribute to my team's/organization's success.

PROFESSIONAL, HIGH-TECH, CANADA, 45–54 YEARS

✿ ✿

My second example that illustrates the need for a new "harmonious order" and "spiritual intelligence" required for our Work-Life Bloom thesis is far more positive. It is no exaggeration to describe it as revelatory.

Alyson Kittler is operations manager at Zipline, an I.T. consulting firm with employees around the globe. During the summer of 2022, Kittler was out walking when she received a call from her CEO, Melissa Wong. As Zipline is a remote-first company—and 99 percent of its communications happen via Slack—Kittler mildly panicked. The company rarely talks on the phone, so Kittler had no idea what to expect. After all, it was the CEO!

The previous weekend had been a rough one for Kittler. She had to put down her 15-year-old dog, Patton. It was a very distressing event for her. Word got back to Wong. That phone call from her? The CEO discovered how much Patton meant to Kittler and simply wanted to check in on her. "I cried for a minute, and then we talked for 20 minutes about animals, grief, and loss," Kittler told me.

"When we hung up, I felt so much better," she continued. "It was a simple act of authentic kindness that made me feel supported and valued. It made me feel that I was more important than the work. When you work for a good leader, you should always feel that way. And with Melissa and Zipline, I do."

When I asked Kittler why that call from Wong was so important, her answer spoke volumes about several of the *Work-Life Bloom* factors. "It speaks to humanity," she said triumphantly. "Prior to Zipline, I worked in several office jobs where there was a clear sense of boundaries. You could go through a breakup, but the expectation was that you'd cry about it in the bathroom, not in your cubicle. It wasn't a place to be a human being; it was a place to get work done. Now I'm at a company where the opposite is true, and it's literally changed everything about how I work and how I show up at work."

Kittler went on to suggest that when employees can relate to others in the workplace through vulnerability—being emotional without judgment—or through acts of reciprocal trust, they want to work harder to help their company and team succeed. If you're a fan of *Batman*, Kittler is doing her best to send you an urgent leadership Bat-Signal.

"Being able to be my best at work is critical," she said. "I'm happier today than I've ever been in my career. I feel personally vested in my co-workers because my company is personally vested in me. My authentic self is what matters the most, and there isn't any time where anyone has ever tried to snuff it out or tone it down."

Kittler began to reflect on how her current employer differed from her previous ones. She said, "Processing my goodbye to Patton at any of those other jobs would have been a very lonely experience. Instead, I had a situation where others reached out to me and helped to open me up so that I could feel not only supported but also validated. Your sadness and pain should never be overlooked. And when your leaders and teammates care about you—I mean really care about you—it has a domino effect. You wind up paying it forward to others, whether you're actively aware of it or not."

The results from the Global Work-Life Assessment Survey that I oversaw provide additional, corroborating evidence to Kittler's viewpoints. I will examine much of the data and insights later on, but for now, let's highlight belongingness at work. A paradox is rather evident:

- Eighty-eight percent of leaders and 75 percent of non-leaders agree or strongly agree that they fit in with their direct team at work. (I'm certain we can agree both numbers are rather good.)

- An alarming 43 percent of leaders and a whopping 65 percent of non-leaders believe their current employer provides average, below average, or no help regarding a sense of belonging at work.

While a substantial portion of team members and leaders believe they experience belongingness, they do not rely on the organization to help them develop it. Between those two data points lies the issue: that sense of belonging and support comes not from the organization or its leaders but from elsewhere.

In sum, we need more leaders like Melissa Wong and fewer experiences like those the trans community at Netflix suffered. If employees do not feel their employer supports a sense of belonging, the chances of a team member blooming diminish.

The following two comments from the Global Work-Life Assessment Survey provide one negative and one positive example:

✿ ✿

During my performance review, I received a promotion. 1.5 months later, they lambasted me saying, "I am inauthentic and a self-promoter, a square peg in a round hole, and extroverted." It hit me out of left field since I just got promoted. It ruined all sense of belonging, psychological safety and caused me to shut down. It's made it difficult to share my career goals. I need trust, a sense of belonging, and psychological safety to bring my whole self to work.

DIRECTOR, CONSULTING, CANADA, 45-54 YEARS

In my current role, I have the freedom to make decisions on the fly. Even if those decisions don't work out, I still have the full support of my boss. I never feel worried about approaching my boss with any questions I have; he is always willing to teach and really enjoys seeing people learn and succeed. Because of his support and teaching skills, I have become an integral part of the team and flourish in the tough situations.

PROFESSIONAL, CONSTRUCTION, CANADA, 35-44 YEARS

✿ ✿

Working Together in Work and Life

If, as I outlined previously, "our lives shape our work; nevertheless, our work shapes us," then I believe leaders have a fiduciary responsibility to adopt this axiom and, by extension, the Work-Life Bloom model. You could think of it as committing to a new social contract with your team members.

Therefore, I believe that you as a leader ought to begin fostering the conditions that permit a) work to flourish, and b) a team member's humanity to grow inside and outside the organization to allow them to *be their best.* Put differently,

A leader's duty of care is to help their team members bloom in work and life, creating value for all.

I THOUGHT IT best to end this chapter on a high note. Not every leader has their head in the soil when it comes to appreciating the importance of the Work-Life Bloom thesis, let alone embodying that duty of care time and time again.

In late winter 2021, I was riding my bicycle in an attempt to lose my COVID weight. Halfway through my outing to Victoria's ferry terminals, I felt my iPhone buzz in my back pocket, indicating a voicemail. When I returned home and parked my bike in the garage, I listened to the voicemail. I couldn't believe my ears. One of my leadership heroes had just left me a message.

Alan Mulally is the former president and CEO of the Ford Motor Company, serving as its most senior leader between 2006 and 2014. For over 30 years before that, he held roles at Boeing, including executive vice-president of the Boeing Company, president and CEO of Boeing Commercial Airplanes, and president of Boeing Information Defense and Space Systems. To say that Mulally has been at the helm of two of the USA's most important and prominent brands would be a wild understatement.

Mulally had read my fourth book, *Lead. Care. Win.: How to Become a Leader Who Matters*, and wanted to talk. Was I dreaming? I phoned him back, sweating profusely during that first chat. We proceeded to have several conversations via Zoom—both recorded and private—over the next 18 months. Mulally had been the CEO of companies that earned billions in revenues and profits under his leadership. He provides us with an important lesson as we continue to unpack the Work-Life Bloom model: whatever it takes, we must *work together*, whether it's work or life.

"Growing up, we had very modest means, very few resources, but we had two parents that just absolutely loved us and taught us that if we learn to work together with people, we can make a big difference to the greater good,"[48] said Mulally, during one of our conversations.

Mulally grew up in Kansas. His parents had an extraordinary impact on his eventual leadership style at Boeing, at Ford, and in life, equipping him with several adages and memorable mantras to live by. One of those was: "Expect the unexpected and then expect to deal with it in a positive way." It's a great insight into Mulally's famously and infectiously optimistic attitude about work and life.

While at Boeing and Ford, Mulally introduced his "working together" model, a management system containing several operating processes, expected behaviours, review practices, value creation methods, governance actions, and stated leadership attributes. Taken together, these components clarify how people should treat and interact with one another. His system is like the central nervous system of an organization; when an axon and synapse are out of sync, everyone can feel the ripple effects.

Long before it became de rigueur, Mulally advocated for a stakeholder-first mindset as part of the "working together" system. It provides a vital hat tip to the Work-Life Bloom topology.

"Think about this," said Mulally of his time at Boeing. "Every airplane has been a tremendous success, meaning that the airlines love it. They operate it; they've done well. They've created value for everybody that uses them around the world. For every airplane we designed, we included the airlines and all the stakeholders in the development of the airplane. So, we're looking at their world. We're seeing where the world is going. They were part of the biggest decisions on every part of the airplane."

In discussing stakeholder inclusion, Mulally subliminally touched on the importance of all Work-Life Bloom factors, including agency, trust, relationships, and organizational norms. Team members generally want the opportunity to be involved, to have their feedback heard, and to be a part of the decision-making, even if the final decision doesn't go their way. This is agency. You have the makings of a winning operation when agency is coupled with a work environment in which everyone trusts one another through solid relationships and a high-performing culture.

Mulally pointed out that the success of his Boeing tenure was partly due to the "working together" principle of involving others. Not only were the airlines invited to the table for feedback and collaboration, but so too were investors, suppliers, and certification agencies, among other stakeholders. He said, "We included them every step of the way. If you include all the stakeholders, starting with all the employees, then you by definition are going to create what people want and value, and you're going to do it in the most efficient way." In sum: Your network cannot be myopic or focused on one type of stakeholder only. To bloom is to be thinking always about others and your strategy and plan to deliver a compelling vision.

There is one other benefit to Mulally's system, and it is highlighted by another important maxim from his upbringing: "Develop an integrated life, and that is your life's work."

The model Mulally so successfully applied in firms like Boeing and Ford can also be applied to family, spiritual, community, and personal influences. "Working together is a way not just to operate Boeing or Ford, but life," he said. "The more you're comfortable being authentic, everybody will love it because they're dealing with the person that is not only authentic but living their beliefs and values."

"To bloom is to mature into realizing one's potential," he said to me. "It's a state of great activity, thriving on achievement, a time of vigour and beauty."

It's as good a setup as we can ask for as we enter the next phase of *Work-Life Bloom*. It's time to introduce the six work-factors that can help people to bloom.

*"Managers are incurably susceptible to panacea peddlers.
They are rooted in the belief that there are simple, if not simple-minded,
solutions to even the most complex of problems. And they do
not learn from bad experiences. Managers fail to diagnose
the failures of the fads they adopt; they do not understand them."*[1]

RUSSELL L. ACKOFF

CHAPTER III

Work-Factors

WHEN SHE WAS CEO of British luxury fashion house Burberry, Angela Ahrendts once said, "Knowledge is power. So, the more the associates know about the strategy, about what's coming, the better. Everyone talks about building a relationship with your customer. I think you build one with your employees first."[2] Those four sentences pack an indelible punch in terms of the six work-factors I am proposing, which will help your team members bloom.

Executives all too often wax lyrical about their leadership prowess, uttering empty phrases like "culture is our competitive advantage" or "employees are our most important asset." In most cases, this is simply corporate lip service or leadership snake oil. The same goes for the organizational values that adorn the entrance to most corporate buildings. Senior leaders may talk a good game about providing a positive employee experience and their self-perceived excellence at doing so, but many fail to understand that they don't actually deliver the goods. It's like offering someone a half-empty bottle of plant fertilizer.

For team members to expertly serve the customer (or stakeholders, or community) and perform at a high level in their role, leaders must address several work-factors. (Of course, six life-factors must also be considered, but we'll explore those in Chapter IV.)

If, as Ahrendts suggested, you should build a relationship with your employees first, you can no longer willfully ignore the features that will help you do this. You must become well-versed in the six work-factors we are about to unpack in this chapter. They are critical to the evolution of your leadership style. Moreover, they are imperative if you want team members to *be their best*.

Let's think about a practical workplace example to illustrate the point.

You find yourself in the emergency room of your local hospital after an accident. It's not life-threatening, but you really shouldn't have been FaceTiming your father while riding a bike. Kaboom! You can still hear the crunch. The unabating throbbing leads you to suspect your shoulder is dislocated, or worse, a surgical repair is in your very near future.

After being processed by the E.R. staff rather quickly, you're now a patient patiently waiting. An hour passes, and you finally hear your name called. Thank goodness, because you don't want to listen to any more moaning from the waiting area. Graciously, you make your way to the radiology ward. When you arrive two floors up from the E.R., you see two signs. One is for the X-ray department, the other for MRIS.

Your X-ray is first, so you open the door to that part of the ward. It's as though you've entered a tomb of melancholy. Even Shakespeare would be proud of the atmosphere. The individual at the front desk doesn't even worry about looking you in the face. Their abject lack of interest is palpable. "Just wait over there," they say, blindly pointing to one of three available chairs. "We'll get to you when we get to you."

After 15 minutes or so, you are summoned into the X-ray room. The two radiologists haven't even bothered to ask how you're feeling. As you're mercilessly draped with what feels like a 75-kilogram lead vest, you overhear one of them say, "What's the point? He never listens to me anyway around here." It seems they are in the middle of a conversation about their boss. The other radiologist responds with "Yeah, as if he even cares. I honestly can't wait to get out of here."

Bruised now not only from your accident but also from the mood of these three employees, you soldier on and head back to the radiology ward waiting area. Another 30 minutes pass. Is your mood ever dark. You're now finally off to an MRI scan of your shoulder. You walk past the X-ray area and think to yourself, "Just how glum can someone be in their job?" and enter the MRI wing. What a difference 20 metres can make.

As you enter the next waiting area, a woman cheerfully says, "Well, that sling doesn't look like a good sign at all. Tell me, what happened?" You notice the room seems brighter, and there is an unmistakable tone of generosity and kindness. There are photos of smiling people on the wall.

You sheepishly explain the cycling mishap. This MRI team member is genuinely concerned for your well-being. She relays a story to you about her father's rock-climbing shoulder accident from a few years ago. She puts you at ease, letting you know he recovered from it fully. And he still climbs. She walks you to the changing room, where you will strip and put on an army-green hospital gown. "Don't worry," she jokes. "We don't take photos for Instagram in here. Everyone looks the same." You smile and disrobe.

Once you're dressed in the hospital's finest sartorial splendour, you are gently guided into the MRI room itself. Two radiologists are waiting for you, both with smiles as wide as the River Nile. "Welcome!" they say simultaneously. They ask about your accident, making you feel like a human being again, and then explain how the MRI machine works and what to expect. "Blissful" doesn't begin to describe their attitude.

After 20 minutes, the test is complete, and the radiologists are back in the room to help you out of the MRI bed. Not only are they ever-so-gentle, but they explain what will happen next with your results too. Seeing you to the door, they wish you the best of luck in your recovery. Their empathy level is off the charts. One begins to kid around with you as you're exiting. "Try not to high-five anyone with your right arm for a while," they joke. You laugh and leave the hospital with a smile, despite the persistent ache in your shoulder. You've already forgotten about the moody X-ray team.

This type of scenario plays out time and time again in our organizations. Just substitute X-ray and MRI for sales and engineering or human resources and I.T. Maybe even sub-teams in the same business unit. Take your pick. The question is: How can one group of individuals be so negative and disconnected while another group—working mere metres away in the same organization—is so positive and engaged?

As you learn more about the six work-factors, you must also keep in mind that there are three pillars underpinning your team members' views on their workplace. Those pillars are the following:

- The team they are a part of.
- The organization as a whole.
- You, the leader of the team.

The first pillar is your team—sometimes colloquially known as your direct reports—the group of people banded together to achieve results. Your team members may even have their own direct reports that they're leading. Thus, you are responsible for creating the conditions in which your team members (and theirs) can perform both positively and productively, whatever their role. Any team's operating methods can significantly impact how people perform, whether they bloom or not. When you think of the first pillar, ask yourself: How do people conduct themselves on their team?

The second pillar is the organization. Keep in mind how the organization might also affect a team member's ability to perform. You may even be in a position to help guide or change various organizational traits. Perhaps you can alter some of the inevitable "We've always done it this way" work-factors. Whatever the case, the organization's operational tactics will negatively or positively impact team members. It's your responsibility as a leader to circumvent any organizational roadblocks that prevent an individual from effectively performing in their role. You can also accentuate the good that the organization already demonstrates. Thus, regarding the second pillar, ask yourself this: How do the six work-factors impact the team member when viewed against the organization's operations and culture?

The third pillar is you, the leader. What you do as a leader in group and one-on-one situations will shape how your team members perform and feel. Greta Mazzetti of the University of Bologna and Wilmar Schaufeli of Utrecht University published research in 2022 that validates this point.[3] After studying more than 1,000 people across 90 teams over two years, they found that the more involved and engaged a leader is with their team members, the higher those team members feel in terms of their optimism, resiliency, self-efficacy, and flexibility.

Similarly, leaders who positively manage their teams appear to enhance overall effectiveness. Mazzetti and Schaufeli noted: "A leader who inspires, strengthens and connects team members fosters a shared perception of available resources (in terms of performance feedback, trust in management, communication, and participation in decision-making), and a greater psychological capital (i.e., self-efficacy, optimism, resilience, and flexibility)." Therefore, in relation to the third pillar, consider the following: How do team members interpret and react to your leadership style in relation to the six work-factors?

In sum, the six work-factors that impact a team member's ability to *be their best* and to perform in their roles can be swayed by conditions affecting their team, the organization, and your relationship. Ultimately, it is up to you as their leader to define, decode, and then address the six work-factors while simultaneously keeping in mind the three pillars.

WORK-FACTORS

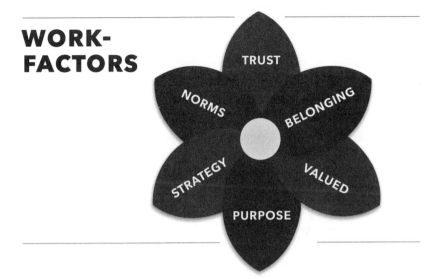

In this chapter, we will examine how each work-factor affects team members. To get us started, let me reintroduce and define them in the context of the Work-Life Bloom model:

✿ **Trust**: The demonstration of authentic and consistent behaviour such that people become an advocate for one another.

✿ **Belonging**: The accumulation of positive experiences that enables people to feel understood, represented, and safe.

✿ **Valued**: The belief that one is paid fairly, consistently recognized for one's efforts, and frequently appreciated for one's impacts.

✿ **Purpose**: The organization's intentions, beliefs, and actions are geared toward serving all stakeholders and advancing society for the greater good.

✿ **Strategy**: The intended direction and related priorities to ensure the short- and long-term focus of team members and the delivery of their objectives.

✿ **Norms**: The operating principles and guidelines that form the culture, providing clear expectations for team members regarding how to interact with one another.

The Canadian business legend Brian Scudamore knew the importance of these work-factors when he launched 1-800-GOT-JUNK in 1989. Scudamore consciously set out to create a company that put employees first. His intuition was that if team members felt a part of the big picture, they would deliver better results. Yes, even in the junk collection business. The success of his first venture was aided by the winning implementation and adoption of several work-factors that we will discuss in this chapter. His thinking is even embedded in the company's vision:[4]

> We know that leadership is the key to growth — leadership as a brand, as a team, and by our actions and values: Passion, Integrity, Professionalism, Empathy (PIPE).

When a customer service agent or an on-site junk removal specialist greets you on the telephone, you will find they are highly engaged, motivated, and enthusiastic. The franchise owners are of the same cast. Scudamore's attention to the work-factors and overall employee experience has helped him launch two additional home services over the years: WOW 1 DAY PAINTING and Shack Shine, a home cleaning service. He has since established a parent company, O2E Brands, where all three successful ventures sit. Annual revenues are more than US$500 million.

Your leadership is about how you nurture and support the work-life factors to help people *be their best* in every interaction. Indeed, as Ahrendts pointed out in a 2010 interview, "If the end result is that someone, somewhere winds up believing they can do something out of the ordinary, well, then you've really made it."[5]

Now let's stick our garden hoe into the work-factor I call *trust* and see what we need to alter so our leadership proficiency becomes something out of the ordinary.

Work-Factor No. 1: TRUST

TRUST

Demonstrating authentic and consistent behaviour such that people become an advocate for one another.

✿ ✿

I lost my trust in leadership. From there on out, I always felt that I had to weigh the consequences of the answer I wanted to give versus still being truthful but shaping it to what I knew they wanted to hear.
DIRECTOR, EDUCATION, USA, 65-74 YEARS

Although one of our values is 'openness,' actually expressing an honest opinion is more likely to get people into trouble. We learn to toe the line.
PROFESSIONAL, HIGH-TECH, U.K., 45-54 YEARS

✿ ✿

In act 1, scene 1 of William Shakespeare's *All's Well That Ends Well*, the Countess is engaged in a conversation with her son, Bertram, who is preparing to leave for Paris. She utters the following to her son:

Be thou blessed, Bertram, and succeed thy father
In manners as in shape. Thy blood and virtue
Contend for empire in thee, and thy goodness
Share with thy birthright. Love all, trust a few,
Do wrong to none. Be able for thine enemy
Rather in power than use, and keep thy friend
Under thy own life's key. Be checked for silence,
But never taxed for speech. What heaven more will,
That thee may furnish and my prayers pluck down,
Fall on thy head.[6]

The Countess provides Bertram—and you—with some critical leadership insights. In essence, she implores him to emulate his now-deceased noble father by letting the good in him guide his conduct. Value power as a leader, but don't abuse it. Respect your colleagues and their lives as much as you value your own life. Speak up, but don't talk to the point of being a nuisance to others. And above all, trust people, particularly those who reciprocate, but be very careful of trusting everyone.

Whether it's your conduct, degree of power, how and when you communicate, or your belief in others, trust might be the work-factor that makes or breaks a team member's faith in your leadership abilities. Similarly, if the organization or leaders from other units act in ways that do not demonstrate or reciprocate trust, you can be assured that team members will find it very difficult to bloom. Take, for example, a situation that played out at West Midlands Trains (WMT) in the U.K.

On April 21, 2021, a managing director of WMT sent an email to approximately 2,500 staff. Nothing out of the ordinary there, of course. In the email, he took the time to thank team members for their hard work over the previous year, which had everything to do with a stressful pandemic. The email read as follows:

> Dear All,
>
> Thank you for your hard work. We realise that a huge strain was placed upon a large number of our workforce as a result of COVID-19. This has not been easy for any of us and we would like to offer you a one-off payment to say thank you for all of your hard work over the past 12 months or so.
>
> Please visit the following link which has a personal message from <redacted> as well as the information of your one-off payment: Message From <redacted>.
>
> Again, many thanks for your hard work and I hope that this gift will inspire you to keep up the good work.[7]

How nice! Except it wasn't. Anyone who clicked the link in the email—under the well-intentioned auspice that they were about to collect a financial bonus for their hardship over the past year—was instead immediately sent another email. The return email read as follows:

I am writing to confirm that this was a test designed by our I.T. team to entice you to click the link and used both the promise of thanks and financial reward to try and convince you to provide your details. This test was purposefully designed to closely mimic the tactics that, sadly, are being used on a daily basis by expert criminal organisations to try to gain access to company data and systems.[8]

The entire act was a phishing simulation test designed by the firm's I.T. leadership team. The need for phishing tests inside an organization is essential. However, should leaders use false promises of financial rewards to conduct such tests, pandemic-related or otherwise? It is not only inhumane and appalling, but it also underscores how trust can get exploited by leaders. Furthermore, it points out with aplomb the message Shakespeare communicated through the Countess: conduct, power, communication, and your belief in others—when used in a positive manner—can help build a trusting workplace.

The General Secretary of TSSA—the independent trade union for the transport and travel trade industries across the U.K. and Ireland—Manuel Cortes responded publicly to the stunt:

This was a cynical and shocking stunt by West Midlands Trains, designed to trick employees who have been on the front line throughout this terrible pandemic — ensuring essential workers were able to travel. It's almost beyond belief that they chose to falsely offer a bonus to workers who have done so much in the fight against this virus. Moreover, having fraudulently held out the prospect of a payment to staff, WMT must now be as good as their word and stump up a bonus to each and every worker. In that way the company can begin to right a wrong which has needlessly caused so much hurt.[9]

The bonus payment was never issued. Soon after, the managing director responsible for the stunt exited West Midlands Trains. The entire episode made me think of something Albert Einstein wrote: "Whoever is careless with truth in small matters cannot be trusted in important affairs."[10]

If we want to learn about the importance of trust, the emperor penguin has much to teach us. I'm not kidding.

First off, emperor penguins inherently trust one another. They are on the same team from the get-go, demonstrating reciprocal trust as both part of a male-female duo and part of a waddle, the name for a colony of penguins. They stick with each other through thick and thin, good weather and bad. And there is a lot of bad weather in Antarctica.

The most impressive thing is what happens once their annual egg is laid. For the ensuing two months or so, Mom heads out to the frigid ocean waters to get herself a belly full of fish. Mom needs to feed itself and, in time, the soon-to-be newborn, so Mom jumps off the ice shelf, leaving Dad in charge. It is a beautiful demonstration of trust between the two penguins. "Don't worry, Mom, I got this," says the dad-to-be.

Dad tends to the egg with the rest of the dads in the ice cold conditions of the waddle, nurturing it through its incubation period. Dad does so by placing the egg gently between its feet, which have a unique brood pouch to protect the egg from the $-57°c$ temperatures that are so common in the Antarctic. All the dads of the colony work cooperatively to protect their eggs by huddling in a large circle—like a football huddle or rugby ruck—to block the chilling winds and icy elements. They take turns standing on the outer rim of the circle, rotating so they spend equal portions of time in the warmer centre. That act of community and team trust is lifesaving—and they know it must happen to survive and to incubate the eggs.

When Mom returns, the newborn chick (finally) begins to eat. The new parents enjoy a brief reacquaintance, and then Dad heads out into the ocean in search of a desperately needed meal. Dad hasn't eaten for weeks. Mom trusts Dad will return. It is an almost inconceivable example of a trusting partnership, how working together even over a distance can result in the safe arrival of a new product—in this case, an emperor penguin chick—all while they maintain the relationship between them. Add to that how the dads trust each other in those frigid circles, and you have quite an example of trust and collaboration.

Emperor penguins can teach us how important trust is when we work together to achieve a goal. Without trust, failure and a lack of blooming are far more likely to happen than success. As the author Nilofer Merchant writes in her book *The Power of Onlyness*, "Without trust, we're just a disparate group of individuals who happen to be gathered and hanging out in the same general place; the power of *us* is diminished."[11]

So, what did respondents from the Global Work-Life Assessment Survey have to say about trust?

FARMER'S ALMANAC: **TRUST**

Two significant points stand out among the findings from the global survey regarding trust. First, it is one of the most important work-life aspects of a person's being. Ninety-one percent of people throughout the world consider it an important or very important attribute. Second, leaders and organizations could be doing a much better job when it comes to creating a trusting workplace.

Does your current employer create a trusting workplace?

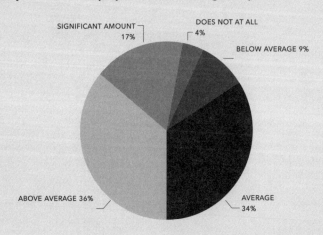

SIGNIFICANT AMOUNT
17%

DOES NOT AT ALL
4%

BELOW AVERAGE 9%

ABOVE AVERAGE 36%

AVERAGE
34%

How important is trust to you?

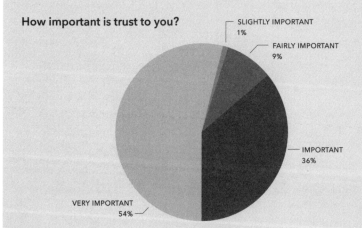

SLIGHTLY IMPORTANT
1%

FAIRLY IMPORTANT
9%

IMPORTANT
36%

VERY IMPORTANT
54%

A Canadian-based vice-president in the mining sector captures the essence and importance of trust very well: "The best leaders provide their reports with latitude and trust to do what they do best and do it in a way that brings out their best selves."

Yet, there is a large gap between leaders' views on trust and non-leaders' views on trust: 58 percent of leaders believe their organizations create a more than average trusting workplace, but only 44 percent of non-leaders believe the same. Not only is this a significant gap, but it also shows us that more than half of all individual contributors feel their workplace isn't a trustworthy one.

Does your current employer create a trusting workplace? (Leaders vs. non-leaders)

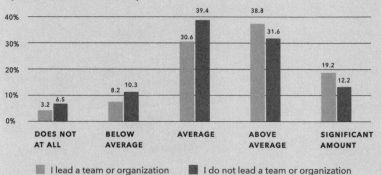

How important is trust to you? (Leaders vs. non-leaders)

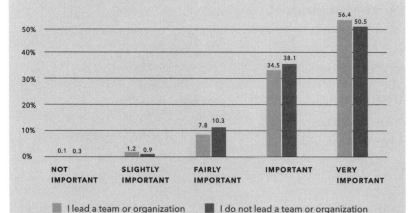

When the data is broken down by generation, a few other surprising revelations emerge. Sixty-two percent of Gen Z employees—those born between 1997 and 2012—believe the workplace is a trusting place, but only 55 percent of Gen X—born between 1966 and 1980—feel the same way. Gen X has the lowest perceptions of workplace trust of the four generations surveyed.

Another large generational gap exists when it comes to beliefs about the importance of trust. Whereas nearly 93 percent of Baby Boomers—those born between 1946 and 1965—believe trust is important or very important, only 83 percent of Gen Z feel the same way. And finally, one point of reference for Millennials, those born between 1981 and 1996. When asked whether the organization promotes trust in the workplace, Millennials scored the highest across the four generations: 71 percent agree or strongly agree that trust is encouraged across their workplace, which is an encouraging sign for this large cohort of current and future leaders.

How do you and your organization create an environment in which team members feel that the trust work-factor is blooming for them? Let's examine a few tactics and techniques you could consider. I promise not to force you to endure a −57°c temperature, but you may find yourself becoming a bit more penguin-like.

The Garden Tools of Trust

Many researchers have spent countless hours studying workplace trust. However, Paul Zak is one of my favourites, and he is perhaps my go-to person on the topic. Zak is the founding director of the Center for Neuroeconomics Studies and a professor of economics, psychology, and management at Claremont Graduate University. He has researched and studied trust for over two decades. One piece of his research points out how much of a positive influence a high-trust organization can have on an employee's well-being and overall performance. Zak writes:

Compared with people at low-trust companies, people at high-trust companies report 74 percent less stress, 106 percent more energy at work, 50 percent higher productivity, 13 percent fewer sick days,

76 percent more engagement, 29 percent more satisfaction with their lives, 40 percent less burnout.[12]

Ron Carucci, an author and a co-founder of consulting firm Navalent, believes our organizations have entered a "trust recession." After conducting a 15-year study with more than 3,200 leaders, Carucci concluded that the gap between a leader's intent and ability to trust is much wider than the average leader thinks. "What we learned in our research," he divulged to me, "is that the definition of honesty is truth, justice, and purpose. You have to say the right thing, do the right thing, and say and do the right thing for the right reason."[13] Trust and its twin sibling, honesty, are not one-time things. While an employee's ability to trust you as their leader is often earned, your demonstration of trustworthy behaviour must be exhibited at all times.

If trust is so crucial to a team member's health, productivity, and overall vibe—if it is fundamental to a team member's opportunity to bloom—it stands to reason that you should be doing something about it as their leader. I therefore recommend three seeds of trust to consider planting within the Work-Life Bloom model: authenticity, consistency, and advocacy.

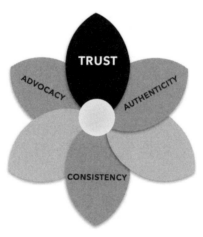

AUTHENTICITY

Much has been, and continues to be, written about being your authentic self and living your authentic life. While this is certainly important, when it comes to workplace trust, leaders must push aside the pop culture bumper stickers and Pinterest quotes and delve deeper. If your ambition is to inculcate a trusting environment in the workplace, leader authenticity is critical. But what is leader authenticity?

Perhaps the French philosopher and author Albert Camus said it best: "But above all, in order to be, never try to seem."[14] There is one you, not two or more. Pretending to be someone else is ill-advised behaviour for anyone who wants to create a trusting environment. You must *be*, not *seem* to be.

If you want people to see through you, go ahead and behave inauthentically. Pretend to be someone else. Lies are a perfect example—even small white ones. Sooner or later, those fabricated stories of your supposedly legendary leadership antics will catch up with you. And then it's on to some profoundly red-faced, embarrassing situations that will haunt you for the duration of your tenure as that team's leader.

Brian Williams lost his job as NBC's *Nightly News* anchor in 2015 for falsifying his in-the-field experience. Williams claimed that his helicopter had been hit by enemy fire while he was covering the Iraq War in 2003. A subsequent investigation found that he had made several other inaccurate statements about his past experience. Not only were viewers duped—which is a terrible place for them to be when the news anchor is to deliver *facts*—but so too were scores of NBC team members who once trusted Williams to lead and act truthfully.

You cannot *seem* to be trustworthy; you must *be* trustworthy. That is the essence of demonstrating authenticity in the workplace. For there to be trust in the workplace and your team, you must always act, lead, and interact with authenticity. Consider these additional techniques:

- **Recognize that transparency is not poisonous**: Don't hide from bad news but be forthcoming with the good stuff, for authenticity requires you to be unambiguous.

- **Be your real self**: Reveal to people that you are more than your work, that you have a life and are willing to share snippets from it.

- **Never be an ATNA**: As I noted in my first book, *Flat Army*, "ATNA—all talk, no action" is an easy way to be inauthentic with team members.

- **Encourage authenticity**: It's not enough for only you to be authentic. Reassure your team of their legitimacy as contributors and that their opinions are always welcome, no matter how much they differ from yours.

CONSISTENCY

During New Zealand's coronavirus-induced national lockdown in the spring of 2020, the country's health minister, Dr. David Clark, was demoted. He then resigned a few weeks later. His demotion came at the hands of then–Prime Minister Jacinda Ardern. His resignation was perhaps his mea culpa. Ultimately, he fell on his sword. But why?

Clark, who had a large say in the decision to send the country into lockdown, was caught ignoring the lockdown rules on several occasions. During the first weekend of the lockdown, for example, he was filmed driving his family 20 kilometres to a beach. The citizens of New Zealand were naturally up in arms about this transgression, but how did Clark's Ministry of Health team feel? How could they trust anything else he might say or do in the future?

It is easy to suggest that anyone acting with such inconsistent trustworthiness is a hypocrite. Clark certainly seems to fit the bill. Boris Johnson, the former U.K. prime minister, demonstrated similar hypocritical behaviours. After relentlessly defending his COVID-19 lockdown office partying, among other ethical lapses, he finally buckled when an entire caucus (and country) demanded that he, too, fall on his sword. As a result, an avalanche of colleagues lost both faith and trust in him as a leader. When you say one thing and do another, you're not only being inconsistent but also acting in the fastest way possible to eviscerate whatever trust existed in the first place.

"Do as I say, not as I do" is an idiom that is likely centuries old. However, it continues to run rampant within leadership ranks across the world. At least Clark did eventually say, "I've let the team down. I've been an idiot, and I understand why people will be angry with me."[15] Boris Johnson, however, seemed nonplussed about his inconsistent behaviour. When he resigned, he commented, "Them's the breaks."[16] Tell that to everyone on his team who had to begin a new job search because of their leader's behaviours.

"Do as I say, *and* as I do" is a far better mantra to adopt, presuming you are interested in creating a trustworthy environment, of course. Your team members need you to be consistent in what you say and do, and to see that consistency is applied in all of your individual and team-based interactions. There is no escaping the need to be consistent if you want trust to remain high among your team members. Consider these additional consistency tools and techniques:

- **Questions and questions:** Trust builds when you consistently ask team members to question the current or future state, as they will feel confident that their curiosities and inklings matter.

- **Verbal and non-verbal communication:** Using a dependable demeanour and tone when communicating—not wildly punishing or overly praising—creates a level of understanding of communication expectations with team members.

- **Remember that integrity is everything:** When you are constantly fair, unswervingly accountable, and reliably honest, you demonstrate consistent integrity in your leadership actions.

- **Walk the talk:** The opposite of ATNA informs us that we must always back up what we say with trust-building, consistent action. Otherwise, we might wind up like Boris Johnson and David Clark, or perhaps worse.

ADVOCACY

In its simplest form, demonstrating advocacy means arguing on behalf of, supporting, or defending another person, place, or thing. To ensure team members feel trusted in the workplace, you ought to become an advocate of trust itself. Advocacy is to organizations what oars are to a rowboat: a vital tool for progression.

Communicating about trust is not enough. You may believe trust is at the root of a great team or organizational culture, but beliefs merely keep the boat afloat. People, we need to cross the lake! Advocacy is, therefore, the enactment of trust. Becoming an action-oriented advocate of trust—rowing that boat across the lake—is a twofold process:

- Advocate for the team member.
- Advocate for trust itself.

Leaders will first earn their team members' trust by advocating for them. I don't mean faking it or advocating only once in a while either. (See the authenticity and consistency sections above.)

By both giving the benefit of the doubt and placing confidence in a team member, you are de facto advocating trust in them and, by extension, all team members. After all, people talk. So, advocating for one particular team member is a surefire way to see your trustworthy conduct spread across the team *as long as you are authentic and consistent with others.*

It really comes down to advocating for a team member's capabilities. Straightforward remarks like "Go for it," "Tell me more," "I like your idea," and "I trust you to do what's right" are easy ways to advocate for an individual and their aptitude. That sort of leadership action then helps build the trust employees seek. You may *believe* your trust in the team member is already prevalent, if not sky-high, but you must act—and thus advocate—with verbal and emotional assurance, doubling down on your confidence in the team member's capabilities if you genuinely want trust to be pervasive across the team. One comment from a South Korean director via the Global Work-Life Assessment Survey captures the point perfectly:

✿ ✿

I want them to trust what I create as much as possible.
DIRECTOR, BUSINESS, SOUTH KOREA, 25-34 YEARS

✿ ✿

Effective advocacy also requires trust to be openly discussed and endorsed. You cannot allow trust to rust, nor can you expect it to materialize out of thin air. Furthermore, it has to become a topic that is not considered taboo. A Paris-based high-tech manager identifies this requirement in the Global Work-Life Assessment Survey:

✿ ✿

My manager always pushes me to make my own decisions even if I might fail. She puts her trust in me and pushes me to get through my ideas and try to make it work.
MANAGER, HIGH-TECH, FRANCE, 18-24 YEARS

✿ ✿

The point about "pushing" is essential. A push can become an opportunity to publicly advocate your conviction about the importance of trust. When the push is clear to the team members, it is the difference between a belief and an action. Remember, belief is critical, but action is a necessary and required follow-up. To push, you openly have conversations highlighting your trust in both individuals and the team as a whole. The beauty of the word "push" in advocating for trust is that it represents equal parts belief and action. The resulting action—that is, the team members either succeeded or failed at their entrusted task—is nearly immaterial. Of course, you want the team to succeed, but being able to assess a failure while acknowledging the learning that came from it will entrench the trust of your team members even deeper. Similarly, recognizing the work of team members who succeed in their task will also help forge strong trust ties.

Push yourself to become unreserved and frank about your advocating for a trusting workplace and team environment. It's how you make it across the lake.

Work-Factor No. 2: BELONGING

BELONGING

The accumulation of positive experiences that enables people to feel understood, represented, and safe.

✿ ✿

I felt like I didn't belong when I first started. Everyone would get along, but I just didn't fit in. I then started to feel welcomed as the days and weeks went on. It's a wonderful workplace where me and my colleagues can collaborate on ideas and come to an understanding.
SUPPORT PERSONNEL, FOOD SERVICES, USA, 18-24 YEARS

✿ ✿

Feeling welcome is something many employees crave. Being open to what makes up a person's character—even if you disagree with their lifestyle choices—goes a long way to helping that person feel understood, represented, and safe.

Stereotyping people based on their looks and what they choose to follow, whether it is beliefs or fashions, is an act of leadership nonsense. A team member who has two arms full of tattoos is not by default a thug. Likewise, somebody's skin colour, gender, or ethnicity should not feature in a leadership judgment card.

A sense of belonging among team members is something that can truly enable great teamwork. But it's also fundamental if you want to establish a more humane relationship between you and your team members. Fostering a sense of belonging makes you a more influential and open-minded leader who accepts team members for who they are. Many employees will ultimately feel happier at work—wherever that is—if they feel like they belong. If people feel like they do not belong or are not good enough, it's hard to be happy and productive—and quite challenging to bloom.

In 2016 the *Guardian* published an opinion piece by an anonymous middle-aged parent titled "Workplace loneliness is a real problem. For 45 hours a week I feel isolated."[17] It prompted more than 800 responses from people who wanted to share their experiences of feeling left out at work. After describing an average morning, helping their kids get breakfast and ready for school, the writer explains why they went back to bed, staring at the ceiling for an additional hour, instead of going to work.

> I did it because I am lonely at work, and staring at the ceiling for an hour was about as much as I could face. I am a different generation to my immediate colleagues, and I'm their manager. They don't want to hear about my troubles; they don't want me being the embarrassing old bloke inveigling my way into their 6pm drinks. And I'm shy and introverted, too . . . so the idea of trying to forge new relationships with people is fraught with horror, even if I know it would be for my own good.

The writer's point is clear-cut: while they know fitting in at work is essential, they do not feel a sense of belonging. This troubling fact underscores the work-factor's importance. It all starts with the leader, who should be signalling that everyone is welcome. And if issues of isolation or loneliness are prevalent, a leader who cares will do something about them. Action like this makes the workplace more inviting while also giving people a greater chance to bloom.

When we're looking for an example of how to create a sense of belonging with others, we need look no further than wolves. (It may seem like

I'm moonlighting as a *National Geographic* contributor, but I'm not. The animal kingdom simply has so many relevant examples of teamwork that it's difficult not to make the most of them.) What can we learn from these animals about the work-factor *belonging*? Wolves help us see the power of community—of feeling understood, represented, and safe—and how you can build it in your team.

Wolves are, first and foremost, complex, brilliant creatures. They are playful, affectionate, intelligent, and, most importantly, devoted to their team. Only a few other species display these characteristics. Like gorillas, dolphins, elephants, orcas, and, yes, emperor penguins, wolves raise their young in family units. That unit provides a sense of community at every stage of a wolf's life.

A wolf's family unit is called a "pack." A wolf pack is an amazingly intricate social structure of parents, children, siblings, uncles, aunts, and sporadic transients from other packs, and its dynamics change at various times. For example, young adults start to assert themselves when older wolves need to be cared for. The pack also makes it possible for its members to form numerous special emotional bonds. It becomes a cornerstone of wolves' cooperative living model. A shared bond is formed by all wolves living in the team. It's analogous to how your team or organization might operate.

Of course, a work team is not a pack of wolves but a group of people with a common purpose who toil together to achieve a set of stated goals. This collaboration is possible because they share a bond that urges them to help and support one another in the face of adversity. Ideally, the team becomes a unit where knowledge transfer, communication, and collaboration occur. The pack structure of wolves facilitates similar actions.

When team members feel a sense of belonging at work, they are likelier to stay with the company. When they feel that they fit in, they will make sacrifices for the greater good of their team and organization. I suppose the bigger question for you to answer is: Are you crafting a wolf pack of belongingness? Or are you accepting that people on your team might feel isolated for 40 or 50 hours a week?

Social belonging is a basic human need hardwired into our DNA.[18] Nevertheless, according to 2020 research conducted by Cigna, over 60 percent of working Americans report feeling lonely at work.[19] Moreover, while firms in the USA spend close to US$8 billion annually on diversity, inclusion, and belonging training,[20] according to 2022 McKinsey & Company research, over 50 percent of people do not feel a sense of belonging at work.[21]

Feeling isolated and lonely exacerbates a sense of not belonging. Dr. Robert Waldinger, whom you met in the previous chapter, agrees. In a 2018 interview, he said, "Loneliness kills. It's as powerful as smoking or alcoholism."[22] Feeling excluded is a profoundly human issue, which is why the repercussions are so severe. Unfortunately, its root causes are difficult to eradicate from even the healthiest of workplaces. Angela Theisen of the Mayo Clinic, for example, points out that depression and anxiety are common mental health conditions associated with a sense of not belonging. "These conditions can lead to social behaviors that interfere with a person's ability to connect to others, creating a cycle of events that further weakens a sense of belonging," she writes.[23]

Susie Lee, senior vice-president of Global Business Transformation and executive officer for Diversity, Inclusion, and Belonging at software company Degreed, shares her insights into how to build a workplace that fosters belonging:

[It] starts with making clear to the entire organization — and repeating the message often — that belonging is an essential value. Through onboarding, all-staff meetings, corporate retreats, messages from executives, and other means of communication, explain what belonging is and why it matters. Some organizations build culture playbooks that lay out their values in great detail and discuss these values at town hall meetings. The more you talk about belonging, the more aware your staff will be that you're committed to helping them feel it.[24]

In other words, Lee is recommending that you create a wolf pack of belonging. There are certainly clear business benefits to doing so.

Colleen Bordeaux, a senior manager in Deloitte Consulting LLP's Human Capital practice, is one of the world's top researchers in the area of belonging in organizations. She co-leads Deloitte's Workforce Experience by Design practice. One of Bordeaux's 2021 studies highlights the value of improving your belonging factor in the organization.[25] She and her team found that 73 percent of leaders indicated that fostering a sense of belonging is crucial to the success of their organization, and 93 percent that possessing a sense of belonging improves organizational performance. Bordeaux and her team's research further highlighted the positive results of a belonging culture: "Belonging can lead to a 56 percent increase in job performance, a 50 percent reduction in turnover risk, a 167 percent increase in employer net promoter score, 2x more employee raises, 18x more employee promotions, and a 75 percent decrease in sick days."

If a team member's sense of belonging is crucial to their health and productivity and delivers solid business results, it stands to reason that you should be taking action to address it. It's time to build your wolf pack. But before we learn how to do that, let's find out how people who participated in my global survey view belonging.

FARMER'S ALMANAC: **BELONGING**

The Global Work-Life Assessment Survey revealed a thought-provoking distinction between Gen Z and the three other generational cohorts, Millennials, Gen X, and Baby Boomers. While 75 percent of the latter generations believed that fitting in at work was important or very important, only two-thirds of Gen Z felt the same way.

How important is it to you to fit in at work?

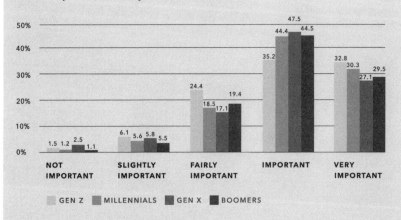

While the difference between Gen Z and the other three generations may seem small or minor, you ought to pay attention to this potentially adverse trend. If your youngest cohort of team members doesn't care about fitting in at work—and cares less and less as time goes on—there is an eventual risk of increased detachment from the workplace and from their older and more experienced team members.

The same scenario might also apply to the next generation, Gen Alpha. These individuals, born between 2010 and 2024, will begin to join the workforce around 2028. Gen Z's and Gen Alpha's apparent ambivalence about belonging could become detrimental in terms of retention, collaboration, performance, engagement, and overall organizational culture in future years.

Another question from the survey—do you feel as though your current employer creates a place of belonging?—lets us dig deeper into this phenomenon. Only 45 percent of all global employees believe their employers create a place of belonging. While that may be shocking, if not disappointing, it becomes more troubling when you remove people in leadership positions from the analysis. For team members who do not lead teams, a paltry 35 percent of them consider their employer as one that provides above average or significant help to create a place of belonging at work.

Does your current employer create a place of belonging?
(All team members)

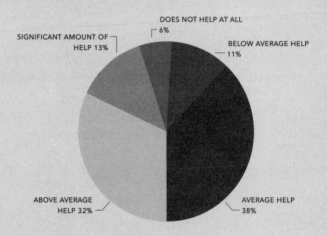

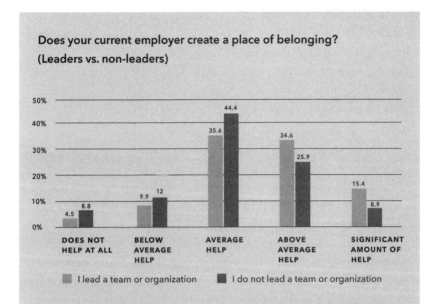

**Does your current employer create a place of belonging?
(Leaders vs. non-leaders)**

Overwhelmingly, people want to fit in at work. That's the good news. However, the belongingness chasm between what people want and what is actually happening inside the workplace is rather grim. While there may be a few vegetables beginning to emerge in the garden box, the soil itself was already contaminated and there is ultimately a low probability of full blooming to occur. The *belonging* work-factor is in need of some serious digging.

The Garden Tools of Belonging

A top-level executive from Sydney, Australia, who works in the not-for-profit sector provides a clear snapshot of the importance of workplace belongingness and the spin-off positive effects when belongingness is enacted.

✿ ✿

I once had an employer that had a strong view about tattoos and ascribed certain personality traits to people with tattoos. I had one myself that she did not know about, and for a brief time, I was worried that I, too, would be judged by her in that way. Or it would prevent me from advancing. I ended up showing her my tattoo and asked if any of the attributes she described applied to me, which she said did not. So, we had a discussion about judging a book by its cover and the importance of people feeling safe to be who they are. This example made me a better manager, and one who openly encourages people to bring their whole selves to work.

EXECUTIVE, NON-PROFIT, AUSTRALIA, 45-54 YEARS

✿ ✿

Imagine being a part of a conversation with your boss whose view on tattoos is so oppositional that you are worried about your chances of promotion or even keeping your current job. Now, extend that to other facets of your work-life relationship. What if your boss had similarly oppositional views about other features that defined you, such as your skin colour, faith, sexual identity, or mobility requirements? It would be downright awful, and your sense of belonging, not to mention psychological safety, would understandably plummet.

The experience of belonging is an outcome of how people feel. It's what team members experience as they circumnavigate their days. Belonging results in an all-pervading personal impression of you, your team, your organization, and society at large. Remember the Netflix example from Chapter II? Belonging matters—a lot.

In addition to the hallmark requirements of diversity, inclusion, and equity, the achievement of belonging is crucially aided by whether people feel understood, represented, and safe. Please note, there is no *or* in that previous sentence. All three are required if team members are to feel that they fit in and thus belong at work and in life.

UNDERSTOOD

When a team member is understood, they don't feel like an alien at work. They are not an outsider; instead, they feel they are an insider. They're "one of us" or, perhaps, "one of the gardeners."

Team members may stroll into work looking, sounding, or acting different than you, but those differences should be recognized as making the team member who they are rather than resulting in estrangement. To be understood is to be appreciated for one's distinctiveness. That is what helps people feel like they belong. It also requires leaders to take proactive stances to understand their team members better.

I once took a chance and asked a Muslim team member if I might join them at Friday prayers. Being Catholic, I've been to my fair share of masses over the years. I've also been to several synagogues with Jewish friends and peers for various services. But I wanted to better appreciate and understand the Muslim faith. Perhaps Friday prayers would be one way to help me do that. "It would be my honour," said my team member. "We'll go next Friday."

Off we went. As with any religious service, Friday prayers has a set of strict rules, actions, and recitations. I did not want to breach protocol in any way, so I stood quietly at the back of the mosque and simply observed. I don't speak or understand Arabic, but what I witnessed provided me with a whole new level of comprehension about Islam. The experience opened both my eyes and my heart. I didn't use it to score points with that team member. I simply wanted to fill a gaping hole in my understanding about Muslim customs, like Friday prayers.

My request to accompany my team member to Friday prayers helped them feel cared for. I don't know for certain if it led to more feelings of belonging, but I felt it couldn't hurt. And while it was a small gesture, I learned later on that it had a significant positive impact on this individual's ability to feel connected to me and the broader team. That itself is the point of the belonging work-factor.

Laszlo Bock, a former Google senior vice-president of People Operations, took a unique yet proactive approach to help him understand his direct reports. During their scheduled one-on-one meetings, he would consistently ask them three questions:[26]

1. What is one thing that I currently do that you'd like me to continue to do?

2. What is one thing I don't currently do frequently enough that you think I should do more often?

3. What can I do to make you more effective?

Open-ended yet specific questions like these create the chance for a team member to feel like they matter because of the empathy being demonstrated by the leader. Ultimately, that empathy opens up connection and a line of understanding.

As a leader, you must remember that not everyone can squeeze into one common definition of the term "team member." After all, we're humans, and each of us is unique. Thus, to better understand people, you must appreciate and endorse their individuality. No team should be built by a bunch of clones—as any fan of *Star Wars* will attest.

Consider using these two tools to help team members feel understood at work:

- **An annual understanding check-up**: As your new operating year begins, ask your team members to outline their current and desired state of belonging by answering the following questions:

    - What experiences from last year helped to make you feel like you belonged on our team/in the organization?

    - What experiences from last year made you feel like you didn't fit in?

    - What changes would you like to see this coming year—if any—so you fit in better with others and with me as your leader?

- **The vent**: To better understand how a team member may be feeling when it comes to a sense of belonging, on at least a quarterly basis, you should give them an opportunity to vent about any situations where they felt as though they did not fit in, be it with you, the team, or elsewhere. But again, your job is to listen and to understand. Don't be reactive or defensive. Validate and take note. If you catch yourself unnecessarily rebutting, employ the WAIT acronym: Why Am I Talking? Even if you see the circumstances differently than the team member does, their *feelings* about the situation are unique to them, and you must accept them without judgment.

REPRESENTED

When individuals see themselves represented within their team or organization, there is one less belonging barrier to overcome. If a team member feels represented at work—be it in terms of gender, race, ethnicity, or age, among other attributes—there is a greater chance that they will feel like they fit in. Easier said than done, of course. And how is this different from diversity, inclusion, and equity? Before we tackle that point and provide suggestions on the *how*, let's look at *why* feeling represented is so important and what exactly it means.

To be represented at work is to feel like you matter and that everyone's differences are appreciated. When a leader and organization respect beliefs, backgrounds, traits, and lifestyles, team members are more likely to feel seen and heard. When they feel included, seen, heard, and thus represented, there is less likelihood of mental or emotional anguish that could impact performance, relations, well-being, and so on. One research study noted that when leaders adequately and genuinely create a framework for team members to feel represented, those team members' stress levels decline and their overall emotional and physical well-being increases.[27]

A team member's feelings about being represented are related but tangential to your organization's diversity, equity, and inclusion (DEI) practices. While the latter are vital, the central point is for leaders to constantly pay attention to and endorse people's differences. How can you as a leader accomplish that?

For example, if you are a white, middle-aged, U.S.-based leader, you cannot change that fact. What you can change, however, are your methods of representation. For example, what illustrations do you use in public meetings or presentations? What about your one-on-one meetings? Are you constantly detailing situations that involve white, middle-aged Americans? If so, why not use examples that encompass Black, Indigenous, and People of Colour (BIPOC)? What about using examples from different countries? (I hear Canada is pretty cool.)

When brainstorming, ideating, or whiteboarding with the team, you may want to examine your frame of reference. Try to put yourself in someone else's shoes while going through any given exercise. For example, if you are heterosexual, male, non-disabled, and Gen X, are you able to publicly consider what it's like to have a different sexuality or gender, to use a wheelchair, and to belong to Gen Z? When you as a leader represent the makeup of people, and not only yourself, it can help the team see that you genuinely care about differentiation.

I'd like you to consider using this simple phrase going forward:

Parity is clarity.

Parity in this sense is the state of being or feeling represented. When your stories, explanations, highlights, questions, and other day-to-day interactions are unequal—when they emanate from one dimension only—there is less chance for team members to feel like they belong. Conversely, when your narratives involve consistently using diverse examples, you are positively articulating a representative culture of the people you serve. "Parity is clarity" will serve as a reminder to operate publicly with equivalence.

SAFE

Harvard Business School's Amy C. Edmondson—the Novartis Professor of Leadership and Management—has studied psychological safety since the late 1990s. If there is a pre-eminent expert on psychological safety in the organization, it's Edmondson.

So, what is psychological safety? According to Edmondson, it is the "shared belief held by members of a team that the team is safe for interpersonal risk-taking." [28] Further, she asserts that safety creates "a sense of confidence that the team will not embarrass, reject, or punish someone for speaking up." [29]

If you want team members to feel like they belong, they must feel safe to be themselves and deploy their voices freely. It is my opinion that you, as the leader, must let team members know that they are understood and represented. Feeling safe to speak up is fundamental to achieving belongingness.

Here are a couple of quotes from the Global Work-Life Assessment Survey that effectively convey my point:

My manager and her manager are often mean. Gossiping to me (or anyone) about others they're frustrated with. Seemingly never telling the person directly. So, I know if they're talking to me about other people, they're also talking to other people about me. It leaves me feeling unsafe and guarded. I don't relax around them.

MANAGER, GOVERNMENT/MILITARY, CANADA, 45-54 YEARS

My current manager is fair and committed to creating a safe workspace for all, ensuring there is no favouritism and that everyone is held accountable for their own words and actions.

PROFESSIONAL, HEALTHCARE/MEDICAL, AUSTRALIA, 25-34 YEARS

While the Australian team member points out how fair and committed their manager is while fostering a safe workplace, the Canadian is obviously discouraged and cautious and feels unsafe at work. Which employee is likely to be the more productive and engaged, and more likely to feel like they belong or fit in? I'm Canadian, but I'm going with the Aussie on this one.

Edmondson's excellent book *The Fearless Organization: Creating Psychological Safety in the Workplace for Learning, Innovation, and Growth*[30] will help you become fully versed on all things psychological safety-related. For our current purposes, however, there are three *safe* actions you should consider taking:

· **Flatten the hierarchy**: A large percentage of organizations are arranged by hierarchical job titles, but for belonging to occur, you must make the hierarchy as invisible as possible. Flattening the hierarchy means making yourself (and potentially other leaders in the organization) more accessible. This creates a balance whereby job titles, paygrades, or office locations don't stand in the way of team members feeling safe to speak the truth.

- **Issue open invitations to offer feedback**: A safe workplace is one where the leader (ahem, you!) urges team members to offer opinions, feedback, and ideas to improve. Invite them to submit constructive criticism or positive comments on anything and everything going on in the team or organization. Think of it as an ongoing and open opportunity for team members to be transparent (and safe) about what they think and feel.

- **Long to be wrong**: No one likes to be wrong, but it's so much worse if no team member feels safe at work because they get reprimanded for screwing up. How can anyone feel safe if you berate them for an error? If something goes awry or a mistake is made, remember that anything and everything has the opportunity to become a learning moment. As often as you can, find the positive in the negative and embrace it.

Work-Factor No. 3: VALUED

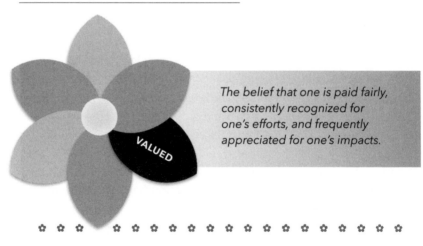

The belief that one is paid fairly, consistently recognized for one's efforts, and frequently appreciated for one's impacts.

Make me feel more valued and appreciated. Sometimes it's important to say thank you to your staff. These are the basics, but my manager never does this.

PROFESSIONAL, HEALTHCARE/MEDICAL, U.K., 35-44 YEARS

Michelle Obama delivered a speech at the Democratic National Convention on September 4, 2012, where, in part, she touched on their family's journey before becoming the presidential family.[31] She said:

> We learned about dignity and decency — that how hard you work matters more than how much you make . . . that helping others means more than just getting ahead of yourself. We learned about honesty and integrity — that the truth matters, that you don't take shortcuts or play by your own rules, and success doesn't count unless you earn it fair and square. We learned about gratitude and humility — that so many people had a hand in our success, from the teachers who inspired us to the janitors who kept our school clean . . . and we were taught to value everyone's contribution and treat everyone with respect. Those are the values Barack and I — and so many of you — are trying to pass on to our own children. That's who we are.

What is Obama really getting at in this short passage? Her words remind people about honesty, gratitude, decency, humility, and respect, of course, but she also points out how many others played a part in their family's success. Obama urges all of us to fully appreciate and acknowledge how other people have contributed to our lives.

Obama sublimely articulates the crux of the next Work-Life Bloom work-factor in just a few words. When we feel *valued*, we have a much greater chance to bloom. But never forget, it is your utmost duty as a leader to ensure your team members feel valued by *you*. So, here is a question for you to ponder:

What are you doing in your role as a leader to make others feel valued?

Unless your job requires constant interaction with the team, it's easy to be oblivious or blind to your team members' contributions. If you do not forge bonds with your team, it becomes difficult to recognize their efforts or appreciate their impact. It also becomes challenging to know if they feel fairly compensated for their contributions. And if they're not feeling appreciated regularly, team members will find it challenging to *be their best.*

Learning how to engage with your team members—making them feel valued—can become the work-factor that makes a difference in how appreciated people feel about their work.

A U.S. administrative support team member in the construction industry captures this point perfectly in the Global Work-Life Assessment Survey: "In my current job, the CEO regularly checks up personally on each employee. That makes us feel valued."

For a costly example of leaders mismanaging this aspect of their duties, look no further than the following bit of alt-rock lore.

Wilco, the Chicago-based alternative rock band, was happily recording their fourth album with Reprise Records, a subsidiary of Warner Brothers Records. Commercially, their albums had not lived up to expectations set after the mild breakout the band had experienced with their sophomore effort. Still, they were forging on. Then, after the better part of a year making their new album, their five-year label rounded on them: the band and their latest effort weren't good enough. Talk about not feeling valued.

The album Wilco had been working on, *Yankee Hotel Foxtrot*, is frequently described in terms such as "legendary." As per their recording contract, Reprise Records paid for the album to be made, including producers, studio time, and post-recording editing. When the final product was submitted to executives at the label, they sent it back to the band with a list of demands for changes. They insisted that the album was not good enough, not poppy enough for audiences of the day.

In an interview with *Rolling Stone* magazine, band leader Jeff Tweedy said, "I felt incredulous. I sincerely believed that this was the most contemporary and accessible record that we had ever made and that it was more likely to be understood and heard by people today than a lot of our other records."[32]

Reprise Records would not budge. Wilco was not feeling valued by their label. After all, the contract dictated that an album was to be recorded. There was no requirement for a particular genre or style. The stalemate ended with Reprise dropping the band from the label but keeping the rights to the album.

Reprise not only pushed Wilco out of its contract but, in its infinite corporate wisdom, also allowed the band to take the recordings of *Yankee Hotel Foxtrot*—even though the record company owned the masters and could have required the band to pay for the privilege of using them. Wilco eventually settled on a two-album deal with a new label, Nonesuch Records, ironically a member of the Warner Brothers Records empire, just like Reprise.

That's right. The parent company, Warner Brothers Records, paid for *Yankee Hotel Foxtrot* twice because the executives at Reprise Records no longer valued Wilco. When the album was finally released, it went on to achieve certified Gold status, more than doubling the sales of Wilco's previous album and landing at No. 13 on the U.S. Billboard 200.

To cement the point of not feeling valued, Tweedy said in that same *Rolling Stone* interview, "They [Reprise Records] ushered us out the back door with an efficiency in the legal department that you would never see if you were on the other end of things. It took longer to finish a contract with Nonesuch [new label] than to finish the contract leaving Reprise."

It's critical to remember that many great ideas are not necessarily great at first glance but, like *Yankee Hotel Foxtrot*, could be impactful over time. Your team members might not create something as noteworthy as a best-selling album, but if you value them, you appreciate and recognize their contributions and ideas. You value their input, extra effort, and desire for open conversations. No matter what people do at your organization, you must believe that they have something to contribute, and therefore they must be valued.

It is pretty clear that Nestlé USA employees feel valued. In a company-wide survey conducted in February 2022, 84 percent of employees said they feel actively encouraged to collaborate with other teams. Another 82 percent said they feel comfortable sharing new ideas with the company leadership. And remarkably, 92 percent said they feel valued at work because of their differences.[33]

Molly Fogarty is head of Corporate & Government Affairs and Sustainability at Nestlé USA. In a 2022 column explaining the organization's application of diversity, equity, inclusion, belonging, and sustainability to feel valued, Fogarty wrote, "Essential to Nestlé's progress is our commitment to a culture of diversity, equity, and inclusion. Bringing together new voices is a vital part of innovating for change . . . This has been a conscious effort at Nestlé, where we've embraced a culture of innovation that invites employees across the entire company to take risks and make real change — from the leadership team, to our manufacturing experts, to those just starting out in their careers."[34]

According to the American Psychological Association's (APA) 2021 Work and Well-Being Survey, a sense of value at work is associated with improved physical and mental health and higher engagement, satisfaction, and motivation levels.[35] The survey also found that employees who are valued at work are likelier to report having a strong sense of purpose and meaning in their lives. (Unsurprisingly, purpose and meaning are two of the *Work-Life Bloom* factors we will examine.) In turn, people who feel valued are likely to experience lower depression, anxiety, and stress levels.

Back at Nestlé, the company introduced an internal crowdsourcing program, Open Channel, to gather ideas from across the organization. They viewed the initiative as a way to not only amass new thinking but also publicly recognize their people.

Those who contribute are acknowledged, and those whose ideas are assessed as stellar receive funding from the company to further their thinking. The theme of Nestlé's first-ever Open Channel innovation challenge in 2021 was investing in and thus inventing new sustainable practices. The firm received more than 1,000 new sustainability ideas from their call to employees. Multiple ideas were funded. That's a whole lot of feeling valued going on at the company.

Nestlé's Open Channel is only one example of how, when a connection can be made between business imperatives, recognition, and employees' desire to feel valued, team members can bloom and the organization benefit.

In the 2012 speech by Michelle Obama I mentioned earlier, she also said, "When you've worked hard, and done well, and walked through that doorway of opportunity . . . you do not slam it shut behind you . . . you reach back, and you give other folks the same chances that helped you succeed."

You are a leader of others. To help your team members bloom and feel valued, appreciate their contributions.

FARMER'S ALMANAC: **VALUED**

I designed the Global Work-Life Assessment Survey such that the data might uncover potential fundamental attribution errors, particularly among leaders. In its simplest definition, "fundamental attribution error" occurs when you're always cutting yourself a break while simultaneously holding others fully accountable for their actions. For example, you might think everyone on the road, whether they're driving or cycling, is a danger to everyone around them, and then you blow a stop sign and hit a cyclist. That's fundamental attribution error in a nutshell. (Also, please don't do this. I'm an avid road cyclist. I really don't want to get hit.)

While the need to feel valued at work is almost universally important across all job types, geographies, and ages, there is a clear demarcation between employees wanting to feel valued and leaders helping to make that happen. When I asked the survey participants whether their current employer helped them to feel valued at work, an argument can be made for fundamental attribution error. In sum, the more senior your role in the organization, the more valued you feel. Yet, the more senior you are, the less your team members believe you create an environment where they feel valued. Look at the results below.

Does your current employer help you to feel valued at work?

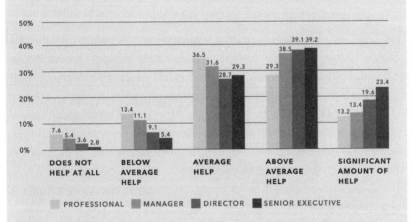

Almost 60 percent of non-leader professionals do not feel their current employer helps them feel valued. Approximately the same percentage of professionals in leadership roles *do* feel that their employer assists their sense of feeling valued in the workplace. Review the leader data below:

• 52 percent of managers believe their employer helps them to feel valued.

- 59 percent of directors believe their employer helps them to feel valued.

- 63 percent of senior executives believe their employer helps them to feel valued.

Compare those responses with the responses from people in non-leader roles:

- 39 percent of administrative/support personnel believe their employer helps them to feel valued.

- 42 percent of individual contributors (professionals/non-leaders) believe their employer helps them to feel valued.

What tactics can leaders use to help more people on their team feel valued? Let's enter the shed and see what garden tools we can use.

The Garden Tools of Feeling Valued

When employees feel valued, they're more likely to report better mental health and physical wellness, as well as higher levels of satisfaction, motivation, and overall workplace engagement compared with employees who don't feel valued by their employers. The American Psychological Association (APA), which conducts an annual Stress in America survey, has been pointing this out since 2007.[36] It's fair to say there is a direct correlation between feeling valued and one's level of stress. The more someone feels valued, the less stress they have to endure. You don't need a doctorate in gardening to understand that one.

If you want your team members to feel valued, there are three critical tactics to adopt. First, adopt a "gratitude attitude." By this I mean that you should regularly appreciate and recognize your team members. Second, acknowledge extra effort. When you apply an "extra effort nod," you call out the contributions of a particular team member for going above and beyond. And third, think about how you reward employees financially. It's one thing to talk a good game about fair wages, but what are you doing to concretely change your wage strategy? Do you "say the pay"? These three tactics are your value-sowing garden tools.

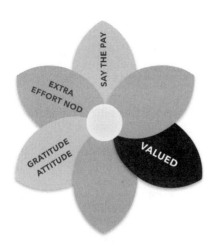

GRATITUDE ATTITUDE

Let me ask you a simple question: Do you constantly and consistently appreciate and recognize your team members? If the answer is yes—and let's be honest, there is hardly a reason for it to be no—how do you do it? How does your demonstrable, action-oriented gratitude attitude manifest?

The following responses from the Global Work-Life Assessment Survey illustrate the importance of being on the receiving end of gratitude, regardless of your seniority:

✿ ✿

I was told by my manager that I was one of the best team leaders on the site, and I felt incredibly valued.

PROFESSIONAL, FOOD SERVICES, U.K., 45-54 YEARS

My leader appreciates my point of view and experience and calls that out often. That recognition empowers me to do the best job I can for myself and the company. It is not all about the money.

MANAGER, GOVERNMENT/MILITARY, CANADA, 55-64 YEARS

It would be nice to feel more like my opinions were valued and taken seriously.

SENIOR VICE-PRESIDENT, MANUFACTURING, CANADA, 55-64 YEARS

✿ ✿

The first two comments are from individuals who are appreciated and recognized by their leader. The resulting impact is positive affirmation. You can almost picture two team members—one in the U.K. and the other in Canada—who have a bounce in their step because of how valued they feel by their boss, a leader who demonstrates a "gratitude attitude." The final comment illustrates the opposite end of the spectrum. Let's call it "unappreciation frustration." If you do not appreciate or recognize your team members, a host of issues are likely to unfold.

Groundbreaking gratitude research conducted by O. C. Tanner[37] in 2019 pointed out that

- 79 percent of employees who quit their jobs cited a lack of appreciation as a key reason for leaving, and

- 65 percent of North Americans reported that they hadn't been recognized by their boss even once in the previous year.

A "gratitude attitude" is rooted in two key leadership actions: appreciate and recognize. I have long been guided by the work of David Sturt, Todd Nordstrom, Kevin Ames, and Gary Beckstrand in their 2017 book *Appreciate* in my efforts to define these two important techniques:[38]

- **Appreciate**: To apply wisdom, sound judgment, and keen insight in recognizing the worth of someone. It is an emotion.

- **Recognize**: To use words to express gratitude. It fuels the feeling of being appreciated.

To appreciate a team member is to identify their worth and bolster their self-worth. If you want to appreciate a team member, call out what they did correctly, how they helped a situation, or when they performed well. To recognize someone is to pass along your thankfulness and to put into words—or even through a small gift, monetary or otherwise—why you are grateful for a team member's contribution. You could, for example, take someone out for a coffee and thank them over those 45 minutes for how they dealt with an over-the-top client.

In sum, deploying a "gratitude attitude" means regularly appreciating and recognizing your team members. It's one step in the right direction of helping people feel valued at work.

EXTRA EFFORT NOD

There is hardly a knowledge worker job on the planet where extra effort isn't required. Whether it's staying late, cracking open a laptop at night, responding to a text or email on the weekend, or working through lunch to address an urgent customer demand, extra effort is as common as the weekly run for groceries. We all do it.

First, let's call out the elephant in the room: extra effort happens. Don't even try to suggest it doesn't. It may not occur every day, but it definitely has its time in the spotlight. However, if you want a team member to feel valued, pinch the tactics from a "gratitude attitude" and appreciate and recognize the extra effort they demonstrate. As their leader, you owe them an "extra effort nod." Read the following anecdotal comment from the Global Work-Life Assessment Survey for a key insight:

Despite exceeding all departmental goals and delivering beyond for clients, management was not willing to recognize my contributions with anything of actual value (compensation, time off, etc.). It was deflating, demoralizing, and left me wondering what the point of my effort was, and thus I should not work as hard as I typically do.

VICE-PRESIDENT, CONSULTING, USA, 25-34 YEARS

This U.S.-based vice-president was exceeding and delivering beyond their stated goals—the very definition of "extra effort"—but they were not being appreciated for it. The failure to provide an "extra effort nod" resulted in a senior leader not only feeling disengaged but also questioning whether to go above and beyond the call of duty the next time a challenging or urgent situation arises. Other repercussions are likely to make themselves known at some point as well.

Sales teams are a good source of inspiration for anyone seeking to learn how to express an "extra effort nod." Many of them already employ excellent such recognition tactics. It's one thing to meet your annual sales quota target; it's quite another to exceed it by 20 percent or more. How do organizations appreciate a sales account executive when they deliver extra effort? By plying them with special recognition packages such as holiday trips, tailored outfits, bonus vacation days, car allowances, or private nights with celebrity chefs.

Not every organization or team is in the financial position to offer such luxurious gifts as "extra effort nods," of course. But the same principles can be applied. If one of your team members has gone out of their way to carry out some action, deliverable, or task that is clearly above and beyond their job description, it is incumbent upon you to recognize their effort. Your recognition will go a long way toward making that individual feel valued in the workplace. Here are some ideas you could use:

- **Public recognition**: Communicate the individual's extra effort to the entire organization. Hotel chains like Fairmont and Marriott post monthly or quarterly photos in the lobby of team members who have gone "above and beyond" their regular duties. See if your team members would like to be publicly recognized.

- **Small gift cards**: Leaders in some grocery stores dispense gift cards to employees who go out of their way to make an extra effort. The gift cards are redeemable at their place of work and can be viewed by team members as recognition of their extra efforts.

- **Time off**: If someone has put in extra hours—maybe over lunch, at night, on the weekend, etc.—to meet a deadline, serve a customer, or just get the job done, they have displayed extra effort. If you acknowledge that effort by making sure the team member gets to take off time in lieu, you not only demonstrate empathy but also show you are humane.

SAY THE PAY

The term "fair pay" gets nearly 10 million hits on Google. Yet when the compensation software and data company Payscale surveyed almost 400,000 employees across the world in 2021, 57 percent of the participants who were paid market rates believed they were underpaid.[39] And 42 percent of those who were paid above the market rate believed they were underpaid. Bottom line? Everyone thinks they're underpaid.

Payscale's analysis further determined that team members who believe they are paid below the market rate are 50 percent more likely to be hunting for a new job than those who think they are paid at or above the market rate.

What are we to make of this dichotomy between being paid fairly and believing you're not paid fairly? It comes down in part to whether or not a team member feels valued. If they feel valued, there is likely corroborating evidence that the individual is a) being paid fairly, but also b) discussing openly and frequently anything to do with their total compensation package (which we'll look at shortly).

Among the thousands of anecdotal comments I collected from the Global Work-Life Assessment Survey, most concerned wages, compensation, salary, or any other term related to pay. Here is a small selection of them:

Pay us more for the work we do especially some of us who put in more for the company. Make us feel appreciated.
PROFESSIONAL, MANUFACTURING, GERMANY, 45-54 YEARS

The number of demands placed on me – being asked to do more and take on more roles without any reflection in pay.
PROFESSIONAL, EDUCATION, U.K., 35-44 YEARS

A salary increase would be welcome and the best motivation.
VICE-PRESIDENT, HIGH-TECH, FRANCE, 55-64 YEARS

There is no significant change in current or past roles, and the salary does not increase even after several years of work. It's hard to find who I am and where I am.
PROFESSIONAL, CONSULTING, SOUTH KOREA, 35-44 YEARS

"Say the pay" is about doing whatever you can not only to pay fair wages—which should be a leadership given in this day and age—but also to openly and frequently discuss with team members all facets of your organization's compensation and rewards programs. It is critical to keep communication channels as open and accessible as possible when it comes to an employee's total compensation. To "say the pay" removes the stigma of discussing anything with team members about pay, benefits, or rewards. There's no reason to discuss a salary bump in secrecy once a year.

Being more transparent and regular with your pay-related information is essential to making team members feel valued. At least twice a year, discuss with your team members the many facets that make up any individual's total pay-based and rewards package, including these:

- **Compensation:** The hard dollars people take home, including base pay and, if applicable, variable remuneration, cash bonuses, stock options or restricted stock units, Spiffs (Sales Performance Incentive Funds), and any-thing else related to cash. Having regular discussions not only about these factors but also about what can be done to increase any of them—or what additional duties or different roles can help to improve any of the compen-sation factors—shows that you value the team member's financial health.

· **Benefits:** Often overlooked by leaders because they're an H.R. or Finance thing, your organization's benefits are an expression of how you value your employees. Having an open dialogue with your team member about your organization's health, mental, dental, and vision plans; parental leave plans; and, if applicable, life and disability insurance and retirement contribution plans offers a perfect opportunity to express how you value the team member.

· **Recognition:** If your organization offers additional modes of team mem-ber recognition, ensure people know about them. For example, does your organization use a rewards program whereby virtual thank-you cards and awards points can be gifted to team members? What about quarterly or annual awards? Is there an appreciation wall? Are there CEO coins rec-ognizing team members who embody your organization's values? These are all examples of how an organization can demonstrate that it values its team members.

· **Learning and development:** Whenever an organization foots the costs of individuals taking time out of their regular duties to reskill, upskill, or cross-skill, it is investing in them. And that investment is another example of showing how you value the team member. If, however, you do not point out the learning investment made in the team member, it can get over-looked by the team member as an investment.

· **Employee wellness:** If your organization supports an EAP (employee assis-tance program), you will be well-served to ensure your team members are aware of what services are offered—for example, physiotherapy, coun-selling, relationship assistance, mental health, nutrition, finances, and so on. Perhaps your organization has links with internal or external col-lectives or resource groups where team members of similar or different backgrounds can meet safely. Or, if your organization has established its DEIB (Diversity, Equity, Inclusion & Belonging) strategy, perhaps there are additional resources for employees to access. But again, the point is to make yourself fully aware of all employee wellness options available to team members so you can adequately communicate how much you value your team members.

- **Social purpose:** Offering team members the opportunity to volunteer in their community—without using their vacation days—is an integral part of a social purpose strategy. In taking such an approach, you signal to team members not only that you stand for something more than day-to-day operations but also that you value them so much that you are willing to pay them their wages to contribute time to the community. It is the very definition of feeling valued.

Consider three additional tactics as you begin to "say the pay":

- **Post the pay bands:** While some organizations, like high-tech company Buffer, are comfortable making details about everyone's compensation package publicly available, others are less willing to be quite so transparent. An alternative is to make known the range of your salaries anonymously, using factors such as years at the organization and total years of experience (among other criteria that may be important to your firm). Your organization's willingness to show the pay range may be a step in the right direction. You could also post the pay bands that your competitors offer to provide direct comparisons. For example, computer science engineers who know that they fall within or outside the pay range for a role with ten years of experience and are located in a city like Paris or New York will be better equipped to have conversations with you about their total compensation package. And so will you.

- **Set up a lifestyle spending account:** Allocate a set amount of the annual budget for team members to use at their discretion. Don't even bother collecting receipts. The lifestyle spending account can be branded as an opportunity for team members to indulge in anything they choose, be it athletic equipment, spa appointments, yoga sessions, art classes, or even a personal trainer. The point is that you are providing a monetary investment outside their normal remuneration. You are helping them to feel valued in a remunerative way that is separate from their regular paycheque and is designed to be spent on their lifestyle.

- **Pay to play**: Not everything in the "pay" category has to translate into hard dollars. Some people consider time off to be more valuable than additional money. When you "pay to play," you offer the team member options outside of a paycheque, bonus payment, or stock options. Consider giving people a set number of wellness days in addition to their regular allotted vacation days. Perhaps your organization could shut down between Christmas and New Year's Day? Have you considered implementing a four-day workweek? Whatever option you choose, giving time back to a team member in the form of days off is another way to make them feel valued.

Work-Factor No. 4: PURPOSE

The organization's intentions, beliefs, and actions are geared toward serving all stakeholders and improving society for the greater good.

✿ ✿

Many times, due to being overworked, I get stressed and feel that I am unable to go to work. But then I remember the purpose of work, and I go without hesitation.
MANAGER, EDUCATION, INDIA, 25–34 YEARS

I feel like too often people forget that first and foremost, there needs to be a focus on results. That said, investing in philanthropy programs, volunteering time, and allowing employees the space to give back to their communities is meaningful and highly valued.
VICE-PRESIDENT, INTERNET, USA, 45–54 YEARS

✿ ✿

William Damon, a Stanford University professor and psychologist, defines "purpose" as "a stable and generalized intention to accomplish something that is at the same time meaningful to the self and consequential for the world beyond the self."[40] He first defined it in 2010 for adolescents, but I believe we might repurpose it for our Work-Life Bloom argument. Two founders and their company examples provide some backup for my claim.

My first example is Hot Chicken Takeover, which opened in Columbus, Ohio, in 2014 to serve the sweet smells and tastes of Nashville's famous hot chicken culture. It did so to make a profit, sure, but it also aimed to give people a second chance. HCT, as it's often called, offers employment to men and women who "need a fair chance at work."[41] Founder Joe DeLoss said in 2022, "Our business was intentionally built to hire folks who have been affected by adversity. That adversity shows up in people's lives as being involved in the justice system, being affected by homelessness, incarceration, addiction."[42]

Seventy percent of HCT staff have spent time incarcerated. Many used to be unhoused. HCT hires people to help get them back on their feet, pushing them to set their sights on what's next. Profit is vital, but so too is operating with a higher purpose. The company now has four restaurants in Columbus and two in the Cleveland area. It constantly strives to "create a sense of belonging, engagement and enthusiasm in each and every one."[43]

My second example comes from Katlin Smith, CEO of Simple Mills, which she founded in 2012 when she was 22 years old. Her mission was clear: make simple, healthy, and delicious food. She realized that purpose is much more than a fixation on profit. In 2017, she said:

> It starts with purpose. At Simple Mills, we are here to positively impact the way food is made, enriching lives and bodies through delicious, convenient foods made from clean, nutritious ingredients. This is the first and most important component of our company and culture. Every piece, every person, must be centered on fueling our mission—from hiring criteria to the way we source ingredients, to the products we make.[44]

Simple Mills earns in excess of US$100 million annually, employs over 100 people, and sells its products in more than 28,000 stores. The company is clear in its intent: "We believe if you don't recognize an ingredient, your body won't either, so we handpick ours with purpose — only including things that nourish you. Nothing artificial, ever."[45]

Research (see, for example, *The Purpose Effect* by yours truly) has proven that purpose-driven organizations like HCT and Simple Mills are more successful if they operate with the long term in mind while simultaneously serving all stakeholders, which include customers, team members, partners, suppliers, the community, and the environment. Other research also proves that people desire a sense of purpose from their work.

According to a 2015 Gallup survey, 70 percent of workers said their work primarily determines their sense of purpose.[46] In addition, the 2022 Alight International Workforce and Wellbeing Mindset Global Study reported that "39 percent of team members believe that meaningful work is more important than pay."[47]

In fact, the research from Alight also found a direct link between productivity and purpose. After reviewing 47 different drivers of productivity, Alight discovered that "four of the top 11 focused on company purpose and values." These are the four drivers:

- I can be myself at work.
- I feel like I belong at this company.
- My personal values align with the company values.
- I feel connected to the purpose or mission of my company.

The pandemic has had an impact on people's feelings about work and purpose as well. In October 2021, Gartner surveyed more than 3,500 employees around the world and found that 65 percent felt that the pandemic had made them rethink the place that work should have in their life, and 56 percent said it had made them want to contribute more to society.[48]

However, over a decade of researching the concept of purpose, I've discovered that there are other reasons why an organization ought to be doing something about creating a sense of purpose for team members. External research supports my case.

A 2017 study conducted by FCLTGlobal and published under the title *Making the Case for the Long Term*[49] demonstrated that firms focusing their business on the long term had 47 percent higher revenues and 36 percent greater earnings. Furthermore, over a 14-year period, these firms added 12,000 more jobs on average than their peers. The study suggested that had all organizations acted in this manner, the U.S. economy would have grown by US$1 trillion, creating more than 5 million jobs.

A 2022 follow-up study by FCLTGlobal, *Walking the Talk: Valuing a Multi-Stakeholder Strategy*,[50] found that organizations using stakeholder-oriented language in their operations generated 4 percent higher returns, delivered 1.5 percent higher sales growth over three years, and invested twice as much in R&D as a percentage of sales.

For every HCT, Simple Mills, or other organization that incorporates a purpose mindset into their operations—to the benefit of society, team members, and customers—it seems there are many more that continue to practise purposeless habits. In return, large swathes of employees find it challenging to bloom because their employer operates with a middle finger firmly drawn to its stakeholders. The stories of Volkswagen AG, Wells Fargo, and Boeing are legitimate examples of companies that seemed to be operating with a singular mission (profit) and a view to only serving the short-term interests of that singular stakeholder.

Volkswagen AG lied to both the public and regulators and became ensnarled in a diesel fuel emissions scandal in 2015. By 2020, the company had accumulated a total of US$34.69 billion in fines and settlements. Unsurprisingly, employees became increasingly unhappy with the company, as reported by the workplace satisfaction firm Kununu.[51]

Starting in 2011, Wells Fargo employees were encouraged by senior leaders to fraudulently open millions of personal banking accounts unbeknown to its customers. The practice went on for several years. In 2016, the company was forced to pay out approximately US$2.7 billion in civil and criminal lawsuits. Thousands of employees were terminated to help pay for the damage, while others voluntarily left the organization because of the company's adverse behaviour.[52] As with Volkswagen AG, it was an avoidable calamity and led many team members to question the company's purpose.

Boeing's infamous cover-up of its known 737 MAX aircraft issues was at best deplorable. A total of 346 people died in two fatal crashes in 2018 and 2019. After a thorough review, the company was found to be fully aware that issues with its Maneuvering Characteristics Augmentation System (MCAS)—a flight stabilizing program—could cause the 737 MAX to crash. Senior leaders of the airline deliberately hid the issue from its customers.

On January 7, 2021, Assistant Attorney General David P. Burns of the U.S. Justice Department's Criminal Division wrote the following scathing judgment: "Boeing's employees chose the path of profit over candor by concealing material information from the FAA concerning the operation of its 737 Max airplane and engaging in an effort to cover up their deception.

This resolution holds Boeing accountable for its employees' criminal mis-conduct."[53] Boeing was forced to pay a total criminal monetary amount of over US$2.5 billion, composed of various penalties and compensation payments to airline customers and relatives of the 346 passengers who died. If only Alan Mulally had been Boeing's CEO at the time.

Between the three examples cited above, nearly US$40 billion was paid out to compensate, in one way or another, for purposeless decision-making rooted in greed. That leads me to three key questions: What might that money have been used for if stakeholders—including their team members—were at the core of their purpose? How much more innovation, creativity, and performance might have resulted from employees if the senior leaders weren't so myopic? And how many more people might have bloomed?

FARMER'S ALMANAC: **PURPOSE**

I have studied the concept of purpose since 2014—publishing a book on the subject in 2016 titled *The Purpose Effect*—and am in a somewhat unique position to discuss it. While countless leaders, pundits, authors, and others have finally discovered the concept of purpose, I can assure you that the garden box was very lonely for many years. For quite a while, it seemed like I had only my friend Aaron Hurst—author of *The Purpose Economy*—to talk to about the concept of purpose. Thankfully the tide has brought in a plethora of positive purpose crests and further thinking. (And Aaron and I still like to talk about purpose.)

Had I asked global audiences specific questions focused on purpose back in 2014, I'm confident the responses would have been ridiculously low. Not only were very few organizations operating with purpose, but also very few people understood how they could incorporate the concept of purpose into their operating culture. The Global Work-Life Assessment Survey provided somewhat encouraging results specific to the organizational purpose work-factor. However, it also revealed some troubling insights.

Review the following three statements regarding the concept of purpose that global team members were explicitly asked if they agreed with. The results have been broken down by country. Notice anything?

Perceptions of Purpose

	MY ORGANIZATION OPERATES WITH PURPOSE IN ITS ACTIONS.	HOW IMPORTANT IS IT TO YOU FOR AN ORGANIZATION TO OPERATE WITH PURPOSE?	MY EMPLOYER'S ORGANIZATIONAL PURPOSE HELPS ME TO PERFORM IN MY ROLE.
Australia	72%	78%	46%
Canada	73%	84%	48%
France	76%	84%	57%
Germany	72%	78%	49%
India	88%	91%	55%
Netherlands	71%	69%	39%
South Korea	70%	70%	38%
Spain	75%	81%	51%
Sweden	68%	80%	46%
U.K.	69%	78%	52%
USA	74%	80%	47%
Average	73%	79%	48%

There is good news and not-so-good news to report. In the good news section, team members around the globe seem to believe that their organization is operating "with purpose in its actions." Sweden scored the lowest at 68 percent positive, and India scored the highest at an astonishing 88 percent positivity. The global average is 73 percent positivity, which I would call a win in the purpose quest. Yes, it can and should get higher over time—I hope it can top 85 percent positivity one day—but we should be proud that it's so high today.

Most people believe that it is important or very important for their organization to be operating with purpose. Sixty-nine percent of Dutch workers believe it to be so—the low mark of all eleven countries surveyed—whereas a remarkable 91 percent of workers in India agree. This is to say that a substantial majority—four out of five employees around the globe—want to work for an organization that embeds purpose in its operating practices. This is a good thing! (Although the South Koreans and Dutch may need a bit more of a push on this one.)

However, I must also highlight a glaring purpose hole. Roughly 50 percent of global team members don't believe their "employer's organizational purpose helps me to perform in my role." As I detailed in *The Purpose Effect*,[54] when there is a misalignment between someone's personal or role purpose and their employer's stated purpose, you wind up not only with increased levels of employee disengagement but also a higher likelihood of attrition, customer dissatisfaction, and revenue stagnation. Not good.

Let's investigate a few purpose garden tools we can use to bring organizational purpose to the fore and help team members bloom.

The Garden Tools of Purpose

Since writing *The Purpose Effect*, I've continued to review what makes one organization a successful purpose-driven one versus those that are not. Organizations that are good at creating purpose consistently use three essential garden tools.

First, they issue a "declaration of purpose" statement and back it up with impact targets whose results are made publicly available. Second, they demonstrate the integrity of their purpose declaration by not only operating with purpose but also making decisions and taking action based on it. And third, they encourage and permit their team members to "do good" in the communities where they work and live. We will discuss each of these three garden tools below. However, one predominant theme encircles these three items: stakeholder capitalism.

Whether the organization is for-profit, publicly traded, not-for-profit, or operating in the public sector, if it endorses the basic principles of stakeholder capitalism, it is much more likely to receive the buy-in of team members. In short, employing a stakeholder capitalism ethos helps team members in their quest to bloom.

"Stakeholder capitalism" is not a new term, and it has been endorsed and misunderstood in equal measures over the years. At its core, stakeholder capitalism implies the organization ought to serve the interests and long-term welfare of many stakeholders, not simply those who deserve a financial return—that is, shareholders, owners, or other investors. (From a public sector perspective, the argument of financial return can be extended to those who hold power in elected or even non-elected offices.) An organization that adopts stakeholder capitalism does not operate solely in the short term for profit or power gains. Instead, its leaders take a long-term and thoughtful approach to their organization's standing and the standing of society at large as well.

So who are the stakeholders in stakeholder capitalism? In a nutshell, all of us. Stakeholders represent society. And society is made up of citizens, customers, owners, suppliers, partners, investors, the environment, and of course, the organization's team members.

If you want to help your team members bloom, your organization should serve the interests of all stakeholders, not only those seeking a financial or power return. HCT and Simple Mills are stellar examples of companies that serve the interests of all stakeholders. The old mindset of serving shareholders or those in power first is an easy way to demonstrate to team members that your organization's focus is myopic and not purpose-driven. Employees are increasingly focusing on issues such as community impact, Environmental, Social, and Governance (ESG) concerns, and social issues such as diversity, equity, inclusion, and belonging.

This book does not aim to solve the issues that arise from stakeholder capitalism or short-termism. They are far too complex. You may want to read my book *The Purpose Effect*, *The Purpose Economy* by Aaron Hurst, or *Deep Purpose* by Harvard Business School's Dr. Ranjay Gulati for further insights on those topics. It is clear, however, that organizations adopting a stakeholder-first approach will be far more likely to help team members reach and stay in the bloom state if they adopt that approach consistently.

When I interviewed Dr. Gulati, he said, "Purpose is only as good as what people in the organization believe it is."[55] If you want your team members to believe that you and your organization operate with purpose—thus giving them a higher chance of blooming—a stakeholder-first model can be supported by three tools I will outline next: declaration and impact, integrity, and service to your community.

DECLARATION AND IMPACT

BVT Engineering Professional Services (now referred to as Brevity) is based in New Zealand and Australia and specializes in interior building design and seismic engineering. Its team comprises roughly 25 people across the two countries. Brevity provides universal bracing solutions for non-structural building requirements and layout and design services for building codes and seismic requirements. Should an engineering firm declare an organizational purpose and align employee impact with it? Brevity believes so.

Matt Bishop is the founder and managing director of Brevity. In 2021, he and the company released both their declaration of purpose and an accompanying impact statement. When asked why these were important to him, Bishop wrote, "I wanted to ensure the company would continue with the essence and energy with which it was founded, and that there would be a clear purpose beyond profit at the heart of the organization."[56]

He went on to state, "The resulting Declaration of Purpose is not a company values statement, nor is it simply a positioning of the company. It formalizes the company's direction and enables our people to test their career and personal goals against it and choose whether they align. And all the team signs the document as part of our annual company get-together."

Bishop's point highlights the first purpose garden tool for you to consider. Your organization's declaration of purpose is critical. It must be at the core of your culture. Team members are demanding that their place of work stand for something more than profit and power: your firm must represent all stakeholders in its declaration of purpose. It helps people to bloom. However, the declaration alone is not enough.

There ought to be a stated intention and, thus, an alignment between the declaration of purpose and its impact. This is where Brevity's declaration of purpose shines.[57] It outlines specifically what is expected of everyone in terms of the purpose-impact outcome alignment. Brevity's five impact statements are as follows (the capitalization is theirs):

1. That if our company is to be successful, our clients must also be successful and OUR SERVICE MUST BE EXCELLENT, AND HIGHLY VALUED BY OUR CLIENTS.

2. That if our service is to be excellent, WE MUST ALL CONTINUE TO LEARN AND EVOLVE, and we must continuously develop our skills and expertise as a company.

3. That we must HOLD EACH OTHER ACCOUNTABLE TO SUCCEED, using evidence-based, data-driven approaches in a high-trust environment.

4. That WE MUST BE ONE COMPANY, ONE CULTURE, with a connected team able to collaborate from anywhere, at any time, regardless of the external environment.

5. That to unlock creativity and innovation, OUR SERVICES MUST BE PRICED ACCORDING TO THE VALUE OF THE OUTCOMES WE CREATE, not time and material inputs.

What can we learn from Brevity from a purpose-based leadership tactic perspective? Consider the following tactics:

- **Declare your purpose**: It seems simple, but if your organization has not taken the time to devise an organizational purpose statement—ideally with the involvement of your team members—it will be best to begin the process immediately. Whether it's a one-line statement or a few sentences, your declaration of purpose signals to the organization what you stand for and how you want to be known. It acts not only as a North Star of principle but also as something everyone can unite around. For example, Canada Post Corporation is Canada's national mail carrier. In 2021, it declared its purpose as "A Stronger Canada — Delivered."[58] Ever since then it has worked with team members across the country to embed its purpose across all functions and job responsibilities—for example, it has embossed the declaration on its delivery trucks and runs enterprise-wide team training forums to discuss it. The CEO Doug Ettinger wrote, "I believe with every delivery, every interaction, and every decision, we can be a positive force for change. We serve all Canadians and know we can do better."[59]

· **Align your impact**: As we will discover in the next work-factor, *strategy*, the goals and targets of your organizational purpose must not be disconnected from the actual work people perform. Therefore, your organizational purpose has to be tightly joined to your organization's strategy so that both the purpose and strategy feel integrated with team members' work. The declaration of organizational purpose must also come with an articulated impact, something Brevity does well. What are the specific outcomes you envisage for team members related to the purpose? What impact can team members have on your stakeholders by enacting the purpose? What expectations do you have of team members to uphold the purpose? These questions—and others you may identify—help to ensure that the declaration of purpose is not merely words on a page. Employees will then begin to see the alignment between your organization's purpose and how they are expected to perform in their roles.

INTEGRITY

Senior leaders frequently use the word "integrity," but it can easily be misused or misapplied. For example, even though it committed one of the worst accounting frauds in history, Enron listed integrity as a core value.

Most of us take integrity for granted. The concept has become so fundamental that many of us fail to celebrate or even notice when it is intact. However, when it is in short supply, life can become deeply unpleasant and disrupted. Just ask the hundreds of thousands of employees and customers of Enron. This is why integrity is so important in your attempts to operationalize purpose.

If you ask me, one of the pre-eminent examples of a company and its senior leaders advocating for integrity while conducting purpose-driven business was—and continues to be—Ben & Jerry's.

The famous ice cream company's purpose is "To operate the Company in a way that actively recognizes the central role that business plays in society by initiating innovative ways to improve the quality of life locally, nationally, and internationally."[60] In 2005, it became the first ice cream maker in the world to use Fairtrade Certified ingredients, and back in 1989 it opposed Recombinant Bovine Growth Hormone use in cows due to "its adverse economic impact on family farming."[61]

Ben & Jerry's CEO Matthew McCarthy said in a 2019 interview, "What you do every day, how you do it, the integrity with which you operate day in and day out, the storytelling that marketers love to talk about, comes from our people. Our people live our ice cream as well as our social mission every day."[62]

The company essentially asks itself daily, Are we acting with integrity when it comes to our purpose? Ben & Jerry's continues to distribute 7.5 percent of its annual pre-tax profits to community organizations around the world. They also donate hundreds of thousands of dollars annually to progressive causes such as climate action, racial justice, and peacebuilding. The company's Project Mootopia pilot program aims to halve greenhouse gas emissions from 15 of its dairy farms by 2024. All these actions were started by decisions—judicious verdicts from the company's senior leaders to operate with purpose, backed by integrity.

The challenge confronting you is considerable: How do you make purpose central to the operating principles of your organization? As I mentioned earlier, that topic is outside the scope of this particular book, but if you want to help your team members bloom, the *purpose* work-factor is one tool you should leverage. And when you uphold your organization's purpose—especially when team members become frazzled during periods of turmoil, disruption, and change—it validates your integrity on the purpose file. Win-win!

SERVICE TO YOUR COMMUNITY

In 2014, the U.S. drugstore chain CVS Health (then called CVS Caremark) became the first U.S. establishment to stop selling tobacco products. Its president at the time, Helena Foulkes, predicted the firm would lose approximately US$2 billion in direct and indirect revenues as a result of the decision. At the time of the announcement, she also said, "We know that the sale of tobacco is extremely inconsistent with being a healthcare provider."[63]

That same year, a pharmacist named Graham MacKenzie stopped selling sugary beverages at his Cape Breton, Nova Scotia, pharmacy, Stone's Pharmasave. "I made this decision to help educate my customers on the effects of sugary drinks," he wrote.[64] MacKenzie used his platform as one of the town's pharmacists to create an environment—at least in his pharmacy—that supported healthy food choices.

In 2005, after witnessing his 12-year-old special needs daughter get shunned by other children while in a hotel swimming pool, Gordon Hartman began to think about how other families were being affected the same way. Hartman decided to sell his investments to start a funding campaign that eventually opened the doors to Morgan's Wonderland, the world's first inclusive amusement park, in San Antonio, Texas. Named after his daughter, Morgan's Wonderland is a 25-acre theme park free for anyone with special needs. Yes, free. Its aim is to be a place of fun for people who have special needs but it is built for everyone's enjoyment.

That same year, the India-based consulting firm Mahindra Group launched its Employee Social Options Program (ESOPs). ESOPs provides Mahindra employees with various opportunities to volunteer outside the organization. As a result of its year-over-year encouragement of ESOPs, the company witnessed its employees donate 362,585 person-hours toward giving back to society, an average of 9.3 hours per team member in its fiscal year 2022.[65]

Since 2000, the Canadian telecom company TELUS has donated over Can\$1.4 billion to charitable and community organizations and volunteered a collective 1.6 million days of service through the efforts of its team members and retirees. The company's team members donate over 1.3 million hours of community service annually through individual and team-based events in addition to its yearly company-wide TELUS Days of Giving campaign. The company's giving strategy is tied to its organizational purpose: "To connect all citizens for good."

The examples of CVS Health, Stone's Pharmasave, Morgan's Wonderland, Mahindra Group, and TELUS encompass diverse organizations connected by one central word: community. The decisions made by each of the respective leaders of these organizations were designed to aid the advancement of the communities in which they lived. You must consider doing the same as you enact the *purpose* work-factor, keeping in mind two distinct facets of community: intention and giving.

- **Community intention**: Employees look to organizations to be purpose-driven, sure, but when your actions demonstrate the *intent* to better the communities you serve, your team members will start to feel purpose is being done as though it matters, that it's being done for the right reasons. When you make decisions to benefit a team member's community—be it directly or indirectly—it furthers their belief in you and the organization. For example, operating as a pharmacy and selling cigarettes is a somewhat incongruent combination. Eliminating the sale of cigarettes signals to employees that the organization holds an intention—and thus the belief—that they are in business to better serve the community in which its team members live. When your stated intention is to help communities thrive, it backs up your organizational purpose and your team members' trust in your leadership.

- **Community-giving**: Any organization that does not dedicate time and dollars to directly support a team member's community will be hard-pressed to have that individual support that organization's stated purpose. A critical component of purpose is to ensure you a) allow team members to volunteer their time in their community during their regular work hours, and b) establish the mechanisms to directly donate organizational funds and/or services toward various community needs. Failing to establish a community-giving strategy as part of your organizational purpose is a bit like going fishing without a rod or bait. A team member will not believe your purpose statement or other stated intentions if there are no mechanisms in place to directly support their communities in need.

Work-Factor No. 5: STRATEGY

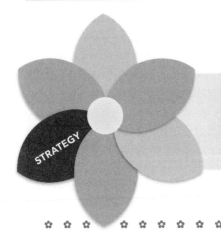

The intended direction and related priorities to ensure the short- and long-term focus of team members and the delivery of their objectives.

✿ ✿ ✿ ✿

I think, as an employee, that income is very important. But, as a manager, following a clear strategy is very important, too.
MANAGER, AEROSPACE/AVIATION/AUTOMOTIVE, FRANCE, 25-34 YEARS

✿ ✿

Aesop was an enslaved Greek who lived between 620 and 564 BCE. He was alleged to have invented many of the fables we still use today, such as "The Boy Who Cried Wolf," "The Hare and the Tortoise," and "The Lion and the Mouse." However, there are varying opinions and theories about whether he was responsible for writing these fables.

Some suggest many different writers have revised his original stories over the years. Others believe that a Greek man named Babrius curated and edited Aesop's thoughts as they were passed down from one generation to the next. Regardless, Aesop, it appears, was a man who spent a lot of time strategizing. His fables were observations of life's simple truths and have stood the test of time. He explored morality through animals' relationships and interactions.

I would like to pay homage to Aesop and explore his fable "The Grasshopper and the Ants," as we can relate it to the work-factor *strategy*. The original legend concerns an army of ants working diligently together to collect and store food for the impending winter and a grasshopper who ignores the coming frost and ultimately seems incapable of demonstrating any strategic behaviours.

The grasshopper was a wee bit narcissistic with a sprinkling of self-ish cluelessness. Instead of thinking, deciding, and then acting upon the required preparations for the upcoming winter, the grasshopper played around, laughed, and due to their self-absorbedness, genuinely failed to strategize. So, when the cold weather set in and doom loomed on the horizon, what did the grasshopper do? They asked the ants for food to survive. In Aesop's fable, the ants were very disappointed with the grasshopper's behaviour but eventually acquiesced. So, let's call the ants good team players.

If we fast-forward to today, we can find many ants in the workplace. They are team members or even other leaders who must put up with a boss who just doesn't understand how important strategy is for everyone. A grasshopper-boss who does not pay attention to or refuses to discuss strategy with the team is bound for trouble.

We might even suggest that the ants that Aesop wrote about in "The Grasshopper and the Ants" make a guest appearance in research conducted by two-time Pulitzer Prize winner and world-renowned biologist Edward O. Wilson, known more commonly as E. O. His work in the 1960s around ant pheromones—a chemical substance produced by an animal that serves as a stimulus to other individuals of the same species—highlighted the nuances of ant ecosystems. E. O.'s findings also map back to a team's need to understand the strategy.

Wilson identified how ant colonies communicated with one another to accomplish their goals. Put simply: ants work collaboratively to think *and* do, two critical components of strategy. While there may be a queen, the workers are fully aware of their role and, thus, the overarching strategy. There is constant communication, consultation, and connection among colony members. There is no confusion. The ants are marching to the same beat.

Years later, Wilson shifted his research to other animals, including humans. In his 1998 book, *Consilience: The Unity of Knowledge*, he wrote: "The greatest challenge today, not just in cell biology and ecology but in all of science, is the accurate and complete description of complex systems."[66] For team members to perform effectively in their roles, they must continuously deal with complex systems. As a leader, if you cannot decode or help them to understand the overarching strategy meant to guide them, you make their jobs even more complicated.

Aesop's grasshopper is the epitome of someone who doesn't grasp strategy's importance and is incapable of helping others. But the ants— both fictional and real—remind us that good things happen when we communicate, consult, and connect with one another. If we want to be leading blooming teams, we must not emulate the grasshopper.

Keep in mind that the work-factor *strategy* is not a process. It's not design thinking. It has nothing to do with Agile or Lean models. It is a behaviour, one that the grasshopper failed to employ. In the Work-Life Bloom model, strategy is about adopting an awareness mindset. There are no steps to follow or sequence of events to check off. There is no methodology. There is simply an attitude that you must espouse.

It is the recognition—your recognition—that you need to continuously help team members understand your team's and organization's strategy. The failure to adopt an awareness mindset—to disregard your team members' needs to be better versed with the strategy—is a sure path toward closed-mindedness and stagnant, if not diminishing, performance.

✿ ✿

When not being sure I was receiving trustworthy information about future planning and the strategy, I felt I needed to guess what was behind what I was being told.

SENIOR EXECUTIVE, CONSULTING, USA, 65-74 YEARS

Please, just support the strategy.

MANAGER, CONSTRUCTION, SPAIN, 35–44 YEARS

I feel engaged when empowered to align my team's strategy to that of the greater organization because I have clarity of what is needed. Communication was (and is) key!

VICE-PRESIDENT, FINANCE/BANKING/INSURANCE, USA, 55–64 YEARS

✿ ✿

FARMER'S ALMANAC: **STRATEGY**

On an aggregate basis, 69 percent of team members at all levels believe their organization has a clear strategy. I wouldn't call that impressive, but it's not awful either. Unfortunately, only 47 percent of global employees believe their employer's strategy helps them perform in their roles. Put differently, roughly half of your employees do not positively connect their performance to your organization's strategy. In my books, that's a problem. A noteworthy pattern—and not the good kind—emerges when we slice the data in two different ways. First, let's examine responses to two statements broken down by the four generations.

My organization has a clear strategy.

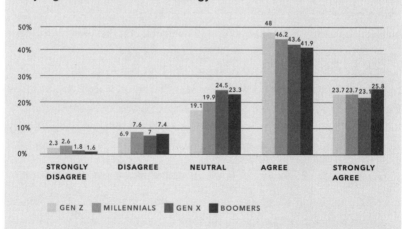

GEN Z   MILLENNIALS   GEN X   BOOMERS

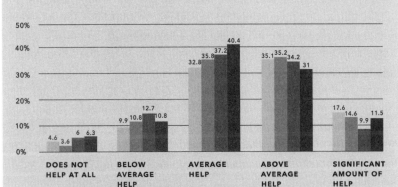

My organization's strategy makes it easier for me to perform in my role.

While the discrepancy between generations is not vast, the younger someone is, the more likely they are to believe their organization's strategy is clear. Conversely, the older a team member is, the less likely it is that their organization's strategy helps that individual perform in their role.

Specifically, 53 percent of Gen Z indicate their organization's strategy makes it easier for them to perform in their role. That's the high-water mark. Unfortunately, it begins to change significantly as people age. Fifty percent of Millennials, 44 percent of Gen Xers, and 43 percent of Boomers feel their organization's strategy makes it easier for them to perform in their role. These results might be construed as follows: as people get older, they become jaded by the organization's strategy, shifting instead toward intrinsic motivating factors to slog through their days on the job. It's about as ideal as a cornucopia of slugs in a strawberry patch.

Furthermore, does an organization want its most senior and experienced people to become increasingly disillusioned with its strategy as they age? Don't we want the performance of our industry veterans to be high and thus intertwined with the organization's strategy? It's a rhetorical question. I know you're nodding yes right now.

Next, let's examine answers to the same two strategy-based statements by leaders and non-leaders.

My organization has a clear strategy.

Categories: STRONGLY DISAGREE, DISAGREE, NEUTRAL, AGREE, STRONGLY AGREE

- STRONGLY DISAGREE: I lead a team or organization 1.9, I do not lead a team or organization 2.9
- DISAGREE: I lead a team or organization 6.5, I do not lead a team or organization 8.7
- NEUTRAL: I lead a team or organization 17.3, I do not lead a team or organization 29.9
- AGREE: I lead a team or organization 47.3, I do not lead a team or organization 40.6
- STRONGLY AGREE: I lead a team or organization 27, I do not lead a team or organization 17.9

■ I lead a team or organization   ■ I do not lead a team or organization

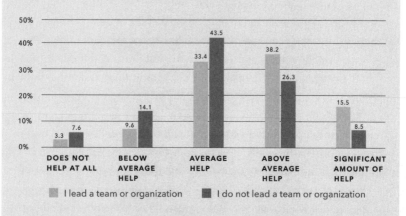

My organization's strategy makes it easier for me to perform in my role.

Categories: DOES NOT HELP AT ALL, BELOW AVERAGE HELP, AVERAGE HELP, ABOVE AVERAGE HELP, SIGNIFICANT AMOUNT OF HELP

- DOES NOT HELP AT ALL: I lead a team or organization 3.3, I do not lead a team or organization 7.6
- BELOW AVERAGE HELP: I lead a team or organization 9.6, I do not lead a team or organization 14.1
- AVERAGE HELP: I lead a team or organization 33.4, I do not lead a team or organization 43.5
- ABOVE AVERAGE HELP: I lead a team or organization 38.2, I do not lead a team or organization 26.3
- SIGNIFICANT AMOUNT OF HELP: I lead a team or organization 15.5, I do not lead a team or organization 8.5

■ I lead a team or organization   ■ I do not lead a team or organization

Houston, we have a problem. Whereas 74 percent of leaders believe the organization possesses a clear strategy, only 59 percent of non-leaders agree. Perhaps worse, a paltry 54 percent of leaders agree that their organization's strategy makes it easier for them to perform in their role. It drops like a space shuttle on re-entry to 35 percent for non-leaders.

What do we make of these insights? First, there are a lot of slugs in the strawberry patch. Oodles. More seriously, leaders must improve their awareness around strategy, not in terms of creating it per se, but in terms of their communication, consultation, and connection habits. These three C's are the garden tools of strategy, which we will discuss next.

The Garden Tools of Strategy

The goal of the *strategy* work-factor is not to create a better organizational strategy. That may seem counterintuitive. Rather obviously, your organization's strategy is critical. But for this particular work-factor, I am not in a position to help you improve your organization's strategic intent or path to success. If that is the dilemma you face, I would start by reading the books I have listed after the Coda that explicitly focus on crafting and enacting a better organizational strategy.

What, then, is the goal of the strategy work-factor for *Work-Life Bloom*?

Your job is to create a better alignment between you, your team members, and the organization's current and intended strategy, related priorities, and deadlines. That alignment will come from how you communicate, consult, and connect.

Keeping team members up-to-date on the organization's execution of its strategy is imperative. But you must also find ways to consult with them related to their specific job function. The average leader has many blind spots. Insights from employees can be vital to enhancements of or revisions to the strategy itself. And finally, you must make the strategy real; you have to connect the dots between your organization's strategy and how it affects team members' ability to carry out their current tasks.

When you adopt the three C's of the strategy work-factor, the end result is team members who better understand the big picture. When team members are plugged into your organization's short- and long-term intentions, the resulting effect is alignment. When team members feel the strategy aligns with their needs, high performance is not ensured but it's far more likely. Thus, the potential to bloom is greater.

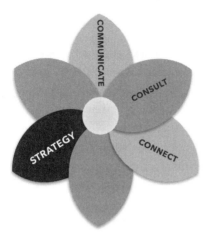

COMMUNICATE

How hard can it be to communicate your organization's or team's strategy and related objectives to team members? That depends on your style of communication. I have learned that an immersion strategy is the most productive approach. What does that mean?

The Canadian Oxford Dictionary's definition of *immersion* provides a clue: "the act or an instance of immersing [. . .] the process of being immersed [. . .] mental absorption in an activity."[67] That's a clear tipoff. It's even a recommendation of sorts. The "activity" I want you to think about is strategy.

Communicating strategy and objectives should not be a one-time or annual tactic. Far too often, however, an organization's strategy gets rolled out at the beginning of the operating year, never, or rarely, to be discussed again until the next operating year begins. Is that good enough? Is it employing immersion? Will an employee absorb the strategy if it's only mentioned in passing?

The answer to both of those questions is, of course, no. If your strategy is to be fully appreciated and understood by team members, you should adopt an immersive communication strategy. Furthermore, your communication must use an immersion technique if you want team members' performance and output to be positively shaped by the strategy. (As we discovered, only 35 percent of non-leaders agree that their organization's strategy makes it easier for them to perform in their role.) In sum, you must find opportunities to communicate and relate the strategy as frequently and as clearly as possible. Here are some tools you can use:

- **Team meetings**: Whatever meeting cadence you may employ, aligning the organization's strategy with your team strategy (and objectives) and communicating that strategy during a set number of annual team meetings can be effective. You don't need to devote an entire meeting to this. You only need a 10–15 minute segment. Take the time during several of your team meetings to a) illustrate where the organization is at with its strategy and results, and b) align your team's progress with it. When you open things up for questions, you also create an opportunity for team members to further cement their understanding.

- **Video summaries**: Crafting a short video solely for your team's use is another dependable way to create alignment. Adopt whatever frequency you believe makes sense. The video's primary purpose is to highlight the team's performance matched against the strategy. The video becomes a reinforcement tool of both the strategy and the team's objectives.

- **Dashboards**: Using an asynchronous tool like Web-based dashboards can also be helpful. As you outline on the dashboard how specific projects, goals, objectives, or tasks are playing out with your team, you can align each one with portions of the organization's strategy. It's another opportunity to communicate the strategy and demonstrate how you are aligning your leadership with the organization's short- and long-term focus.

CONSULT

Your organization's strategy is built around a set of guiding principles, objectives, and tasks to achieve several overarching goals. As I pointed out earlier, this is not a strategy-building book, but let me introduce one strategy feature that you might want to consider implementing to improve your team members' chances to bloom.

If we can agree that a good organizational strategy acts as a guide for all team members—a path that shows everyone in the company where the organization is heading, why, and by how much—would it not be a good idea to occasionally consult with the people who are enacting the strategy? If leaders announce the strategy and team members execute it, it's likely an excellent idea to intermittently check in with the team members to see how it's playing out. That action can create a strategic bond.

The successful implementation of your organization's strategy is heavily dependent on your team members. Yet, few employees ever get

involved in the strategic planning process. This means not only that leaders miss out on critical feedback that could help shape future versions of
the strategy, but also that the chance to reinforce any context between
the employee, their performance, and the strategy is lost. This is perhaps
another reason why two-thirds of team members not in leadership roles
do not believe their organization's strategy makes it easier for them to perform in their role. What to do? You could use one or both of the following
options to engage your team members:

- **One-on-one meetings**: Ask yourself if you take the time during any of your
  one-on-one meetings with team members to discuss the organization's
  strategy and talk over what is working and what's not. Feedback from
  your team members provides the chance for alignment and future organizational strategy modifications. Even if you're not in a senior leadership
  role, your request for feedback and the dialogue that ensues could provide
  you with input and ideas to help the senior leadership team with future
  strategic direction changes. It's your chance to be proactive and provide
  feedback to senior leaders on what's going on in the trenches. At a minimum, it shows that you care about the team member's opinions—one for
  the win column of *Work-Life Bloom*.

- **Anonymous surveying**: It's one thing for organizations to issue their
  annual or quarterly employee engagement survey, but it's quite another
  to specifically ask your team members for thoughts about your organization's strategy via an anonymous survey. Once or twice a year, you may
  want to conduct a simple survey or poll that asks team members for their
  ratings and feedback and allows them to be anonymous. Receiving quantitative and qualitative feedback in summary form via the entire team will
  help you better understand trends specifically related to the strategy. By
  taking this consultative action, you're also establishing another opportunity to create context between team members' performance and their
  understanding of the strategy.

CONNECT

This one is super simple: your role as a leader is to *connect* the organization's strategy to your team members' roles and objectives as often as it
makes sense. By making this connection, you are providing an essential
perspective for each individual. While you may think this is redundant

given you are "connecting" while you *communicate* and *consult*, connecting is very definitely a pillar of its own.

What good is it to a team member if an organization's strategy only sits on a website or annual report PDF document? It's no good. For team members to bloom, they have to feel the strategy is relevant to them. They should feel *connected* to it. One foolproof way for that *not* to happen is to rely on the "hopes and prayers" approach. You can't hope the team member is going to make that connection. And praying for it to occur is a pretty immature leadership tactic. How do you connect? There is one specific way that makes the most sense:

- **One-on-one meetings**: As I note above, while *consulting* with your team members for feedback on the strategy, you can easily use the same time slot to connect their roles to the strategy. Not every one-on-one meeting requires this to happen, but ignoring it outright is ill-advised. Moreover, it's not a hard leadership lift. Open-ended questions can do the trick. Start a dialogue with the team member by asking how they think their role has recently contributed to the organization's strategy. From there, you can infuse the conversation with your leadership insights regarding what else they are doing to help achieve the strategy. Doing this for 10–15 minutes two to three times a year is all it takes.

Work-Factor No. 6: NORMS

NORMS

The operating principles and guidelines that form the culture, providing clear expectations for team members regarding how to interact with one another.

❀ ❀

In my current role, my team leaders give collaborative feedback and work with me to make processes easier and more efficient for everyone.
ADMINISTRATIVE, HEALTHCARE, USA, 25–34 YEARS

When faced with a challenge or problem, the current organization does not look for someone/something to blame; instead, they simply move to pull in the expertise from within the team to look at possible options to resolve the situation. All input is received, and exploration of the possible decision to implement takes each of the perspectives into consideration, even if previous decisions need to be changed, given the new information at hand.
ADMINISTRATIVE, GOVERNMENT/MILITARY, CANADA, 45–54 YEARS

❀ ❀

The pandemic provided us with many leadership lessons, both good and not-so-good. Perhaps more interesting, however, is that some organizations made changes prior to the pandemic and leaned on those transformations to help them navigate through the pandemic. The software giant Autodesk was one of them.

First, let's start by defining "norms." At their core, norms are a set of operating principles and guidelines that help form the culture of any team or organization. They act as expectations for everyone. Norms are the tenets through which people conduct their tasks with one another while at work to achieve the objectives of the role, project, or opportunity. They are not your organization's purpose, mission, or vision. While important, purpose, mission, or vision are separate from norms. Think of norms as behavioural parameters that everyone across the organization is supposed to observe.

Autodesk has nearly 11,000 employees worldwide who design and manufacture software products and services for industries such as architecture, manufacturing, engineering, construction, entertainment, and education. Annual revenue exceeds US$3.5 billion.

Rita Giacalone, the former vice-president and global head of Culture, Diversity & Belonging, worked with Autodesk to help shift the company's operating culture. And this was pre-pandemic. After months of focus groups, workshops, discussion forums, and feedback loops, Giacalone and her team finalized what is still known as the "Culture Code." This code serves the purpose of defining employee expectations when working with others, be it peers, customers, partners, or other externals. In other words, it defines norms.

Autodesk's Culture Code contains several key components that make Autodesk a "Customer Company."[68] In particular, its "Ways We Work" factor helps team members to understand what it means to act as "One Autodesk." Key behaviours include empowering team members to be decision-makers, acting authentically, and demonstrating integrity. The principles and related attributes underpin the firms' policies and procedures. The Ways We Work have become the operating norms of what Autodesk employees expect of themselves and their colleagues.

On paper, it looks fantastic. The ultimate test for any team or organization, however, is whether the ostensible goodness of something like the Culture Code can make a substantial difference to the organization's conduct and results. Throw in a pandemic, and you've got yourself an amazing litmus test.

Giacalone said during an interview with me, "Informed by the Culture Code, our guiding principles were to care authentically, establish inclusive work practices, over-communicate, and create a sense of belonging."[69]

In response to the uncertainty and stress of those first few weeks of the pandemic, Giacalone's team created various resources for leaders and employees that "specifically called upon our Culture Code as a source of guidance and strength."

"For example," she continued, "as part of establishing inclusive work practices, we advised teams to develop new virtual norms. These could include things like defaulting to video for Zoom calls, reminding everyone it's okay for kids, roommates, and pets to barge in, or asking for all team calls to take place between 9:00 AM and 3:00 PM, with a break from noon to 1:00 PM. By establishing these simple agreements, teams better understood expectations and how to work with one another."

The Culture Code was also used to help leaders at all levels adopt an over-communication strategy. "When you're not sitting at a desk near others, communication becomes even more crucial," said Giacalone. "We encouraged employees to clarify expectations with managers, like what work should be prioritized." Autodesk also suggested that employees and managers be transparent about challenges they were facing and when they might need extra support.

It became apparent, however, that because the framework of the Culture Code was already in place, many Autodesk employees were prepared to utilize the company's Ways We Work norms to endure the initial disruption of the pandemic. The corporation believed it handled the initial phases of the pandemic successfully because of its established norms.

Norms act as a behavioural compass of sorts for team members across an organization. They should be considered well-defined expectations in the workplace, outlining what's acceptable and what isn't in terms of interactions between people. From there, leaders and team members should hold each other accountable in the context of those expectations. Norms are a way to help your team understand what is behaviourally expected of them. As their leader, you should be not only inclusive in the establishment of the norms, but clear about them too. It's equally important to be consistent when enforcing them.

If we were to visit certain Indigenous groups in the Amazon rainforest, we would discover that some of them have no leaders. Instead, the group members make decisions communally. They have a collective identity, and each person has a place and a purpose within that identity. Everyone has something to offer, and their contributions are equally valued. The groups will typically have discussions in which all their members are allowed a voice. Their time-immemorial traditions, customs, and practices (their norms) act as their compass. Everyone is in the know. If those norms fell by the wayside or were misunderstood, the culture of the group might fall apart rather quickly.

In 2006, Dr. Jeff G. Hart from the University of Nebraska conducted a study involving over 1,600 members of the Winnebago Tribe in Nebraska.[70] One of the aims of the study was to learn about the group's customs and norms. Through interviews, observations, and other methods, Hart aimed to examine the group's long-established interconnection between their culture and established norms.

He discovered that while the Winnebago Tribe had an inherent and respected leadership hierarchy, the norms helped build community and extended understanding among its members. The norms act as a way to pass on traditions, language, and other essential characteristics of the Winnebago People. One Tribal Council member relayed the following to Hart: "Leadership is based on the knowledge of knowing your community, knowing your people, knowing the visions, and knowing the culture." All of this *knowing* does not magically happen. There has to be a foundation of norms for it to be passed on, understood, and applied.

The Winnebago People employ a leadership model that is backed by norms. But the model only works if consistent norms are applied across all facets of the group's operations. Hart writes in his research paper that "all are part of the sacred circle. This shared role binds the People as one and provides a role model for leadership."

In sum, norms are the operating system components acting like a compass that allow your culture to succeed. They require your leadership to be defined, implemented, and continuously practised. The cue you can take from the examples above is that culture can become your competitive advantage only if consistent norms are applied.

FARMER'S ALMANAC: **NORMS**

I have found throughout my career that there is a strong correlation between an organization's or team's culture and their proper use of norms. When team members and leaders are not aware of the norms or the norms have not been consistently applied, the culture tends to suffer. And when the culture is one in which team members feel less than inspired, performance can also fall off. It's the quickest if not easiest way to fall from a blooming state to become one of the other three personas.

Despite the annual alarm bells issued by corporate culture research firms Gallup, Aon Hewitt, and the like, when I asked people if they felt their organization was a great place to work, 71 percent of global workers responded in the affirmative. I found that to be a rather phenomenal statistic. I was expecting far worse, given the repeated issuance of corporate culture concerns by these firms and employee disengagement data points. It's not perfect, and there is certainly room for improvement, but it's not dire either. But, as I pointed out earlier, any survey is but a moment in time and our work-life personas will ebb and flow based on our current interpretations of the work-life factors.

My organization is a great place to work. (All employees)

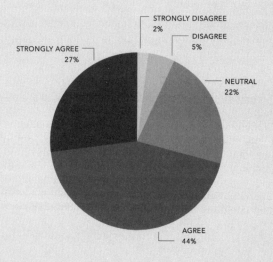

STRONGLY DISAGREE
2%

DISAGREE
5%

STRONGLY AGREE
27%

NEUTRAL
22%

AGREE
44%

Opinions about how great a place an organization is to work vary widely across industries. Over 80 percent of employees in the entertainment, media/printing/publishing, and telecommunications industries believe their organization is a great place to work. Conversely, just over 60 percent of employees in industries such as food services, government/public sector, and legal say the same.

My organization is a great place to work. (By industry)

INDUSTRY SEGMENT	AGREED	NEUTRAL/DISAGREE
Aerospace/Aviation/Automotive	71%	29%
Agriculture/Forestry/Fishing	70%	30%
Business/Professional Services	76%	24%
Construction	75%	25%
Consulting	75%	25%
Education	68%	32%
Engineering	67%	33%
Entertainment	81%	19%
Finance/Banking/Insurance	74%	26%
Food Services	62%	38%
Government/Public Sector	60%	40%
Healthcare	66%	34%
High-Tech Related	78%	22%
Legal	62%	38%
Manufacturing	67%	33%
Media/Printing/Publishing	86%	14%
Non-Profit	71%	29%
Research/Science	76%	24%
Retail	68%	32%
Telecommunications	82%	19%
Transportation/Distribution	68%	32%
Utilities	75%	25%

When the data is delineated by leaders and non-leaders, a somewhat more troubling picture emerges. Whereas 74 percent of leaders state that their organization is a great place to work, only 64 percent of non-leaders say the same. It could be argued that for almost two-thirds of non-leader employees to say their organization is a great place to work is a good, if not great, response. However, when you then look at the statement they were asked to rate, "My employer's organizational culture helps me to perform in my role," things are less positive.

My organization is a great place to work. (Leaders vs. non-leaders)

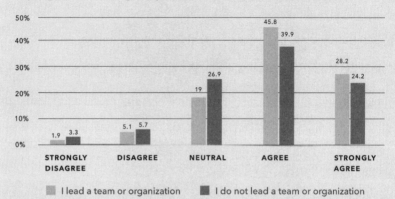

I lead a team or organization ▪ I do not lead a team or organization

My employer's organizational culture helps me to perform in my role. (Leaders vs. non-leaders)

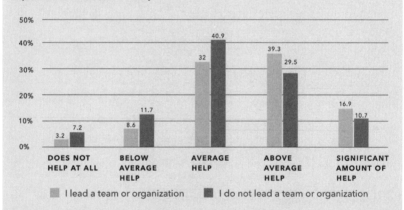

I lead a team or organization ▪ I do not lead a team or organization

With only 56 percent of leaders and a paltry 40 percent of non-leaders agreeing that their organization's culture helps them perform in their role, you can see that improved norms might help more people to bloom. So, let's open up the garden shed and see what can be done differently from a culture and norms perspective.

The Garden Tools of Norms

"Culture is the shared set of norms and interpretations that people normally have that drives what they think is the right thing to do."[71] Roger L. Martin shared those words with me during one of our conversations. He is the former dean of the Rotman School of Management at the University of Toronto, a best-selling author, and a strategy adviser to CEOs and senior executives. Martin was named the top management thinker in the world by Thinkers50.

When Martin works with companies, he often instructs senior leaders on the importance of norms. "Every single interpersonal interaction you have is going to be critical to making culture. And you need to be intentional so that it's the culture that you want to have. Not the culture that you might dream about." I believe wholeheartedly that norms are crucial to the day-to-day operations of your organization as well as the culture you desire. I should know. I've had a front row seat to the importance of norms and how they ought to be thought of as your organization's operating system.

When I joined TELUS in 2008 as its global head of Leadership, Collaboration, and Learning, there were ample opportunities to think about how team members might work better with one another. One key component of the company-wide culture change we undertook was the introduction of norms. We had to consider both organizational and team norms.

Organizational norms were those implemented standards expected of everyone across the company, regardless of location or title. Flexible Work Styles—the company's pioneering concept officially launched in 2009 that gave team members the choice to work from home, in the office, or a combination—was one example of the organizational norms. It's still going strong many years later, updated to reflect current times, of course.

Fair Process, an organization-wide collaboration and decision-making framework, was another organizational norm that we introduced. (I provide more analysis of Fair Process when I talk about the *agency* life-factor in Chapter IV.) Other organizational norms included the systemic use of collaboration tools and technology. After these organizational norms were introduced, the culture at TELUS dramatically improved. To look at just one measure, over five years, the firm's employee engagement score skyrocketed from 53 percent to 87 percent. Of course, I'm biased, but it felt like many people were blooming during those days at the organization.

Team norms were another dimension of the culture change at TELUS. It is essential to measure culture not only at the organization-wide level but also at the team level. While organizational norms are critical in terms of culture, individual teams have unique operating methods. What works for the sales team may be quite different to what works for engineers or people working in finance, and may even be considered quite unorthodox. A marketing or public relations team may decide it's okay to answer texts and emails at night because of the nature of their jobs, whereas a group of university professors in the faculty of Dentistry might consider the prospect anathema. This is precisely why team norms have become a twin to organizational norms.

Over the years, I have gone through many organizational and team norm exercises inside and outside of TELUS. While there is no one way to conduct the practice, it essentially comes down to identifying and answering a few questions. Furthermore—and this is imperative—it's not a one-time exercise. Norms must be re-examined reasonably regularly at both the organizational and team levels. If you define them once and hope for the best, you're more likely to be bitten by a shark than to witness sustained cultural success. (By the way, the odds of getting bitten by a shark are 1 in 3,748,067.[72])

Next, let's discover the questions that you must continually ask (and answer) regarding organizational and team norms. Of course, you'll likely have your own questions, but the list I've devised will help kick-start the collaborative conversations you need to have with team members on the creation of said norms. The questions have been broken down into three categories: what and how, who and who else, and where and when.

One more point that can't be stressed enough: norms are a decisively important component of your culture. And as you should begin to recognize by now, when your culture is humming, you create the opportunity for more team members to bloom.

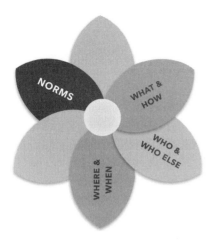

WHAT AND HOW

The what and how of norms centre on two actions: define the norm and then characterize the behaviour associated with it. The norms may change, but documenting them is essential. It's also best to involve members far and wide as organizational norms get created or updated. As for team norms, the bare minimum standard is to involve all of your team members in creating and updating them. That's how great cultures get built. Some what and how questions to consider are as follows:

ORGANIZATIONAL NORMS: WHAT AND HOW

WHAT	HOW
What are our decision-making methods across the organization?	How should the organization collaborate to make decisions?
What do our customers, clients, or citizens expect of us?	How will we put those we serve externally first?
What do we expect of our CEO/top leaders?	How must our CEO/top leaders show up for team members and others?
What collaboration technology do we standardize across the organization?	How will we ensure that all team members can seamlessly connect and collaborate?
What is our organization-wide philosophy on learning and development, career development, and a skills-based culture?	How will we hire, promote, develop, and shift people into roles and projects across the entire organization, and terminate people when necessary?

TEAM NORMS: WHAT AND HOW

WHAT	HOW
On our team, what do we expect of each other as we work together?	How will we support one another to accomplish our goals and deliverables?
What do we expect of our direct leaders as they lead us?	How will our leader back our team's operations and norms?
What does our leader expect of team members?	How will we be expected to support the team leader in our operations?
What is our team's strategy to collaborate with other teams?	How will we be known as we work with different teams?
What is our team's philosophy regarding new roles, assignments, or projects?	How will we ensure team members can apply their skills to new opportunities on the team?

WHO AND WHO ELSE

The who and who else dynamic of norms concerns an aspect of corporate culture that is far too often missed: who needs to be involved AND who else needs to be involved? Organizational and team norms must not be crafted in isolation. Furthermore, care must be applied in terms of whom the norms directly and indirectly affect. Here are some who and who else questions to consider:

ORGANIZATIONAL NORMS: WHO AND WHO ELSE

WHO	WHO ELSE
Who is primarily affected by the introduction of this org norm?	Who is secondarily affected by the introduction of this org norm?
Who stands to benefit from this org norm?	Who stands to be negatively affected by this org norm?
Who must be included in the adoption of this org norm?	Who is a secondary stakeholder in the rollout of this org norm?

TEAM NORMS: WHO AND WHO ELSE

WHO	WHO ELSE
Who from our team is affected by the introduction of this norm?	Who from outside of our team is affected by this norm?
Who from our team stands to benefit from this team norm?	Who from outside our team stands to benefit from this team norm?
Who from our team will be upset with this team norm?	Who from outside of our team will be negatively affected by the norm?

WHERE AND WHEN

The where and when of norms focus on two critical facets of work: place and time. Whether you were aware of it or not, we were hurtling quickly toward a showdown between employees and employers about where and when right before the pandemic took off in 2020. The results of various lockdowns and other pandemic-induced mindset changes expedited the reality of the where and when of work. Thus, careful thought ought to be invested in the organization and team norms that deal with place (where the work happens) and time (when the work occurs.) Some where and when questions to consider are as follows:

ORGANIZATIONAL NORMS: WHERE AND WHEN

WHERE	WHEN
Do we have a flexible work styles standard across the organization? (Where can people work?)	Does our organization support standard hours of operation? If so, when does our organization operate?
What are our standards to equip team members to work effectively if working from home?	Do specific roles require flexible hours? If so, when do certain roles operate? Has it been communicated?
If team members are working remotely (at home, in the office, and in between), what are our standards to equip them so they can work effectively?	Do we support the "right to disconnect"? If so (or if it's the law), have we communicated our policy of when people can or should disconnect?

WHERE	WHEN
What are our standards to equip team members to work effectively if working solely from the office?	Do we support time shifting so team members can work flexible hours? If so, what is it and has it been communicated to team members?
Do we wish to employ organization-wide "anchor days" so team members are expected to be on-site and in the office on certain days of the week? (Combination of where + when)	

TEAM NORMS: WHERE AND WHEN

WHERE	WHEN
In addition to any organizational norms, does our team require team members to be on-site?	In addition to any organizational norms, when does our team require team members to be on-site?
Does our team require team members to be online for particular meetings or occasions? What platform will we use?	When will these sessions occur if we require team members to be online for particular meetings or occasions?
Does our team desire certain times or days of the year, quarter, or month to hold training, recognition, or team bonding events? If so, where will these be held and when? (Combination of where + when)	

You can download a copy of the Organizational and Team Norms What and How, Who and Who Else, and Where and When questions at www.worklifebloom.com/extras.

In the Greenhouse: WORK-FACTORS

There is much for you to unpack and apply regarding the six work-factors. I never suggested it would be easy. In reality, leadership is pretty difficult. To become a better leader and help your team members to bloom, you should thoroughly consider the lessons and tactics I've presented across the six work-factors. The work may be challenging, but it is essential.

I began this chapter by recommending that—as you learned about each work-factor—you also keep in mind the pillars on which your team members base their view of their roles. As a reminder, those pillars of a team member's perspective were the following:

- The team they are a part of.
- The organization as a whole.
- You, the leader of the team.

Make no mistake, your team members not only regularly scrutinize, interpret, and assess how effectively the work-factors get handled in terms of the three pillars, but also constantly question their role and responsibility in each one. Which is to say, there is one additional viewpoint to introduce: the team member themselves. Maybe that seed was already planted for you.

The Global Work-Life Assessment revealed that for team members to bloom, they need most—not all—of the work-factors to be viewed positively. So, while the work-factors are only one half of the Work-Life Bloom model, the more you can have conversations with team members about their views on the six work-factors against the backdrop of the team, organization, you, as well as themselves, the more everyone will benefit. Therefore, consider these final questions about how you can measure your success as a leader as it relates to each work-factor.

TRUST

✿ Does the team member feel the majority of their interactions are authentic and consistent and that people advocate for one another?

BELONGING

✿ Does the team member feel understood, represented, and safe, and that they are continuously awash with positive experiences?

VALUED

✿ Does the team member believe they are paid fairly, consistently recognized, and frequently appreciated for their impacts?

PURPOSE

✿ Does the team member agree that the intention, beliefs, and actions of the organization and its team members are to improve society?

STRATEGY

✿ Does the team member understand the organization's direction, priorities, and focus so they can positively function in their role?

NORMS

✿ Does the team member understand the operating principles and guidelines for interacting with peers and colleagues?

You may choose to use a dashboard of some sort to help keep tabs on your team members' opinions or perspectives across each of the six work-factors and pillars. For example, you could make notes or use a 5-point Likert scale. Feel free to use something like the chart below (or visit www.worklifebloom.com/extras to download a copy).

	THE TEAM	ORGANIZA-TION	ME/LEADER	TEAM MEMBER
	How does the team member view their peers in terms of enacting or living up to this work-factor?	How does the team member view the organization's efforts to endorse this work-factor across the culture and operations?	How does the team member view my leadership style specific to this work-factor?	How does the team member view their own conduct specific to this work-factor?
TRUST				
BELONGING				
VALUED				
PURPOSE				
STRATEGY				
NORMS				

NEXT, WE'RE SETTING our sights on the other side of the garden box: the six life-factors. Before you dig in, keep in mind one important point. I stated earlier that there is no such thing as work-life balance. While I'm standing by that point, I want you to reflect on the word "balance" for a moment. What if we looked at it not as a fulcrum or teeter-totter but as a bank account? Don't we all want a positive or high *balance* in our savings account? Don't we all experience anxiety if our bank account *balance* drops to zero?

Of course we do. So, I want you to think of the six life-factors as six positive investments, not in a bank but in an individual's personal account. We want the balance of that account to be as high as possible. And when it is, we bring those positive vibes into our work and lives. Win-win!

Like the six work-factors, the life-factors are not about work-life balance but they can help people achieve a positive *balance* in their personal account. And as you will discover, the six life-factors are the attributes that help to develop the character of a team member.

*"You are the storyteller of your own life,
and you can create your own legend or not."*[1]

ISABEL ALLENDE

CHAPTER IV

Life-Factors

IRST PUBLISHED IN 1988, Brazilian author Paulo Coehlo's novel *The Alchemist* is at its core a story about transformation and the relentless pursuit of one's "Personal Legend." It is an ideal starting point for this chapter, which focuses on the six life-factors of the Work-Life Bloom model.

The allegorical novel follows an Andalusian boy named Santiago, whose parents' dream is that he enter the priesthood. Santiago's dream, however, is to travel. He becomes a shepherd, wandering the southern Spanish countryside to appease his need for constant movement. A conformist he is not.

Santiago's penchant for peripatetic ways continues. Answering a call he hears in a recurring dream, he heads to Egypt in search of a treasure. That search is a metaphor for Santiago to discover his "Personal Legend" and live life to the fullest.

In his youth, Santiago seems to fully comprehend his "Personal Legend." Yet, as he ages over years of travel to Egypt, he recognizes that things can get in the way of remembering (and further developing) one's Legend. The team members under your leadership may be having a similar experience. How many were blooming in their younger days and now seem to have checked out or become disinclined to pursue their "Personal Legend"? How many are dealing with significant obstacles in life that are getting in the way of their efforts to further develop themselves to *be their best*? This is an important point for you as a leader to contemplate.

While on the road to Egypt, Santiago realizes that many people become stuck, blockaded, and even blinded by a diverse assortment of issues along the journey of life. Antagonists, inclement weather episodes, anxious moments, and terrifying scenarios can all stall or inhibit the quest to achieve one's "Personal Legend." Santiago recognizes this quandary in one particular passage:

> Everyone, when they are young, knows what their Personal Legend is. At that point in their lives, everything is clear and everything is possible. They are not afraid to dream, and to yearn for everything they would like to see happen to them in their lives. But, as time passes, a mysterious force begins to convince them that it will be impossible for them to realize their Personal Legend . . . To realize one's Personal Legend is a person's only real obligation.[2]

Throughout his journey to the pyramids—and, spoiler alert, the trek back to a very noteworthy sycamore tree in Andalusia—Santiago discovers how important it is to remain true to yourself and to constantly develop yourself throughout the quest to achieve your "Personal Legend." Giving in to the expectations of others is no way to live a life, according to Santiago. Nor is settling. Good is just not good enough.

We could argue that through the character of Santiago, Coelho is imploring us to live a life that is not solely chockablock of meaning but also has respect, healthy passion, connections, constant growth, and the courage to make decisions. People should feel it is their duty—an intimate responsibility—to reach and thus fulfill their "Personal Legend." However, there is a plot twist toward the end of the novel when Santiago experiences an epiphany.

A full life is not accomplished from the achievement of the "Personal Legend" but rather from the daily pursuit of it. The adage "to learn is to live" is important, sure. But "to live is to trek" is vital. Coelho's big reveal is that the most significant learning in life comes from the journey itself and not the achievement of some end-state. When you calibrate that message against the Work-Life Bloom theory, there is an underlying argument to consider. As I mentioned in Chapter I, "Our lives shape our work; nevertheless, our work shapes us." What is the argument I encourage you to mull over?

Will you become a positive force and assist in your team members' life-journey?

Coelho's hidden message is powerful yet also poignant. For however long you may be their leader, you have a pivotal role to play in helping the individuals under your direction both pursue and achieve their "Personal Legend." To be clear, you are not responsible for your team members' lives. That much is obvious, partially because you cannot make decisions for them. You're not about to weigh in on the nitty-gritty, like a home purchase or the preparation of a will. But you can positively impact them and their interpretation of the lessons they learn along the way. In this regard, you are helping them to *be their best*, and maybe even pushing them closer to realizing their dreams.

Metaphorically speaking, you play a crucial part in each team member's journey to Egypt and back. As the alchemist points out to Santiago:

> Before a dream is realized, the Soul of the World tests everything that was learned along the way. It does this not because it is evil, but so that we can, in addition to realizing our dreams, master the lessons we've learned as we've moved toward that dream. That's the point at which most people give up. It's the point at which, as we say in the language of the desert, one "dies of thirst just when the palm trees have appeared on the horizon." [3]

A former letter carrier for the U.K.'s Royal Mail provides some profound first-hand and non-allegorical insights into the significance of every employee's journey—their "Personal Legend." Furthermore, his story highlights the importance of several life-factors that can affect one's role, which we will unpack throughout this chapter.

In 1981, Phil Goddard became an apprentice engineer with British Telecom (BT). Over the years, he moved up the ranks, eventually landing in a pre-sales role, where his technical acumen helped him land major deals for the company. In his later years at BT, Goddard became an account manager and sales executive, leading both accounts and teams of BT team members, and handling multinational clients.

His had been an excellent career to this point. Goddard was not only a hard worker and respected leader at BT but also a dedicated networker. His Rolodex of internal and external contacts was vast. He felt supported by his peers, his team, the clients he served, and leaders across the company.

In 2006, after 25 years at BT, he was offered a voluntary redundancy package. Once he finished mulling over the pros and cons of the offer, he accepted it. In doing so, Goddard was now free to think about what might come next. "As you get older," he told me, "the pace, the energy, and the demands become a challenge."[4] He moved roles and companies three times during the next 14 years. It's fair to say these were hit-and-miss career stops. Then, in 2020, the pandemic hit. A private equity firm unexpectedly bought the company Goddard was working for, and he was immediately furloughed. Eventually, he was made redundant.

"I had gone from having a really great career," Goddard thoughtfully offered, "feeling really important, having a team of sales professionals, and having a sense of purpose to suddenly facing life in the scrap heap." Goddard was 55 years old and worried about what he would do next in his career and life in general. Was the journey over?

Using his network, Goddard landed a position at TalkTalk—a national telecom carrier in the U.K. However, by Christmas of 2020, Goddard realized he was completely unhappy in his new role. Moments of stress, a lack of support, and an inability to sleep led to serious self-reflection.

"As life goes on, your tolerance for suffering fools diminishes," he quipped. Goddard weighed the good paycheque against his misery, grappling with what to do. He asked himself some serious life questions. He wondered out loud to me during our interview, "Do I work to live, or do I live to work?"

That is one of those existential questions we must ask ourselves—and ask of our team members—if we desire a blooming state. However, in order to answer it, we need a sense of ownership of our journey. Brené Brown writes in 2017's *Rising Strong*, "We are the authors of our lives. We write our own daring endings."[5]

Remember, though, that you are the leader of a team. I would add to Brown's passage that every author—that is, you and your team members—could do with an editor. Maybe even a few. Might you play the part of your team members' editor? Can you help them develop factors that permit them to answer that most existential question from above? Could you lend a hand so they might successfully write their "own daring ending"?

Goddard eventually resigned from TalkTalk. "I admitted to myself that I was unhappy, and I then felt two feet taller," he remarked. While he was working through his three-month notice period, his wife told him, "Royal Mail is recruiting. Why don't you apply to be a postman?"

He applied for the letter carrier job, answered some online situational-based questions, and almost instantly landed an interview. "Careful what you wish for," joked Goddard, quoting Confucius. "I was offered the job."

What did Goddard learn through this part of his life's journey?

"If you let life dictate to you, and you worry about it, your brain will stimulate hormones and make you feel bad," said Goddard. He believes that everybody's situation is unique, but a humble moment during his shift to becoming a postman was the global response he received. After his story went viral, thanks to an article in a U.K. newspaper, it seemed that the entire world was behind him.

"I had messages from every continent, all sorts of people saying you've really inspired me," Goddard added. He wondered why people were so moved by his decision to become a mail carrier after so many years of being an executive. "When you dig under the surface," he said, "people say, 'I want to be able to do that.'"

In my opinion, the "that" Goddard suggests people desire is having the gumption, fortitude, and means to continue fulfilling a "Personal Legend." At 55 years of age, Goddard was determined to continue being the author of his life, writing his own daring story.

He seems to have achieved that aim. In early 2023, he left Royal Mail for a position at Social Value Portal, a company that helps organizations in the pursuit of social, economic, and environmental well-being. "I now feel that I am contributing to something meaningful in society," he said to me in a follow-up conversation. Its mission as a social impact company is to prevent greenwashing by instituting methods to accurately measure and report social purpose value. Goddard proved again the importance of the "Personal Legend," its alignment with the Work-Life Bloom model, and—as we will discover in this chapter—the six life-factors.

Goddard's vulnerable recounting of his journey—like Santiago's revelation in *The Alchemist*—provides you with something to consider. How much support does your direct leader provide as you journey through life and, by extension, work? And, how willing and prepared are you as a leader to create the conditions that will help your team members successfully carry out their own journey?

These questions are at the crux of this chapter and the life-factors, six unique elements that focus on the self and help to create the conditions for people to bloom. The life-factors complement the work-factors from the previous chapter but are unique in that they focus on an individual's identity, their self.

The life-factors are attributes that develop a person's character and are used in life, of course, but they also help an individual in the workplace. So it's a win-win scenario for the crops in the garden box. By extension, when you help team members successfully develop their life-factors, your garden box becomes that much easier to manage as well.

In this chapter, we will tackle each life-factor, exposing their impact on team members and looking at practical techniques to apply them to help team members develop their proficiency. The six life-factors aligned with the Work-Life Bloom model are as follows:

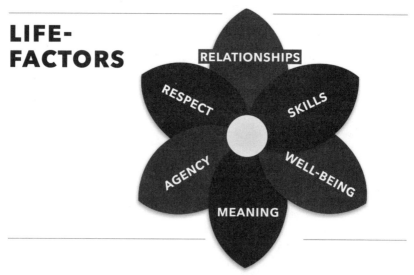

LIFE-FACTORS

RELATIONSHIPS
RESPECT
SKILLS
AGENCY
WELL-BEING
MEANING

✿ **Relationships**: The community of strong and weak ties—your full network of connections—which facilitate a willing exchange of assistance.

✿ **Skills**: The attributes you develop and the aptitudes you gain to perform confidently at work and in life.

❁ **Well-being:** The emotional, social, physical, and financial health of your present state.

❁ **Meaning:** The feeling and articulation of self-worth on a daily basis.

❁ **Agency:** The ability to make decisions and take action that results in positive outcomes.

❁ **Respect:** The expression of appreciation and admiration for who you really are.

Before I dig the spade deep into the soil of the *relationships* life-factor, take a few moments to think carefully about the following words from author Kathleen Winter in her 2010 novel, *Annabel*:

> People are rivers, always ready to move from one state of being into another. It is not fair to treat people as if they are finished beings. Everyone is always becoming and unbecoming.[6]

Keep this passage in mind as you begin to deliberate the life-factors of *Work-Life Bloom*.

Life-Factor No. 1: RELATIONSHIPS

The community of strong and weak ties–your full network of connections–which facilitate a willing exchange of assistance.

❁ ❁

Please promote relationships between colleagues.
PROFESSIONAL, BUSINESS/PROFESSIONAL SERVICES, SPAIN, 18-24 YEARS

Get people together to build teams outside of work. Meaningful programs in the community are great team-building initiatives that gives
employees broader perspectives and also builds relationships. Managers need to ensure there are career/life goals in place, not just corporate
goals. Worthy for management teams to discuss.
VICE-PRESIDENT, INTERNET, USA, 45-54 YEARS

✿ ✿

With all due respect to the 1980s Norwegian band, you're bound to
have a few "a-ha" moments when you change roles and companies. I
joined TELUS in late 2008, a few months after leaving SAP. One of the first
events I participated in at TELUS was the annual Retirees Holiday Lunch.
Despite its current-day international prowess across multiple business
lines, TELUS started in 1904 as a British Columbia-based, publicly run
telecommunications company. Given its history, retirees are an essential
part of the culture.

The Retirees Holiday Lunch is just as you might expect. In a very large
room that accommodates hundreds of people, former TELUS team members arrive just before noon to be feted and served by current executives
and leaders. The meal is turkey—with all the trimmings—complemented
by holiday goodies, egg nog, and hot chocolate. The current leaders revel
in the opportunity to put on festive aprons and ridiculously oversized oven
mitts, taking orders and delivering hot plates to the retirees' liking. Lovely
thank-you gifts are distributed at the end of the shindig.

During my inaugural Holiday Lunch, I had a conversation with an older
woman that sticks with me to this day. It was a festive "a-ha" moment, a
gift that keeps giving.

After a few small-talk questions and answers, I realized that I was talking to a 40-year veteran of the company. She was a former director who
had held several different roles and responsibilities over her tenure. She
had been retired for over a decade. Somehow, we then got onto the subject of networks and relationships. I'm paraphrasing, but the end of the
conversation went something like the following:

I love coming to this lunch every year. It reminds me how important
my friends were to me at BC Tel [former name of TELUS]. I was busy but
happy. There was a lot going on. But I was never bored, never lonely.

And then, without prompting, she offered me some advice, knowing I had only been at the company for about six weeks.

Find your people: it's the best thing you'll ever do.

I often think about that exchange, and in the context of this book, I wonder if today's leaders fully comprehend how important it is for team members to *find their people*. Perhaps more significantly, are leaders aware of the impact they can have when they help to create such an outcome?

Research suggests, however, that large swathes of people are lonely. Many individuals have no network, not even a small one. We might construe loneliness as the opposite of finding your people. If a person doesn't have a vibrant network—when there are no strong relationship ties in their orbit—the chances for loneliness increase. If strong ties are lacking, the likelihood of the next tier of contacts—oftentimes referred to as one's weak ties—dramatically diminishes too.

Not only does loneliness create negative consequences in one's life, it creates deleterious workplace effects too. The whole situation is about as stimulating as occupying the middle seat on an airplane, sandwiched between two obnoxiously intoxicated first-time flyers during a five-hour flight. It's that bad.

Nobel Prize winners Daniel Kahneman and Angus Deaton discovered through their 2010 research, for example, that loneliness was one of the top factors preventing life happiness and satisfaction. Unsurprisingly, people who are lonely demonstrate a high incidence of sadness, stress, and anxiety.[7] In addition, research conducted by the University of Chicago psychologist John Cacioppo in 2014 suggested that loneliness can increase an older person's chances of premature death by 14 percent.[8]

From a work perspective, in a 2022 study of several hundred hotel employees, researchers showed that workplace loneliness leads to psychological detachment from people's jobs.[9] The research also revealed that workplace loneliness contributes to emotional exhaustion, creating adverse effects on the home front. A similar 2020 study in New Delhi found that loneliness at work "was negatively associated with psychological well-being and self-esteem" and that managers suffering from loneliness at work reported "increased feelings of work alienation."[10] Maybe Paul McCartney was onto something when he wrote the song "No More Lonely Nights." Or maybe Drake was with his song "I Get Lonely." Or heck, his follow-up, "I Get Lonely Too."

As if things weren't bad enough, the pandemic has done us no favours on the loneliness front. For many workers in roles not deemed essential or frontline, the shift to a home-based office was swift and even distressing. Steven Van Cohen and Ryan Jenkins, who wrote the 2022 book *Connectable*, found that 72 percent of all global workers experience loneliness monthly, and a shocking 55 percent feel lonely at least weekly.[11] As the loneliness numbers continue to increase and strong and weak tie relationships plunge, research firms have assessed the costs.

A massive 2017 study of thousands of U.K.-based employees conducted by New Economics Research indicated that loneliness costs employers roughly £2.5 billion annually.[12] Cigna, a U.S. healthcare and insurance company, suggests loneliness costs U.S.-based employers more than US$154 billion annually in stress-related absenteeism.[13] The Bankwest Curtin Economics Centre says it costs Australian employers AU$2.7 billion.[14] Wherever you look, loneliness and a lack of relationships cost organizations billions. It's like an omnipresent weed in the garden box.

In 2018—long before COVID-19 took over our lives—the U.K. Government created a Ministry of Loneliness in response to the loneliness crisis. It has been in operation ever since. Its purpose is clear: "Supporting people to have meaningful social relationships is not just crucial to people's physical and mental health. It also affects their engagement in the workplace and wider community cohesion."[15] It's looking out for both the wellness of its citizens (life) and the organizations that employ them (work). I'd go so far as to say the Ministry of Loneliness could be considered the first adopter of at least part of the Work-Life Bloom framework.

A few other people are trying to fix this loneliness and relationship plight too. Aaron Hurst, whom I mentioned earlier in the book, is the founder of Imperative, a company that believes "meaningful human connection at work is the key to unlocking transformational benefits both to the business and individual employees."[16] Hurst is one of the good guys doing good things to help solve the predicament I outlined above.

During our discussion on my *Leadership NOW* program,[17] Hurst pointed out that leaders must take responsibility for getting employees out of their loneliness cycle. In addition, he's adamant that leaders must help their team members by encouraging them to have meaningful relationships.

"At the junior level, a lot of it is tied to how we design jobs, all the interactions are transactional, and there's no real place for human interaction in the workplace anymore," said Hurst. "It's all transactional interaction. As you get more senior, there actually is more human interaction."

It's a salient point. As a leader, you're likely very busy and in multiple meetings with different people daily, while also possessing a vast network of LinkedIn contacts. The same may not be true for your team members. It might do you some good to check in with your team to see just how wide and deep their networks are, not only to help combat loneliness but also to build up team members' self-esteem, access to information, and sense of meaning. That in turn can help eliminate potential sadness, stress, anxiety, and exhaustion at work and home.

"We are wired to naturally be drawn to and thrive when we are with other people and where we feel protected by the group," Hurst said. "We are optimized neurologically to crave that, and when we don't have it, we start to shut down and operate out of fear. It's when you feel like you are part of a group of people, where it's meeting your neurological need for a tribe. And when you don't have that, you start to move into an 'us versus them' mentality, losing empathy and shutting down your willingness to take risks. Unfortunately, I think that's happened in the workplace, and the pandemic exacerbated it."

In today's fast-paced world of rapidly advancing changes, creating space for human conversations and connections is critical, especially in the workplace. Leaders must acknowledge that networks and relationships are vital components of team members' well-being. When those components are flourishing, so too will both the organization and the individual. In other words, the life-factor *relationships* helps team members in life and work.

Obviously, you are not the U.K. Government (unless you are reading this book and are, in fact, part of the U.K. Government), so you're likely not about to set up a Department of Loneliness at your organization. Instead, something more practical—let's say relationship tools—is required to help your team members find their people and stem the tide

of loneliness by building better networks. But before we get to those relationship garden tools, let's open up the Farmer's Almanac and see some
good and not-so-good results from the Global Work-Life Assessment Survey regarding the *relationships* life-factor.

FARMER'S ALMANAC: **RELATIONSHIPS**

In 2022, the author Scott Stratten shared the following with me: "If you
believe business is built on relationships, make building them your business."[18] Stratten is spot on.

The good news is that a large proportion of leaders (73 percent)
and non-leaders (59 percent) polled in the Global Work-Life Assessment Survey also believe that relationships are an important element
of one's ability to bloom. Incidentally, male and female participants
polled identically at 69 percent, and there was no discernible difference between Gen Z, Millennials, Gen X, and Baby Boomers. Between
68 and 70 percent of each generation surveyed on the topic responded
that meaningful relationships were important.

How important is it to you to have meaningful relationships at work?

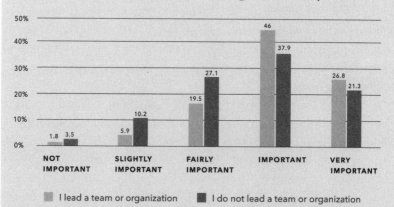

If relationships, and thus a robust network of strong and weak ties,
are important to a majority of team members, I maintain that leaders bear partial responsibility for nurturing relationships. Not only are

relationships good for business, as Stratten suggests, but they also combat loneliness and improve employee performance. Furthermore, a strong network can create a built-in support network for the inevitable times of life and work dodginess. A U.K. director in professional services provides some fantastic context for the latter point:

I have very close relationships with the people that I work with. We are a very close-knit team. Because of this, we speak very candidly about personal situations, mental health, well-being, and support each other through any challenges.

DIRECTOR, BUSINESS/PROFESSIONAL SERVICES, U.K., 35-44 YEARS

The sad reality that I discovered in my research, however, is that leaders are not creating the conditions for relationships and networks to form. At the same time of my survey, only 43 percent of leaders felt that their current employer had helped them develop their network and relationships, which is relatively feeble. The situation is positively dire for non-leaders. A paltry 23 percent believed they were being provided with above average or significant help in this area.

Has your current employer helped in the development of your network/relationships?

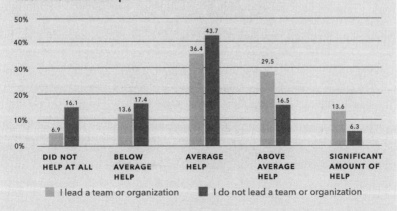

To recap: Most employees, regardless of their level, gender, and age, believe that relationships are important, yet a huge majority don't believe their organizations are doing much to make that happen. It is time to open up the shed and determine what garden tools you need for the *relationships* life-factor.

The Garden Tools of Relationships

It is clear that social community has declined over the past several years. With that decline comes both concern and opportunity. You ought to be concerned, because a lonely person in life is likely to be a lonely worker. And, as we've discovered, loneliness is a costly expense. However, on the glass-half-full front, you can create the conditions at work that allow a team member to feel part of something. You may argue that being connected to a community of workplace peers is a given. Being employed is enough. I counter-argue that when you treat the workplace as a social community, far greater benefits can accrue for team members at work and in life.

Before I outline the relationships garden tools for you to consider, step back for a minute and think about a few of the community-wilting stalks in society. We discussed loneliness earlier in this section, but there are other examples of how our social relationships are declining. For example, U.S. church membership among adults was 76 percent at the end of World War II. It now hovers at less than 50 percent.[19] In the U.K., the Church of England admitted in 2018 that Sunday service church attendance had fallen by roughly 300,000 people since 2009.[20]

In 2021, Enso Group and Quadrant Strategies discovered that only 35 percent of Americans strongly agreed that they fit in with their local community. To drive home the consequences of that, the authors stated: "Low community belonging is likely to mean less happiness, lower health, and shorter life outcomes."[21] And let's not forget the 80-year Harvard Study on Adult Development (Grant and Glueck), which I cited in Chapter 11. So what was the one factor from the Harvard Study that primarily distinguished if someone was happy or not? Drumroll, please . . . Relationships!

The collapse of local community newspapers is potentially another sign of the *relationships* life-factor quagmire. Since 2005, the USA has lost more than 25 percent of its community newspapers. That figure is on track to reach 33 percent by 2025, according to Northwestern's Medill School of Journalism.[22] The same trend can be seen in Canada. Since 2008, 344 community newspapers have shut down (with 66 new ones starting) for a net loss of 278 publications.[23] As handy as it might seem, Facebook Marketplace is no substitute for community-building. Local newspapers—be they online, physical, or both—are one more reason people's relationship quotients are dwindling.

The decline in people's community—and the related consequence of loneliness—was sublimely pointed out by the author Robert Putnam. First, in a prescient 1995 article, "Bowling Alone: America's Declining Social Capital," and later in his 2000 book, *Bowling Alone: The Collapse and Revival of American Community*, Putnam revealed that Americans were becoming less and less connected with one another. For example, attendance at various community meetings had dropped by 58 percent, family dinners had declined by 43 percent, and there was a 35 percent falloff of get-togethers with close friends.[24] And this data was collected before Y2K!

Leaders must create a sense of community at work, because that may be all an individual has. It is vital that you—as the supporting leader of your team—create the conditions in which people can build and nurture both strong and weak ties inside and outside the organization. Your leadership in the context of this life-factor is crucial. As the authors John Hagel III, John Seely Brown, and Lang Davison wrote in 2010: "The edges of our social networks represent the weak ties that connect us to people who can provide us with access to new insights, experiences, and capabilities that provoke us to improve our own game."[25] But the reality is, your team members need strong ties if you ever want them to develop their weak ties.

I recommend you employ a three-prong relationship-building approach for your team members: inside, outside, and online. Let's tackle *inside* first.

INSIDE

Christine Porath is a professor at Georgetown University's McDonough School of Business. She is the author of *Mastering Community: The Surprising Ways Coming Together Moves Us from Surviving to Thriving* and defines "community" as "a group of individuals who share a mutual concern for one another's welfare." Porath believes that to reach a community state, we must always be looking out for each other's well-being. She suggested to me that a better community is achieved when we care about one another.[26] In turn, this can create a better corporate culture.

I agree. And in fact, I'll go one step further. As a leader, you demonstrate care when you help establish community *inside* the organization. *Inside*, therefore, refers to the people on the team you lead and team members from other parts of the organization.

Helping team members develop their *inside* network is vital. A strong community and organizational networking ethos cannot be enjoyed by only a few people. The renowned management thinker Henry Mintzberg says it best: "Companies are communities. There's a spirit of working together. Communities are not a place where a few people allow themselves to be singled out as solely responsible for success."[27]

Here are some ideas that you could use to support team members in building their internal (*inside*) relationship:

• **Networking 101:** You likely got to where you are today as a leader in part because you know how to network *inside* the organization. It's time to pass on that wisdom. Take a moment to ask your direct reports what they do by way of internal networking. Use an open-ended question for this so they can answer freely. Regardless of their answer, invest the time to help them understand the basics of internal networking and how to make connections that might currently seem out of reach.

- **Skip-level meetings**: These are formal or informal one-on-one or small group sessions that involve team members who report to your direct reports. If your current leadership hierarchy is structured this way, skip-level (or skip-skip-level) meetings can build relationships with people inside your unit. This in turn helps your bond with the team members you meet to grow and helps them by giving them exposure. In addition, they will likely pick up a few networking tips along the way.

- TMRGS: Team member resource groups (TMRGS) not only can assist with the *belonging* work-factor from the previous chapter but also can act as a beautiful relationship-building medium. At its root, a TMRG is a team member-led group whose aim is to connect others to causes and issues they support. In 1970, the Xerox CEO Joseph Wilson helped launch the world's first TMRG by supporting the Xerox National Black Employees Caucus. This group permitted Black team members to discuss their experiences at the company. If your organization does not have a TMRG strategy, I suggest you remedy that immediately. Your direct support of TMRGS (and ideally participation in them) will build strong and weak ties over time and support the *belonging* work-factor. A Canadian vice-president shared this comment in the Global Work-Life Assessment Survey about the value of TMRGS: "My company has an Indigenous Ally Networks employee resource group. Being part of this group enables me to think about how to better contribute to a healthy society both within and outside the work environment."

- **Peer-to-peer (P2P) learning groups**: Unlike TMRGS, P2P learning groups (sometimes referred to as forums) are managed instances of employee teach-backs and sharing. They're a form of collaborative education—typically held face-to-face but sometimes held virtually—that usually does not involve a formal instructor. Instead, team members come together and work together on the content or problem to solve. Because these groups are cross-functional, involving members from across the organization, they help team members form new relationships.

- **Annual mentor**: Arrange an annual mentor for each of your team members. Over one year, the mentor provides guidance and counsel on items that matter most to your team member. The two of them establish the frequency of their meetings. Working with someone in a leadership position—but outside your direct management—establishes a new relationship and provides the opportunity for support different from your views and biases.

- **Mix-and-match hour (part 1)**: Once a month or quarter, set up each team member with a one-hour informal chat with someone from a different part of the organization. Use your leadership skills to help make the arrangements with the other leaders. There's no preparation required or meeting minutes to take. It's simply a good old-fashioned connection session, helping to develop weak ties into strong ones.

OUTSIDE

The best-selling author Dorie Clark once offered me sage counsel on the topic of external network building, also known as establishing relationships *outside* the organization. When people begin to network externally, they are adopting one of the most effective habits around to help them achieve long-term success. "When it comes to changing the course of your outcomes," Clark said, "other people are one of the biggest factors that contribute to that."[28]

Paying homage to the importance of weak ties, she also told me that external "acquaintances" could be equally vital to one's long-term success. Clark introduced me to a new type of networking: infinite horizon networking. I found it fascinating. Infinite horizon networking, as Clark described, is a "pure, no-agenda relationship-building" type of networking. It's about having zero goals or expectations in the external relationship. You're building the *outside* connection simply out of personal interest in the person as, well, a person. The concept here is that you just never know if your paths may cross at some point in the future when something completely organic may come to fruition.

I reflected on Clark's point and analyzed my *outside* relationships to see a) if they fit the parameters of her concept, and b) if so, what I did to create them. I realized that a couple of times a month, I reach out to complete strangers on LinkedIn. I introduce myself, provide some light context, offer to send them a signed book, and ensure they know there are no strings attached. I quickly realized I'd been hired several times to deliver keynotes because I'd been unwittingly using Clark's strategy for years.

However, helping your team members to build their *outside* network is not solely about reaching out to strangers. Consider these additional tactics to help them develop their external (*outside*) network:

- **External events (part 1):** It may seem obvious, but COVID-19 played havoc with corporate budgets. Consequently, many team members have missed meeting new people because opportunities for external face-to-face training or conference events have been reduced or cut altogether. You can fix this. Quit being such a penny-pincher. Invest in your people's development. By doing so, you are also encouraging their external network growth. Win-win!

- **Community volunteering:** Whether it's organized by your workplace or your direct team, or you allow individuals to arrange it on their own, volunteering in the community is another way to meet new people outside the workplace and the home. It doubles as a way to give back to those in need, which aligns with the *purpose* work-factor.

- **Special interest groups:** Persuading your team members to join special interest groups (SIGs) outside the organization can help them build contacts with people in a variety of professions. Toastmasters, for example, started in 1924 and is still going strong. It's a chapter-based organization devoted to helping people in local communities with public speaking and communication without a care for what industry people come from. International people development and talent organizations like ATD and SHRM also have regional chapters that people can join. Whatever the scenario, promoting SIGs to your team members is yet another way to help them meet new people outside your firm.

- **Mix-and-match hour (part 2):** In this version of the mix-and-match hour, you set up each member of your team to have a one-hour informal chat with one of your contacts from outside the organization. That may mean you reach out to another leader who connects one of their team members to yours. Two or three times a year is ample. It's yet another simple connection session, helping again to develop weak ties into strong ones.

ONLINE

A comment from a U.S.-based director via the Global Work-Life Assessment Survey explains what *online* can look like:

☆ ☆

I'd love to see more social time on our calendar. For example, we're working to create a virtual book club that supports developing personal relationships between global employees outside the professional persona. That peer-to-peer opportunity would establish more emotional connections and foster a stronger foundation of trust.

DIRECTOR, GOVERNMENT/MILITARY, USA, 25–34 YEARS

☆ ☆

Online is all about online relationship-building. Virtual book clubs are one way to go. I've been invited to more than a few virtual book clubs where I've been fortunate to meet some incredibly talented people.

As we have progressed through the *relationship* life-factor, you may have noticed that I have not articulated any online examples or tactics. That was deliberate. I'm not against online relationship-building. On the contrary. I have met heaps of brilliant people online, to shake their hands in a face-to-face setting only years later. Some I have never met face-to-face.

What I am against, however, is having online networking as the sole relationship-building option in your leadership toolshed. It should be used in addition to *inside* and *outside* networking. I do not recommend an online-only relationship-building approach.

Having said that, to help your team members build their online networking skills, consider using the following ideas:

- **Public channels**: The Internet is awash with nonsense, but reputable organizations with verified content contributors and lively public discussions are an excellent way to discover people. LinkedIn is a prominent platform that you should encourage team members to use to meet others. So, too, are publishing platforms like Medium and Substack, in part because you cannot be anonymous or use a pseudonym in them. Encouraging, or indeed teaching, your team members to participate in and build networks in online public channels will help them enhance their relationships through Web-based means.

- **Internal channels:** Online internal channels offer a unique opportunity to connect with colleagues across departments, locations, roles, and even countries. Many organizations use internal social platforms, such as Slack, Yammer, or Microsoft Teams, where team members can share ideas or comment on old ones and make new connections. You can encourage your team members to use these platforms by participating yourself and highlighting the benefits of engaging with colleagues online. Online interest groups, hobby groups, and team member networking groups (TMNGs) can be a great way for people to connect with others who share similar interests. You can facilitate the creation of these groups and encourage team members to participate, which may even strengthen existing bonds. After he reviewed this section of the book, my editor started a Slack channel for parents who work at Figure 1 Publishing. Kudos, Steve!

- **External events (part 2):** If we learned anything from COVID-19, it's that we're pretty good at virtual events. With CFOs continuing to watch their travel budgets, external online events will remain cost-effective ways to meet people outside your organization. While I did suggest above that you invest in your people by encouraging them to attend face-to-face events, that does not mean I believe live online events should be scrapped. For example, during a 2022 event for accountants that I keynoted, two-thirds of the attendees were online rather than with me in the conference centre. I showed a QR code on my last slide via the online platform that people could use to sign up for my online community, Bloom Friday, if they wished. (Go ahead and try it out with the QR code found below.) That nifty piece of technology meant I wound up connecting with nearly 100 people who weren't even in the room. Your team members can also leverage the benefits of technology in this way. When they participate in online events, encourage them not only to get connected with a speaker or facilitator but also to engage in the platform chat or the virtual networking rooms to meet other virtual attendees.

- **Mix-and-match hour (part 3):** You could also set up an *online-only* introduction between your team members and people from within your network who can act as online mentors or connections. They could correspond by email or direct message, or have a text-only relationship where the mentor provides small bursts of asynchronous assistance.

Now that we've finished with the *relationships* life-factor, let's tackle another important one: *skills*. I purposely placed these two factors back-to-back because there is such a complementary alignment between one's relationship-building capacity and what I will outline next in the *skills* life-factor.

Life-Factor No. 2: SKILLS

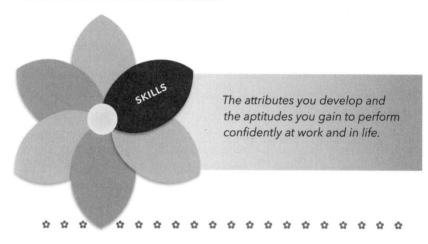

The attributes you develop and the aptitudes you gain to perform confidently at work and in life.

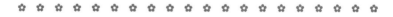

In a previous company, I was given the opportunity to change skill sets and positions. I was always learning, and it made the job more fun. I think professional development makes me feel supported.

PROFESSIONAL, EDUCATION, CANADA, 45-54 YEARS

Many people feel that their life ambitions are misaligned with the career development and talent management models they encounter at work.

While career progression conversations and the managing of talent will never go away for leaders, you must consider something else. What if team members no longer seek to climb the proverbial career ladder? What if they're looking for something more in their life than ascension to the corner office? Could it be a portfolio of some sort? Succession planning and merit promotions will continue to be necessary for you, but what happens when upward mobility is no longer central to a team member's life satisfaction quotient? What might they be interested in instead?

In a word, *skills.*

Three employees from three different work sectors in South Korea, Australia, and France who participated in the Global Work-Life Assessment Survey provide some candid assessments about their pleas for skills development.

✿ ✿

I feel stagnant at work and have no opportunity to develop my skills.
MANAGER, RETAIL, SOUTH KOREA, 45-54 YEARS

I am part of a newly formed team. I haven't been able to develop any new skills over the last year, and it is disheartening.
PROFESSIONAL, CONSULTING, AUSTRALIA, 25-34 YEARS

I am happy when my boss gives me the possibility to develop all my skills.
SENIOR VICE-PRESIDENT, ENGINEERING, FRANCE, 35-44 YEARS

✿ ✿

Some team members won't necessarily want to move up; they may, however, want to grow. They long for experiences. They seek juicy new lateral roles or special assignments and yearn to learn, connect, and develop. Building off the previous life-factor, *relationships,* they also crave new contacts and interactions that will help them become more well-rounded and affiliated human beings. These points are at the root of the *skills* life-factor.

Importantly, such team members will want to use their new skills not only at work but also in life. As a leader, you should therefore avoid focusing solely on workplace *vertical ambition* and instead consider something I call *horizontal ignition.* This will require you to adopt a horizontal skills-building mindset. If you don't, you may discover that your team members find their way to a different organization and at that point you may be finally forced into changing your mindset. But it will be too late.

An organization's reliance on a jobs-only talent model—and by association its entrenched job description and job family ideology—is an additional inhibitor to the successful implementation of the *skills* life-factor. In their 2023 book, *The Empathy Advantage*, Heather E. McGowan and Chris Shipley write: "Job descriptions are often little more than a portrait of the last person to hold that position. They tend to be filled with irrelevant requirements and, often, requirements for outdated skills. That's because we tend to think of jobs as a set of relevant skills learned at a university or in a training program, and that worked when skills had a reasonable shelf life. That's rarely the case these days."[29]

Not everyone wants to stay in a job family, waiting for a promotion based on merit, tenure, or both. If an organization solely uses the construct of job families—which denotes upward classification of job roles for a cluster of functions, for example, a job family of marketing or engineering roles—it prohibits people who want to develop themselves outside of the job family from ever believing they might be suitable working in an entirely different function. Embracing *horizontal ignition* is one way to evolve your *Work-Life Bloom* leadership game.

Thus, specific to the *skills* life-factor—and to help your people bloom—you have a threefold leadership task ahead of you related to *horizontal ignition*:

- Expand your team members' capabilities laterally across the organization.
- Invest in your team members' portfolio of skills.
- Mature your thinking to adopt a skills-based ecosystem mindset.

I will tackle each of these *horizontal ignition* components in the Garden Tools section, but first, I want to give you another example of the importance of the *skills* life-factor.

Ravin Jesuthasan is the author of *Work without Jobs*. He is also a senior partner and global lead for Transformation Services at the asset management firm Mercer. I discussed with Jesuthasan the importance of skills and why leaders and organizations need to develop new muscles and introduce new behaviours related to them.

Jesuthasan believes two central ideas will reshape the world of work. Both have something to do with skills. "First, how we redesign work to enable talent to flow as seamlessly as possible while sending it the signals, the assets, and the resources, to enable that talent to perpetually reinvent itself. And second is how we envision that talent experience so that we meet people on their individual terms instead of forcing them to fit our 'one size fits most' model."[30]

In a nod to his recommended elimination of the "one size fits most" scenario, Jesuthasan pointed out that organizations will eventually have to do away with their use of job descriptions. (That will certainly make McGowan and Shipley happy.) He sees a future where "skills become the most important asset" of both the organization and team members. The elimination of job descriptions will allow people to reinvent themselves, shifting into roles or assignments that motivate them to perform. (And when this happens, people will also feel good away from work.)

It's not as though people crave monotony in their roles. On the contrary, monotony is a leading indicator of disengagement. The continued practice of managing by job descriptions will wind up boxing individuals into routine tasks when they crave a continuous skills development environment.

The global healthcare giant Novartis is all in when it comes to adopting a skills-based ethos. The firm employs over 110,000 employees and earns annual revenues in excess of US$51 billion. Every year it touches the lives of 770 million patients worldwide. When I sat down with Simon Brown, the chief learning officer at Novartis, he pointed out that the company's shift to a skills-based operating system was crucial to properly aligning roles, people, and content to skills. "Everything hangs together through a common skills ontology and technology that provides a common language and framework to understand skills across the company. If we're looking at what we need to deliver against a certain business need or requirement in one area, we can assess what skills we have to fill the role gaps or we can even serve short-term gig assignments," he told me.[31]

Brown pointed out that the Novartis skills operating system not only facilitates the company's internal business operations but is being used for external purposes too. "We use our skills approach as people volunteer their time for NGOs and charities," he said. "We find that rather than people simply volunteering their time, for example, painting, we can properly match them to an organization that could take advantage of their core skills, such as someone having strategy planning as a core skill." He admitted Novartis will not realize the full benefits for a while as it's a multi-year strategy, but it is clear that the company's skills operating system has become a cornerstone of its overarching talent, culture, and workforce strategy.

Michael Griffiths is a senior partner, principal, and lead in Deloitte's Workforce Transformation Practice. He is another revolutionary skills thinker. Griffiths believes leaders need to move toward a skills-based operating system much like Novartis leaders have. In particular, he sees a trend where team members are bridging their skills development for life *and* work purposes. In an interview with me, he said, "We are finding that people are able to bring their skills [to work] and then have adjacent skills identified for life as being a part of the conversation of how to match their skills to their work."[32]

Griffiths and his Deloitte colleagues have spent quite a bit of time researching the importance of skills. For example, in a survey of 1,021 global workers and 225 executives across industries in June 2022,[33] the firm reported the following:

- 77 percent of executives indicated that moving to a skills-based ethos is critical to navigating future business disruptions.

- 12 percent of workers said they are able to customize their work responsibilities based on their current skills, capabilities, and interests.

- 14 percent of executives agreed that their organization uses their workforce's skills and capabilities to their fullest potential.

There are many opportunities to fix the gaping hole in the *skills* life-factor. Griffiths suggested, for example, that leaders must better understand how to utilize skills throughout the organization. In his opinion, leaders ought to be doing a much better job of matching people's skills to roles or, better, to specific projects and opportunities. Ultimately, the organization will need to use the composite skills data of its team members to devise an entirely new talent process mechanism.

"You have to create value for the individual and see the person for their skills, not what they look like," said Griffiths. "Take out bias and create a transparent marketplace where people can see opportunities as they go and then get matched. Skills enable you to see the full person and their potential without bias. Likewise, leaders can see employees for who they are and who they could become."

You cannot continue tailoring your talent management strategy to preserve "bench strength," the forced development of people simply to ensure you can fill the next open job. This myopic approach is the very reason many employees leave organizations. Moreover, if you fixate solely on career development paths for your team members—code for tenure or time-based promotion tracks—it will exacerbate the exodus of employees seeking development that does not necessitate job promotion. This is no way to support a blooming state. It's not even a balanced state.

A significant number of employees are not making their place of work central to their existence. It's an essential part of their life, sure, but not the focal point. What they seek from their employer is an investment in their human potential. As a result, employees have begun to call the shots on what will make them stay. And it is most definitely not H.R.'s antiquated job descriptions or job family practices.

It has become abundantly clear that skills and the organization's talent marketplace strategy are becoming critical components of the future of work. "Not only do they uncover the skills that people already have," remarked Jesuthasan, "they're able to match those skills to emerging bodies of work and able to stretch the capacity of the workforce."

As Griffiths explained, "Skills enable you to see the whole person. Skills-based organizations are 79 percent more likely to have a positive workforce environment experience."

FARMER'S ALMANAC: SKILLS

A positive factor emerged from my survey. Regardless of role, seniority level, geography, age, or gender, people are highly confident in their skills and abilities. That's the good news. The not-so-good news? The skills people currently possess are not being used to their fullest extent inside the workplace. In addition, most workers do not feel that their employers are assisting in the development of their skills.

Let's look in detail at the good news first. I presented the survey participants with two different but slightly related questions about skills. In both cases, the responses were overwhelmingly positive. People are bullish about their abilities. I've presented both sets of results below through leader and non-leader dimensions. The first was a general question framed as a statement about how confident they felt about their skills and abilities, and the second focused on the context of the workplace.

I am confident in my skills and abilities.

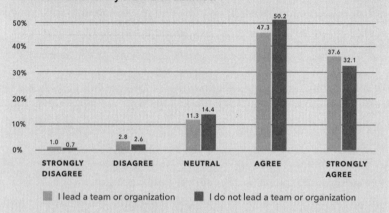

How confident are you in your skills and abilities at work?

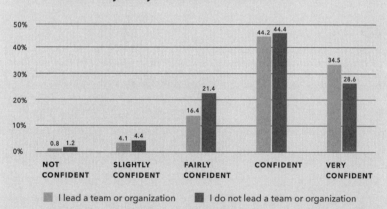

Eighty-two percent of non-leaders and 85 percent of leaders are confident in their skills and abilities. When I asked the same question in the context of the workplace, there was a drop in confidence, but it was not off the charts. Whereas 73 percent of non-leaders are confident in their skills and abilities at work (a nine-point drop), leaders only fell to 79 percent (a six-point drop). In sum, the majority of employees—regardless of rank—are highly confident in their skills and abilities in life and at work.

People were not shy about explaining their perceived difficulties with their organization's lack of leadership on the skills and abilities file. Review the following comments from five employees in five different countries:

✻ ✻

When I was reorg'd into a new team where they made assumptions about my experience and skills and never bothered to learn more about me – I was pigeonholed into a role where I felt underutilized skill-wise but inundated with meaningless work. Also felt like I had to fight to get noticed, and I hate "tooting my own horn," just to prove that I could do things I already knew I had experience in.
DIRECTOR, COMPUTERS, CANADA, 45-54 YEARS

Speak to individuals and ask them if there are ways they could assist their departments – genuinely, and possibly even providing formal examples so they know individuals were serious in their endeavours. Some skills they possess may not be in their job description but they could be an ideal development opportunity for individuals and senior leaders alike.
PROFESSIONAL, GOVERNMENT/MILITARY, U.K., 25-34 YEARS

Consider all of the skills, knowledge, experience, and other attributes being brought to the workplace, not just what they have seen in the most recent year since joining the team. The lack of formal credentials does not take away from years of experience that provide much more credibility than just an academic credential.
ADMINISTRATIVE, ENTERTAINMENT, USA, 45-54 YEARS

Give me training for better chance to earn more for the work I am doing. I like to have good training that is related to my work and gives me more to develop my skills.

PROFESSIONAL, INTERNET, GERMANY, 25-34 YEARS

Create a personal rapport and provide more tools and training for building skill sets that helps in future career path.

DIRECTOR, FINANCE/BANKING/INSURANCE, INDIA, 35-44 YEARS

These comments represent but a sliver of the importance people place on their skills and abilities. They not only covet continuous skills development but also want leaders to recognize the skills they already possess—perhaps developed elsewhere—and let them use them in their current role. In addition, there is a desire for leaders to fully appreciate the entirety of an individual's skill set, not just the skills that got them the job. People long to be appreciated for their entire repertoire of skills, rather than being pigeonholed by one or two main skills.

Unsurprisingly, only 38 percent of non-leaders and 53 percent of leaders felt that their employer provided above average or a significant amount of help in developing their skills and abilities. I urge you to ponder those data points as we enter the next section, The Garden Tools of Skills.

Has your current employer helped in the development of your skills and abilities?

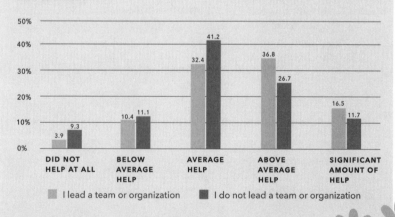

The Garden Tools of Skills

The concept of *horizontal ignition* is key to helping you adopt a successful approach to all aspects of skills going forward. Moreover, it's key to getting the *skills* life-factor correct for team members.

For far too long, leaders have relied on *vertical ambition* as the basis of someone's desire to develop. In fact, a hidden bias against *horizontal ignition* has existed for years. For example, in 1974, Edwin E. Ghiselli of the University of California, Berkley, published an article in *American Psychologist* titled "Some Perspectives for Industrial Psychology." Ghiselli's inability to comprehend anything but upward mobility as it relates to desire led him to diagnose others not fitting this archetype as having "hobo syndrome." I'm not kidding.

> ["Hobo syndrome"] can be defined as the periodic itch to move from a job in one place to some other job in some other place. I have seen this syndrome in all manner of people, from those engaged in occupations that require little by way of training or skill, to those in substantial managerial positions. This urge to move seems not to result from organized or logical thought, but rather would appear more akin to raw, surging, internal impulses, perhaps not unlike those that cause birds to migrate. Floaters readily provide socially acceptable explanations for their peripatetic activity, but under careful examination these explanations turn out to be little more than rationalizations. The simple fact is that after being in one place for a matter of months, or perhaps a year or so, depending on the strength and periodicity of his itch, the individual is impelled to pack up and move to another place and another job.[34]

I want to be clear: Ghiselli's thinking is about as antithetical as you can get when it comes to the skills-building mindset you should espouse.

To combat the ignorance of Ghiselli—or, for that matter, anyone who still believes that skill development is only for those who wish to climb the corporate ladder—there are three tactics I urge you to consider. Each has the potential to help individuals feel positive about their *skills* life-factor, which could in turn help them bloom. The three factors are as follows:

- **Lateral hopping**: Establishing the conditions that permit people to develop their skills through various assignments and opportunities.

- **Portfolio investing**: Bettering a team member's skills through stretch and non-core subject matter areas.

- **Skills-based rationale:** Developing a mindset that considers skills and attributes rather than simply job descriptions and opens the way for gig-like appointments.

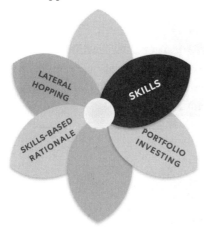

LATERAL HOPPING

Lateral hopping takes a cue from Roger L. Martin's integrative mindset model. In his 2007 book, *The Opposable Mind*, he defines "integrative thinking" as follows: "The ability to face constructively the tension of opposing ideas and, instead of choosing one at the expense of the other, generate a creative resolution of the tension in the form of a new idea that contains elements of the opposing ideas but is superior to both."[35]

I believe that it ought to be perfectly acceptable for you to bridge the gap between employer needs and team member desires. This bridging is at the core of lateral hopping and the *skills* life-factor. As a leader, you have objectives to meet. And you need people to perform in order to meet said objectives. Many people do not want to be pigeonholed into a permanent job. They want a variety of experiences, networking connections, and skill-building opportunities. Per Martin's integrative mindset model, how do we balance the tension of these two opposing ideas to design something that results in a new idea, superior to each entity's requirements?

Consider creating a gig economy inside your organization. Establish an internal free agent marketplace open to full-time team members, and perhaps also retirees and alumni looking for a part-time opportunity. Think of it as an internal version of Upwork, Fiverr, Guru, or Toptal—you are creating a form of job crafting. You can accomplish it through role-based and project-based actions.

- **Role-based actions:** The Government of Canada—not exactly a high-tech global powerhouse headquartered in California or Germany—is an example of an organization that permits role-based lateral hopping through its Free Agents program, first piloted in 2016. The program now acts as an incredibly creative option for the federal government's departmental workforce mobilization ambitions. It offers a space where public servants can take charge of their careers and acts as a skills-building mecca through short-term role-based assignments for employees. It is horizontal ignition integrative thinking at its finest and works as follows.

  First, employees are already full-time federal government team members. They have an original role and home department and have been working for a set amount of time. They discuss with their direct leader their desire to join the Free Agents program.

  Departments post assignments to a central portal. The assignments range in size, scope, and duration. Employees who have signed up as free agents review the postings. If they're interested in a posting, they contact the manager associated with it to find out more. Interestingly, free agents may also be pursued by hiring managers directly. After all, Government of Canada workers are on the same team: the country of Canada.

  Because the free agent has the support (and job guarantee) of their home department, they can accept assignments without fear of punitive action. They won't be fired for taking on a short-term gig. And if they don't like the assignment, once it concludes they are guaranteed employment in their home department. But they have to finish the gig that they signed up for.

  What's brilliant about Canada's Free Agent program is not only the job guarantee commitment but also that free agents can accept new assignments after they've completed one. So, in theory, the free agents can remain free agents for quite a while. In addition, some short-term assignments turn into full-time positions, and free agents have the option to accept the full-time position if it's offered to them.

- **Project-based actions:** Let me illustrate project-based lateral hopping with an example. Beth is a sales leader. She wants a short video to be produced for an upcoming client meeting. Beth thinks it should be short, punchy, and fewer than two minutes. There isn't a media team in the firm and her video skills are non-existent. She needs it in two days. What to do?

Beth visits Fiverr, an external gig platform, and effortlessly posts the details of what she needs online. She receives multiple offers of service in less time than it takes to say "lateral hopping." One day later, Beth has the video link in her inbox, and the client meeting goes fantastically.

Let's imagine the person who took on the project is employed at the same firm as Beth. The employee who took the gig via Fiverr is named Humaira. Beth and Humaira are unaware that they're colleagues.

Humaira took the gig—even though she figured out it's for someone in her own company—because she loves the opportunity to expand her knowledge. She's not even in sales. Humaira is a customer support agent. Beth is happy that her project was completed, but due to privacy requirements, she has no idea that Humaira is a team member at her company. Furthermore, she has no idea that Humaira possesses such talent or wants to grow. What a waste.

What if Beth were able to post the gig inside her organization through some version of an internal Fiverr system? What if the organization had a mechanism to tap into the hidden talent among the people it employs? No, it may not increase Humaira's paycheque, but it will assist her *skills* life-factor quotient. Moreover, it will help her bloom.

There is a treasure trove of hidden talent inside every organization. If you were to tap into it through an internal gig or project platform—giving all team members a chance to dedicate a certain percentage of their time toward in-house gigs—you would not only improve engagement but also give someone an opportunity to develop their skills.

Role-based and project-based lateral hopping options are two of the most straightforward ways to help your people grow their skills.

PORTFOLIO INVESTING

Developing your team members is analogous to crafting a financial retirement plan: a portfolio investment strategy is critical. In the context of the team, you want to invest in your team members' skills through core, stretch, and non-core subject matter areas. And when you do, the investment crosses over into their personal lives, making the opportunity to bloom much more likely.

During my time as chief learning officer at TELUS, I was an enthusiastic proponent of something we coined "in-role" and "next-role" skills development. Essentially, it is the responsibility of a leader to work in partnership with a team member to assess their skill level, not only in terms of how it relates to their current job but also by how it fits with their future aspirations. From there, the leader and team member work on a skills development plan together.

Were I still a chief learning officer, I would most definitely upgrade my thinking to augment "in-role" and "next-role" skills development under the banner of a skills portfolio. In-role and next-role would be further delineated by core, stretch, and non-core skills. The resulting skills portfolio would be kept up-to-date and look something like the following, albeit in an online format of some sort:

SKILLS PORTFOLIO

	IN-ROLE	NEXT-ROLE
Core Skills		
Stretch Skills		
Non-Core Skills		

- **In-Role/Core Skills**: I hope you agree that if any modifications are made to the core functions of a team member's role, the organization has to train the individual to accommodate those changes. Any change is not the employee's doing. They didn't ask for it. For example, a new software system alters how customer service agents handle client complaints. The In-Role/Core Skills category addresses mandatory skills development. Hopefully, it lines up with what organizations have been doing for decades. Training people in new skills when business processes change is pretty much Leadership 101. This is not new news.

- **In-Role/Stretch Skills**: When considering the In-Role/Stretch Skills category, you begin looking past the stated objectives of the role, working with the team member to identify two key areas of supplementary development. First, identify what functions in the job description itself can be improved by mutually agreed-upon adjustments. These, of course, might require a skills upgrade. Think task efficiencies. Second, identify which of the individual's skills or abilities could be further developed to increase their effectiveness in their role. For example, a sales account executive

may be good at negotiation but not great. By investing in their negotiation skills, you are bolstering their In-Role capabilities yet stretching them
toward even better performance.

- **In-Role/Non-Core Skills:** It may seem somewhat asinine even to consider
developing non-core skills for your team members. I beg to differ. In-
Role/Non-Core Skills development is a surefire way to demonstrate that
you care about team members and want them to *be their best.* I once had
a boss who encouraged me to shadow account executives for a year. Not
every day, but frequently enough to understand what it takes to sell. At
the time, I not only knew nothing about the sales profession but also had
no responsibility tied to sales training or selling products and services.
Sales was about as close as Tokyo is to Toronto on my skills development
radar. (That's 10,345 kilometres.) But my year of shadowing was sublime.
It stretched my thinking and understanding of the sales profession. About
15 years later, I could use those stretch skills in a completely different role.
When you have skills conversations with your team members, think about
areas that are tangential to their current role as well. My sales shadowing
example demonstrates that it doesn't have to cost much either.

- **Next-Role/Core Skills:** If you are a leader who cares about team members *being their best*—helping them to bloom in their current role—you
are also looking out for their long-term career. You pay attention to and
have conversations about their next role. Maybe even the role after that.
A team member's core skills will likely need to be developed before they
are offered or can accept a new position. Are you willing to be that team
member's coach to help them achieve those delta skills? With that responsibility comes your leadership investment. What will you do to assist the
team member in pursuing their next role?

- **Next-Role/Stretch Skills:** The Next-Role/Stretch Skills are competencies that are supplemental or secondary to a team member's future role
desires. For example, let's say you have a team member in a quality assurance role, but they are seeking a programming job in one to two years.
They're relatively young. The QA role is their first job, and they've occu-
pied it—and been out of university—for two years. You see their potential
and are happy to help them reach their next-role aspiration. You're having
Next-Role/Core Skills conversations, of course, but you also want them

to succeed in their next role as a programmer, so you offer up additional skills advice. You're thinking about both the programmer role and the one after it, perhaps product management or R&D manager. As such, you help guide your young QA team member to consider stretch skills, including presentation skills, report writing, or executive communication traits. These skills are developed on their own time, but you're there acting as a stretch skills Sherpa.

• **Next-Role/Non-Core Skills:** It may seem even sillier to consider developing Next-Role/Non-Core Skills for your team members. But I beg to differ again. As with Next-Role/Stretch Skills, it's not as though you are permitting time in-role for the team member to develop these stretch or non-core skills. This is on the employee's time. You are, however, continuing to offer counsel and guidance on developing these critical non-core skills. You can home in on the topic area during your one-to-one conversations. Next-Role/Non-Core Skills conversations are discussions about long-term character or behaviour enhancements. For example, what might help that team member become a more holistic human being later in their career? Once when I was attending my son's basketball game, a similarly aged man to me pulled out some yarn and started knitting a sweater. I asked how long he had been knitting. "About five years now," he said. I had to ask what had gotten him into knitting. "My old boss," he answered. "About 10 years ago, he said it would help with my creative thinking." By the end of the basketball game, I had discovered I was talking to a high-ranking official in the provincial government, an individual who had made three seniority jumps over the past decade. I'm not suggesting everyone needs to knit, but I am saying it's a good example of a non-core skill that could potentially influence the possibility of a future role.

A healthcare professional from South Korea summarizes the opportunity that a skills portfolio presents:

✿ ✿ ✿ ✿ ✿ ✿ ✿ ✿ ✿ ✿ ✿ ✿ ✿ ✿ ✿ ✿ ✿ ✿ ✿ ✿

I was able to develop my abilities and be recognized for my abilities by finding out the abilities I had that I did not know.

PROFESSIONAL, HEALTHCARE, SOUTH KOREA, 35-44 YEARS

✿ ✿ ✿ ✿ ✿ ✿ ✿ ✿ ✿ ✿ ✿ ✿ ✿ ✿ ✿ ✿ ✿ ✿ ✿ ✿

SKILLS-BASED RATIONALE

Shifting to a skills-based rationale merits a book unto itself. In the meantime, you and the H.R. or People and Culture team should begin paying attention to and studying organizations, like Novartis and the Government of Canada, that are making the cultural shift from jobs to gigs, assignments, and projects. I'll call it the "skills-collar workforce."

As Deloitte researchers presciently wrote in their 2022 paper, "The Skills-Based Organization: A New Operating Model for Work and the Workforce," "Confining work to standardized tasks done in a functional job and then making all decisions about workers based on their job in the organizational hierarchy, hinders some of today's most critical organizational objectives: organizational agility, growth, and innovation; diversity, inclusion, and equity; and the ability to offer a positive workforce experience for people."[36] A skills-based rationale portends far greater benefits than just developing an employee's skills. For example, Deloitte also advocates for the introduction of "serial specialists," when team members go deep on a specific skill or tasks for three years and then move on to do something entirely different in another part of the organization for another three years. In 2013, LinkedIn co-founder Reid Hoffman called these opportunities "tours of duty."[37]

Let's look at what Unilever is doing. On the subject of short-term internal gigs—as part of its skills-based rationale—Patrick Hull, vice-president of Future of Work at Unilever, pointed out to *Business Insider* in 2021 that "we just see that there's all this opportunity that we can unlock for people that maybe we wouldn't have been considering because, as with many organizations, we would have been more in our functional silos. There's a huge benefit that we can unlock capacity in the organization by having people from different functions and departments, even different countries, working on critical projects in the organization."[38]

While the change curve may be steep, your organization's skills-based rationale strategy will become critical to your team members' skills lifefactor quotient.

However, what actionable things can you do *right now* as a leader for your team? I'd suggest that one of the easiest—and even most fun—things you can do is to actively engage your team members in talking about their hobbies and other extracurricular activities with you. Does one team member chair the PTA? Perhaps another is a wiz at using video-editing software. Is somebody an incredible painter? Whatever it may be, there are likely core competencies underlying those things your team members do for fun that could have positive impacts on work-related items in the future. Skills-based workforce for the win!

Life-Factor No. 3: WELL-BEING

The emotional, social, physical, and financial health of your present state.

✿ ✿   ✿ ✿ ✿ ✿ ✿ ✿ ✿ ✿ ✿ ✿ ✿ ✿ ✿ ✿ ✿ ✿ ✿

Make it ok to not be ok. Start not only talking about mental health but be real. Employees mirror the behaviours, actions, emotions and repeat the thoughts of their leaders. Give us/me a chance.

DIRECTOR, MANUFACTURING, USA, 35-44 YEARS

✿ ✿ ✿ ✿ ✿ ✿ ✿ ✿ ✿ ✿ ✿ ✿ ✿ ✿ ✿ ✿ ✿ ✿ ✿ ✿

Well-being is a must-have, not a nice-to-have. While it is but one of the six life-factors, it really is difficult to bloom if you're constantly suffering. Absorbing persistent anguish of any sort is terrible. Imagine not being able to eliminate a pesky weed from your garden box. How frustrating would that be? When something is difficult to eliminate or you find it impossible to feel positive, ominous thinking can become the norm.

If a team member is unwell at home—whether the unwellness is emotional, social, physical, financial, or any combination thereof—be assured it will have an effect on their performance at work. The reverse is true as well. When work becomes the cause of any form of unwellness, the team member's life outside their job is bound to be negatively affected. The anguish weed, however, is running wild across society. Our subjective well-being is not well.

The pandemic did not give us much to celebrate, but it did shine some much-needed sunlight on well-being. Research and consulting firms noticed this change too.

In 2022, for example, Gallup reported that "44 percent of employees experienced stress a lot of the previous day," a sharp increase from 2009, when it sat at 31 percent, and only 33 percent of all global employees described themselves as thriving, in a state of well-being in their lives.[39]

According to Mind Share Partners' 2021 *Mental Health at Work Report*,[40] 76 percent of U.S.-based leaders and team members report at least one symptom of a mental health condition and 84 percent say their workplace conditions have contributed to at least one mental health challenge.

Deloitte released research in 2022 that also reinforces the rather grim prospect of weeds running rampant in the garden box of well-being. C-Level leaders and employees are not prioritizing well-being, whether it's their own or other people's. What do leaders and team members alike point their fingers at for this predicament? You guessed it: work. Work usurps a focus on well-being, yet not being well is caused, in part, by work.

According to Deloitte's research, members of the C-Suite and team members possess alarming levels of unwellness.[41] Examine the following:

UNWELLNESS LEVELS

	C-LEVEL LEADERS (% WHO SAID THEY ALWAYS OR OFTEN FEEL THIS WAY)	TEAM MEMBERS (% WHO SAID THEY ALWAYS OR OFTEN FEEL THIS WAY)
Stressed	41	42
Overwhelmed	40	35
Exhausted	36	43
Lonely	30	24
Depressed	26	23

It's frightening to think that more than one-quarter of the C-Level self-describe themselves as depressed while more than one-third feel stressed, overwhelmed, and exhausted. Ironically, more than two-thirds of C-Level leaders admit that they do not take enough action to safeguard employee well-being.

A stressed, overwhelmed, and exhausted senior leader not only struggles to make essential strategic and financial decisions but also has less
in the proverbial leadership tank to support employees. How are leaders
supposed to help team members bloom if they are struggling with their
own well-being?

No one deserves to live an unhealthy life because of their job. Anyone
who is some combination of emotionally, socially, physically, or financially unwell because of their role is not being adequately supported at
work. This will clearly hit them in their life too. That's why I've classed
well-being as a life-factor. This predicament is a huge problem if you want
your people to bloom. Heck, it's a huge problem if *you* want to bloom.

A leader who is absent from their team members because of their
unwellness exacerbates the rot in the garden box of well-being at work.
How can you model good well-being—let alone implement well-being
solutions for your team members—if you are miserable? You need to model
well-being, not suffer from a lack of it.

Arianna Huffington pointed this out to me in an interview when we
got onto the topic of well-being: "We believe that when leaders take care
of themselves, they are much more able to take care of their employees to
be empathetic, creative, and inspiring. But when they're depleted, running on empty and burnt out, it's much harder to lead from what is best
in them. Modelling is key because we are changing an entire culture that
used to believe that burnout is simply the price you pay for success."[42]

Three comments from the Global Work-Life Assessment Survey confirm both my thinking and Huffington's astute observation:

✿　✿

Many employers have forgotten the meaning of staff well-being and
everyone is expected to just put up with what is placed in front of them
these days and it is wrong.
PROFESSIONAL, PHARMACEUTICAL, U.K., 18-24 YEARS

Walk the talk on mental health and deal with workload issues. Stop saying buzzwords about mental health and keep asking [us] for impossible
deadlines.
DIRECTOR, GOVERNMENT, CANADA, 45-54 YEARS

I am 61. I can't talk about health issues at work.

PROFESSIONAL, MANUFACTURING, USA, 55-64 YEARS

While well-being may be a problem, it is our right as human beings. If someone's job is creating the conditions that cause unwellness, leaders owe it to their team members to remedy the situation. If burnout is the effect and work is the cause, one of your rights that come with being human has been ignored. I encourage you to adopt the following well-being edict:

Employers possess a duty of care to protect the health and well-being of their team members.

It may not have used the same language as above, but the Office of the U.S. Surgeon General seems to agree. In late 2022, the Office released a powerful 30-page positioning report entitled *Framework for Workplace Mental Health & Well-Being.*[43] The framework included five must-haves for well-being to materialize. Vivek H. Murthy, vice-admiral of the U.S. Public Health Service and surgeon general, wrote the introduction letter to the framework. A particular passage caught my eye:

> The pandemic has presented us with an opportunity to rethink how we work. We have the power to make workplaces engines for mental health and well-being. This may not be easy. But it will be worth it, because the benefits will accrue to both workers and organizations. A healthy workforce is the foundation for thriving organizations and a healthy community.

Murthy laid clear the importance of the *well-being* life-factor. A healthy and sound team member is good not only for the organization but also for society. As a leader, you have the garden tools that can help you build up well-being with your team members. In doing so, you will ben-efit both your workplace and your team members' overarching life. And the better their life in and out of work, the greater their chance to bloom.

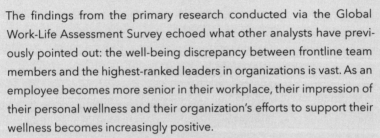

FARMER'S ALMANAC: **WELL-BEING**

The findings from the primary research conducted via the Global Work-Life Assessment Survey echoed what other analysts have previously pointed out: the well-being discrepancy between frontline team members and the highest-ranked leaders in organizations is vast. As an employee becomes more senior in their workplace, their impression of their personal wellness and their organization's efforts to support their wellness becomes increasingly positive.

One question that I asked was whether employers had assisted their team members with their current state of well-being. As you will note from the data points below, drawn from a range of frontline team members (professionals), managers, directors, and senior executives, the belief that their organization provides above average or significant help to support their well-being increases commensurate with a person's role. But let me make one thing clear: the numbers are not high in general.

Does your current employer assist with your well-being?

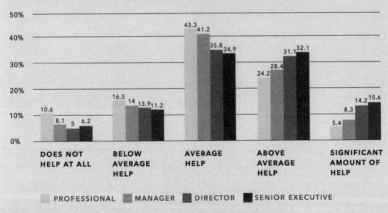

Only 48 percent of senior executives feel their organization supports their well-being. That drops to 45 percent for directors, 37 percent for managers, and an incredibly low 30 percent for professionals/frontline team members. Put differently, 70 percent of professionals/frontline team members do not believe their organization provides satisfactory assistance with their well-being.

When the data is viewed by gender, only 35 percent of female participants responded positively, whereas male participants came in slightly higher at 38 percent. When the question is broken down by generations, it would seem my generation (Gen X) is particularly negative about their employer's provision of well-being assistance. In fairness, though, no generation was more than 40 percent positive about this topic.

Perceptions of How Much Employers Assist with Employees' Well-Being: By Generation

GENERATION	DOES YOUR CURRENT EMPLOYER ASSIST WITH YOUR WELL-BEING?
Gen Z	38%
Millennials	40%
Gen X	32%
Baby Boomers	34%

Before I introduce the *well-being* garden tools, let's look at how important well-being is to people at work.

How important is well-being to you at work?

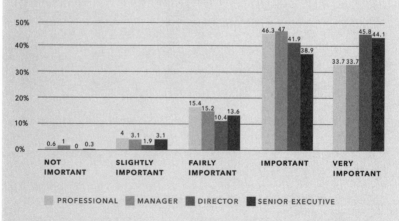

Across the same four role classifications as we used in the previous question, people place well-being very high in terms of personal importance. Eighty percent of professionals/frontline team members believe it is important, as do 81 percent of managers, 88 percent of directors (the highest), and 83 percent of senior executives. From a gender perspective, 83 percent of female respondents rank well-being as important and 80 percent of male respondents feel the same. I found it interesting that Gen Z ranks it lowest and the other three generations are tied in a dead heat.

The Importance of Well-Being at Work: By Generation

GENERATION	HOW IMPORTANT IS WELL-BEING TO YOU AT WORK?
Gen Z	76%
Millennials	82%
Gen X	82%
Baby Boomers	82%

Whichever way the data is sliced, it is essential to point out that an attitudinal shift around the concept of well-being is of the utmost importance. As I said at the beginning of this life-factor's section, well-being is a must-have, not a nice-to-have. We'll look at the required attitudinal shift in the next section.

The Garden Tools of Well-Being

There is a plethora of well-being tactics that you might as well Google. Just don't do it right this second. I've got some critical advice to share first.

Here we go. We need a leadership *well-being* mindset shift. While your staff might appreciate your extending them a few wellness days in recognition of their hard work, it's not enough. Giving them a $500 wellness credit in their first paycheque in January or providing fresh fruit in the breakroom doesn't cut it either.

I have learned from both my research and my personal experience that well-being must become an attitude. Tactics are important, but attitude must be entrenched before anything else. We've become inundated with stories of toxic workplaces, burnout, excessive workloads, rising quit rates, depression, and employee stress. All of these stories point to a deteriorating level of health among team members—at work and in life. And that's why you must prioritize a well-being attitude before you start to deploy any tactics. Without the attitude, you run the risk of deploying organizational party tricks without any systemic purpose. The methods become the proverbial lipstick on a pig.

The well-being attitude comprises three components for your consideration:

- Forthright and open
- Committed culture
- Flexible mind

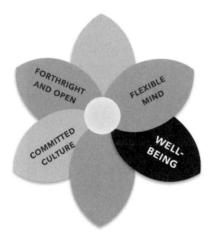

FORTHRIGHT AND OPEN

Lee Chambers is a U.K.-based organizational psychologist and the founder of Essentialise Workplace Wellbeing. Chambers has been at the forefront of helping organizations advance their well-being practices. He has witnessed a lot of companies struggle to attract and retain the talent they need to prosper. Why? It has to do in part with the employer-employee social contract.

"I see a shift in the employer contract and employee expectations," he said to me in an interview.[44] Chambers maintains that well-being is now at the top of an employee's essentials list. That shift is having a profound impact on the nature of organizational talent. "Employee well-being and its practical implementation for businesses has become a must-have for many team members," he added.

To introduce and maintain a well-being strategy that resonates with team members, authenticity is key. Leaders must become forthright and open about it. The employer-employee social contract must evolve, and so too must your willingness as a leader to embrace it. After all, according to 2021 research from IPSOS, 79 percent of people around the world now say their mental health is as important as their physical health.[45] Employee well-being demands your legitimate candour.

With over 100,000 employees globally and more than US$47 billion in annual revenues, GSK (formerly GlaxoSmithKline) operates across three businesses to research, develop, and manufacture pharmaceutical medicines, vaccines, and healthcare products. Sharon Wilkie, head of Operations, Employee Health and Wellbeing at GSK, divulged at a 2021 conference that the company's well-being strategy is openly embedded in its operational conduct with team members.[46]

GSK employs three team member operating pillars: be you, feel good, and keep growing. The feel good pillar provides a worthy example for your consideration. Not only is the organization *forthright and open* about well-being but it also emphasizes the importance of this principle in both work and life. Its "feel good" pillar is backed by the following adage: "When we focus on our well-being and have the flexibility to manage our lives, we can thrive and do great things at work and home."

GSK walks the talk when it comes to its well-being openness and that has translated into uptake and results. The company has over 1,500 active well-being champions who are trained to help propagate the feel good principle. Furthermore, as of 2020, GSK counted more than 10,000 team members in its Health & Well-Being Workplace group. In that same year, over half of the company's leaders took its Mental Health Matters and Managing for Resilience training courses. GSK consistently receives awards and distinctions in recognition of its efforts. Its Glassdoor rating is also very high for a company of its global size, sitting at an average overall score of 4.0 out of 5.0 at the end of 2022.[47]

HSBC is another *forthright and open* organization. The financial services firm earns in excess of US$55.3 billion annually from more than 40 million clients in over 60 countries. It does so through the efforts of 230,000 global team members. HSBC wanted it to be known across its workforce that well-being was deemed mission critical and that it would become central to its operations. The company took the time to rework its corporate values, with a priority on well-being chief among the revisions. It's hard to get more *forthright and open* than making well-being a corporate value of your organization, especially a company with nearly a quarter-million employees. The corporate value is "We help our people enhance their own physical, mental, and emotional well-being. We support work-life choices where we can."[48]

Like GSK, HSBC has earned a number of awards for its well-being efforts. In addition, the results of surveys conducted across the company suggest its well-being leadership is having an impact. Look at the following data from HSBC's 2021 employee survey:[49]

- 81 percent of HSBC global employees rate their mental health as positive.

- 70 percent of HSBC global employees are confident talking to their line manager.

- 7 in 10 HSBC global employees say their work-life balance is positive.

- 7 in 10 HSBC global employees say their physical health is positive.

- 6 in 10 HSBC global employees say their financial health is positive.

There's no step-by-step guide to instilling well-being forthrightness and openness. You either agree that as a leader you're going to be *forthright and open* about well-being, or you don't. And if you choose the latter, I and psychologists like Lee Chambers will be wondering about your long-term talent success.

In the meantime, if you're not in a position to instill well-being or wellness into corporate values like GSK and HSBC did, consider the following two tactics:

- **Initiate open and forthright dialogue**: Stop shying away from asking your team members about their mental, physical, and emotional wellness. Make it a point to specifically query these concepts in your one-on-one meetings or during other informal exchanges.

- **Conduct assessments**: Encourage your team to assess their well-being, while also having a conversation about the results. You might try the Work-Life Bloom assessment (www.worklifebloom.com/assessment) or other free assessments such as the Human Flourishing Program at Harvard University 40-Item Well-Being Measure.

COMMITTED CULTURE

CGI is one of the world's largest I.T. and business consulting firms, with over 85,000 employees in 400 different cities delivering over US$12 billion in annual revenues. If you truly want team members to understand and feel the life-factor of *well-being*, you will think about what CGI does before every meeting. Wellbeing has become a part of its culture. In fact, it has an all-encompassing commitment to well-being. CGI kicks off all internal meetings with what it calls a Mental Health Minute. This minute signifies the importance of well-being at the company as well as the need for self-care.

Suzanne Bossy, director of the Health and Well-Being Center of Expertise at CGI, discussed this well-being culture tactic during a webinar called "Making Mental Health & Wellbeing a Global Priority" in October 2022.[50] Bossy also admitted something about the company's past well-being performance: "Before the pandemic, 60 percent of our employees had never discussed their mental health or well-being." Thanks to the company's culture commitment to well-being, that statistic is steadily improving.

CGI's commitment to a well-being culture didn't end with the Mental Health Minute. In fact, it didn't even start there. Back in 2009, CGI established its award-winning well-being rationale with something called Oxygen. How perfect a name. But note the year it was established: 2009. This Montreal-headquartered firm has long been ahead of many organizations in terms of being committed to a culture of well-being.

Oxygen provides a range of well-being services, resources, and messaging for CGI team members globally. With 400 different offices across the world, CGI also designs initiatives at a global, regional, and local level, not solely at a corporate level. It all comes together because senior leaders made the commitment long ago to foster a culture of well-being. One of CGI's employee commitments helps to illustrate how important well-being is to the company: "CGI is committed to fostering an environment focused on health and well-being where members can thrive personally and professionally."[51]

Notice the use of the word "committed." On the CGI Oxygen portal, senior leaders regularly publish videos of themselves waxing lyrical about their well-being efforts. The company has more than 800 trained mental health ambassadors who "foster a culture of openness and provide adequate support to their peers."[52]

Your commitment to ensuring well-being is a part of your organizational culture—or at the very least, your team's culture—is indicative of your maturity as a leader.

Establishing the environment (aka your commitment to a well-being culture) is an important practice to adopt. When you commit to a culture of well-being, you have signalled to team members that you're for real. It's an extension of how *forthright and open* you are, both as a leader and organizationally.

When team members feel comfortable discussing well-being—emotional, social, physical, or financial— at work, it's a sign of how committed your culture has become to supporting well-being. And if they feel that you are committed to well-being in the culture of work, it can only pay dividends on the home front too.

FLEXIBLE MIND

Read the following quote from a book and see if you can figure out a) when it was written, and b) by whom:

> One of the top five worst moves a leader can make when it comes to leadership is to ignore the changing face of where work can be performed. If the role is conducive to remote work—and your team member has proven their worth—why on earth are you not allowing them to either permanently or occasionally adopt a flexible work style? It makes no sense to not be flexible.[53]

The quote is from *Lead. Care. Win. How to Become a Leader Who Matters.* The book was published in 2020, but the words were written in the fall of 2018. I have first-hand knowledge of this fact because it was me who wrote the book. The paragraph was written 18 months before our world turned upside down and stupidly sideways due to the pandemic. In that same book I defined "flexible work" as follows: "Permitting team members the flexibility to work when and where they are most effective."

I reference my previous writing not for vainglorious reasons but to illustrate a point of reflection. For the purposes of the *well-being* life-factor—and to help team members to bloom—I no longer believe permitting *flexible work* is enough. It is, of course, hugely important. However, it has been several years since I wrote that passage—and we've been through one of modern society's most horrific periods thanks to the pandemic—and leaders have to progress their beliefs. Your thinking has to evolve from merely permitting *flexible work* to enacting a *flexible mind*. I define a *flexible mind* as follows:

Providing the means for team members to feel fully supported whenever and wherever they are working.

A comment submitted to the Global Work-Life Assessment Survey from a female vice-president in the telecommunications sector captures the essence of a *flexible mind*: "Continue to provide a flexible workstyle that allows my kids to show up during calls and for me to take calls from their sporting events."

While the survey respondent alludes to my original definition of *flexible work*, what she is really getting at concerns the definition of a *flexible mind*. Her well-being is positively affected not solely because she's permitted the opportunity to work from home or while she's at her child's sporting event, but also because she feels unilaterally supported. It's one thing to work whenever and from wherever. It's quite another to know you won't be reprimanded if a child unexpectedly enters a video call. This particular survey respondent feels safe to partake in a conference call while simultaneously watching a teenager's volleyball game. That illustrates a huge difference between a *flexible work* ideology and a *flexible mind* one. This respondent's leader is providing both the means and the support the respondent needs. And it aligns nicely with the allyship I brought up earlier in the book: *our lives shape our work; nevertheless, our work shapes us.*

Furthermore, you may have noticed that for the first time in this book, I've identified the gender of the person whose comment from the Global Work-Life Assessment Survey I'm quoting. Up until this point I've refrained from identifying anyone's gender in the survey comments. Why is that? you may wonder.

As I've mentioned, I conducted interviews, surveys, and focus groups and studied all sorts of secondary research for this book. There is an elephant in the room whose presence has yet to be acknowledged, though: while organizations need to adopt a *flexible mind* approach for the benefit of all employees, deploying this tactic to help working moms is long overdue.

A comment from a different female senior leader—one working in retail—helps to define the elephant and reinforce the need for a *flexible mind*:

✿ ✿

When people are honest about wanting flexibility and more time with family it makes me feel more human at work, that I'm not the only person who wants this in today's workplace. It's OK to talk about the reality of work and life.

MANAGER, RETAIL, U.K., 35-44 YEARS

✿ ✿

Two more insightful comments from senior female leaders—in the pharmaceutical and educational sectors respectively—offer glaringly painful examples of the need for a *flexible mind*:

✿ ✿

As a woman and a mother, I have often been asked to work long hours at the expense of missing family activities. This has prevented me from being able to be my whole self at work as the expectation was for me to walk off my family to accomplish work goals.

DIRECTOR, PHARMACEUTICAL, USA, 55-64 YEARS

In my last workplace, returning from maternity leave I saw a change in the way the organization supported me. I felt let down by the way the company treated me.

MANAGER, EDUCATION, U.K., 45-54 YEARS

✿ ✿

A *flexible mind* is ultimately about empowerment. You have it in you as a leader to endow professional responsibility on your team members while you continue to look out for them. They are in charge of their actions. Empowerment does not result in abandonment. Quite the contrary, in fact. You should continue to fully support team members in conducting their professional responsibilities whenever and wherever it is reasonable to do so.

For working moms, the *flexible mind* is long overdue. Permitting people to work when and where they are most effective is one thing; endorsing their need to amalgamate work with life is next-level leadership. Working moms may just be at the front of that list.

Of course, it's tricky for an airline pilot to work from home. It's rather difficult for janitorial staff to do their job from the confines of a park bench. And restaurant servers might find it challenging to deliver food to a table when they're slumped over a laptop at a coffee shop that's not their place of employment.

As a leader, you need to be careful to make certain that no team member feels left out because of their job description, personality, pay grade, or any other workplace difference. Having even one of your team members feel inferior because of where or when they work runs counter to the *flexible mind* approach. It reeks of exclusivity.

Remember, we are aiming to assist the well-being of team members in this life-factor. When adopting the *flexible mind* approach, leaders are observant of and potentially taking action to remedy certain situations in a team member's life (and work). *Flexible mind* goes nowhere fast unless you can understand what your team members are going through, while sympathizing and ultimately taking action. This is at the core of a *flexible mind,* and it's a well-being step I strongly urge you to consider taking.

Life-Factor No. 4: MEANING

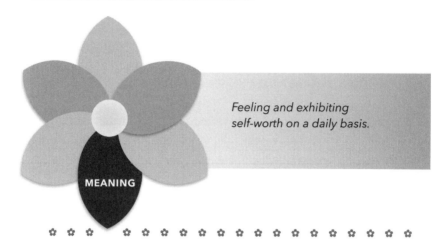

*Feeling and exhibiting
self-worth on a daily basis.*

MEANING

When I am empowering my team, working collaboratively with challenging work and in an area of competence, then I have meaning.
DIRECTOR, CONSULTING, CANADA, 45-54 YEARS

In 2022, I was fortunate to stumble upon Eloise Skinner while I was conducting research for this book. What a shining light she is. Skinner's story is reasonably representative of what many people go through in their lives. We often question whether we can achieve a sense of meaning and self-worth in our lives. Naturally, our job and choice of industry can have a tremendous impact on whether or not we achieve them.

Having studied at venerable institutions like Cambridge and Oxford, East London-born Skinner entered the law profession. It was a vocation she had chosen halfway through her teens. Then, after spending just over a decade learning about and practising law, she had an epiphany.

"Is this what I want to do with my life?" she said to me in an interview.[54] "Maybe this choice I made when I was 16 years old isn't the right thing to carry through."

Skinner had the wherewithal, indeed the gumption, to look within herself and determine if law would provide a sense of meaning for the whole of her life. Unfortunately, upon further review—and a few sidebar consultations with friends and family—she recognized that it would not.

"There had been a long process of figuring out what I could do in the world and how I could contribute or use my skills for something that was meaningful to me," said Skinner. "Law was everything that I had wanted from my first career, but I got to the point where I wasn't sure if it was the role that I could contribute in in the most effective way. And so, I've gone on a professional career journey trying to find purpose and meaning, but also a personal and a spiritual one as well."

What's extraordinary is that Skinner embarked on a path to improve her sense of meaning, only to discover that her purpose in life was to help others determine and enact theirs. "I want to give people a toolkit or the ability to go and do that work for themselves," explained Skinner. "That's really my work. It is very practical and focused on giving people the ideas, frameworks, tools, and guidance such that they can go out and do their own exploratory journey."

Skinner's current quest is to help facilitate a deeper exploration of what it means to be both a human being and an employee. "Cultures that are more open and welcoming—authentically creating space for employees to find their own paths—are going to be the ones that have a direct impact on that employee's own journey," she said. Her 2023 book, *But Are You Alive? How to Design a Life Worth Living*, is a smashing example of her new direction. Putting pen to paper and writing an entire book about the importance of meaning speaks volumes about Skinner's passion for the *meaning* life-factor.

Skinner's story tells us something important. Leaders need not be afraid to discuss the concepts of meaning and self-worth with their team members. Regardless of age, every single one of us is on a naturally meandering path of self-exploration—we are Santiago, the Andalusian shepherd from *The Alchemist*, on our way to Egypt. We are perpetually surveying not only what brings us meaning but also what can deliver self-worth. Each of us is unendingly participating in a personal discovery journey. And each individual's discovery of meaning will vary.

Unsurprisingly, an individual's career choice can significantly affect whether or not they achieve meaning. Therefore, I have classified *meaning* as a life-factor and not a work-factor. (And remember, almost everyone brings their lives to work.) Professors Gary Reker, Edward Peacock, and Paul Wong of Trent University provide a very useful definition of "meaning" that I think applies well to my Work-Life Bloom argument: "Meaning refers to making sense, order, or coherence out of one's existence."[55]

If your team members can't make sense of their role at work, it stands to reason they'll be hard-pressed to find meaning in life. Their existence becomes incoherent, their discovery path disjointed. Thus, there is little chance for self-worth to develop. That is why you must take the *meaning* life-factor so seriously for the purposes of the Work-Life Bloom model.

Eloise Skinner's story is but one example of how this can play out. Why is her story so pertinent? People who seek meaning in their lives often derive it in full or in part from their work. Researchers from the University of Florida discovered a similar pattern that reinforces the relationship between work and life meaning. Doctors Blake Allan, Ryan Duffy, and Richard Douglass wrote:

> Individuals who have found meaning in work are much less likely to be searching for general life meaning, especially for middle and older adults. Work may play such a central role in life meaning that the need to find other sources of meaning is low. Individuals in their prototypical working years (ages 20–50) who find meaning in work were more likely to experience heightened levels of life meaning.[56]

This is precisely why you should enter into a dialogue with your team members specifically about the *meaning* life-factor. There are undoubtedly many Eloise Skinners in your midst, coveting more meaning in their role and, by extension, life. And remember, it's a daily act. After all, I define "meaning" simply as "the feeling and articulation of self-worth on a daily basis."

Meaning is not the same for everyone. It emanates from different places. Our experiences and history can inform it. So too can our likes and dislikes. And let's not forget the influence people's relationships have on it. That includes your relationship with your team members as their leader. (See this chapter's earlier discussion of the *relationships* life-factor.)

All of the above suggests that work plays a prominent role in your team members' discovering meaning. So, what can you do to help them achieve a sense of meaning? That is to come in the Garden Tools of Meaning section. But first, let's once more enter the Farmer's Almanac and excavate the current state of meaning in people's lives.

FARMER'S ALMANAC: **MEANING**

It would be imprudent to go any farther without a word from the psychiatrist Viktor E. Frankl. Globally renowned for his classic volume, *Man's Search for Meaning*—a book that has sold over 16 million copies[57]—Frankl wrote an astonishing total of 39 books. He could be called Captain Meaning.

Frankl's research and related book writing defined the concept of *logotherapy*. He maintained that our chief motivation in life is pursuing what we find meaningful. He was not a man to mince words. One passage of his cuts right to the chase on the matter of meaning: "Life is not primarily a quest for pleasure, as Freud believed, or a quest for power, as Adler taught, but a quest for meaning. The greatest task for a person is to find meaning in his or her life."[58]

A Canadian Gen X manager in healthcare subliminally paid homage to Frankl by providing an insightful expression of meaning in one of their survey responses. For this manager, operating with a sense of meaning does not materialize from a quest for pleasure or power. Instead, they find meaning from several work- *and* life-factors:

I currently have an amazing cast of characters in my personal and professional life. I feel fulfilled with meaning outside of work due to my interests, hobbies, and relationships. I feel like the work I do is equally meaningful and fulfilling. Even though I'm as busy as I've ever been, I feel like I'm able to bring not only my whole self but the best version of my whole self to work.

MANAGER, HEALTHCARE/MEDICAL, CANADA, 35-44 YEARS

Specific to the survey results, many more people than I expected were operating with a clear sense of meaning. Perhaps Frankl's work has paid off. Seventy percent of all respondents agreed or strongly agreed that their life has a clear sense of meaning. The gaps between groups were not wide either. Female and male respondents reported a five-point disparity, with 72 percent of male respondents and 67 percent of female respondents reporting agreement or strong agreement. The variance was slightly wider between leaders and non-leaders. Seventy-three percent of leaders agreed that they are living a meaningful life, compared with 64 percent of non-leaders. Still, nearly two-thirds of non-leaders indicated they're living a life of meaning. That's quite good, given the world's circumstances during the summer of 2022.

Unsurprisingly, Gen Z scored lowest among the generations on living a meaningful life—likely due to their lack of life experience—coming in at 60 percent. In contrast, Baby Boomers scored the highest, at 72 percent. Because Baby Boomers are on the other end of the experience spectrum from their Gen Z counterparts, that makes sense.

Research conducted by the Government of Canada in 2022 corroborates the point. In its annual Canadian Social Survey, Statistics Canada found that 65 percent of people aged 65-74 reported having a strong sense of meaning, while only 52 percent of the population aged 15-24 reported the same.[59]

From a country perspective, only five percentage points separate the majority of nations surveyed, including Canada, the USA, the U.K., Germany, France, Spain, the Netherlands, Sweden, and Australia. In these nine countries, an average of 70 percent of people have a clear sense of meaning. The two outliers—India and South Korea—measured 81 percent and 57 percent, respectively.

Specific to the question "Does your current employer help you achieve a sense of meaning?," whatever way you slice the segment, aside from India, the results suggest that most people do not rely on their employer as a driver or assistant of meaning. Again, aside from India, where an astonishing 72 percent of people feel that their employer positively affects their sense of meaning, the results range from a low of only 29 percent of non-leaders to a high of only 44 percent of leaders. The high mark—if that's what you want to call it—of 44 percent was also achieved by male respondents and the USA independently.

Put differently, most people do not believe their current employer helps them achieve a sense of meaning. What does that, ahem, mean? In part, it means there is a gigantic opportunity for leaders to not only help fill the meaning void for many team members but also bolster it for those who have already defined their meaning situation as a bloom state. If people derive a sense of meaning in part from their work, there is *meaningful work* for you to take on as their leader.

SEGMENT	MY LIFE HAS A CLEAR SENSE OF MEANING.	DOES YOUR CURRENT EMPLOYER HELP YOU ACHIEVE A SENSE OF MEANING?
All employees	70%	39%
Female	67%	42%
Male	72%	44%
Leaders	73%	44%
Non-leaders	64%	29%
Gen Z	60%	41%
Millennials	70%	41%
Gen X	69%	35%
Baby Boomers	72%	39%
Australia	70%	40%
Canada	73%	38%
France	71%	43%
Germany	70%	38%
India	81%	73%
Netherlands	73%	32%
South Korea	57%	32%
Spain	68%	40%
Sweden	73%	35%
U.K.	68%	37%
USA	68%	44%

Achieving and Experiencing Meaning

Next, we'll bring out the Garden Tools of Meaning from the ole garden shed. These tools should allow you to both initiate and fortify the *meaning* life-factor for your team members.

The Garden Tools of Meaning

If meaning is derived in part from our work and a significant portion of people do not feel supported by their employers to achieve it, should you be more worried about your leadership legacy or more focused on what you can do to help your team member's discovery of meaning today?

The work-meaning disconnect will continue if you decide to fret over the engravings on your leadership monument. Instead, this is your chance to shine some much-needed sunlight on the garden box of meaning for your team members. There are three meaning garden tools that I'd like you to consider:

- Micro meaning
- Macro meaning
- Mega meaning

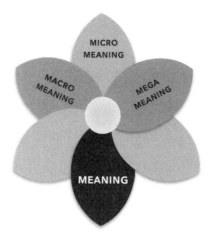

MICRO MEANING

Goodable was founded in 2020 by the former CNN and ABC war-zone correspondent Muhammad Lila. It might be one of the best things to emerge from the pandemic. In a world drunk on negativity, polarization, and egregious use and abuse of power, Goodable is a good news company.

Lila was previously put into some genuinely horrific situations. Chased by terrorists? Check. Fleeing gunfire? You bet. Evading militia and warlords out to kill? Too many times to mention. "The biggest achievement in my life is that ISIS, the Taliban, Russians, and Egyptians all tried to kill me,"[60] he said to me with a straight face.

While he dodged death and waited for many hours in international airports, Lila reflected on what brings him a sense of meaning, repeatedly asking himself two questions: "Why is it we only consider bad news as news? And why doesn't good news count as news?" It may have been an existential crisis of meaning for Lila while he was stuck in some of the world's deadliest situations, but his self-reflection hatched a positive and viable business, something no one has ever tried to do on a global scale.

Goodable is beyond a success story. It's a phenomenon. Goodable reaches an average audience of 40 million people per month across its proprietary channels, plus nearly 50 million more via various display screen partnerships it has negotiated. In addition, its good news content is displayed in over 38,000 venues globally. In 2022, the company announced the launch of "Goodable in the Classroom, a free resource for educators that includes a digest of positive news, printable worksheets, discussion prompts for classrooms, trivia questions, and more."[61]

Lila's various points of self-reflection about the meaning of news are a *good* introduction to the first garden tool in this section: *micro meaning*. What exactly is it?

This will be the third book of five where I have written the following phrase. That's a reflection of its importance:

How do you want to be known when you leave a room?

This line is at the core of *micro meaning*. The word *micro* in our particular context signifies you (micro meaning = *you* meaning), the individual. Without Lila's self-reflection, Goodable may never have gotten off the ground. Worse, Lila could have been captured by the Taliban!

What can you as a leader do to help your team members develop their *micro meaning*, to help them become "how they want to be known when they leave a room"? First, consider having a few *micro meaning* conversations with each of your team members, using some of the conversation starter questions below to elicit a dialogue. The intent is to openly discuss how they individually feel about their personal sense of meaning—the *micro meaning* that results from their role at work.

- What factors help you achieve a sense of meaning in your role?
- What, if anything, is getting in the way of you having meaning at work?
- Are there people or groups you'd like to help now or in the future?
- Could I introduce you to others in and out of work who might help create your path to meaning?
- Are you aware of how others view you and how that might impact your personal level of meaning?
- Is there anything I can do to help you derive a sense of meaning in your role?

Muhammad Lila was smart enough to ask and answer many of these questions independently. He is a worldly and astute leader, of both himself and others. Now he is helping to build up meaning in the team members who make up Goodable. Your team members may not be at his level of independent meaning definition awesomeness. Thus, setting up the time to have meaningful conversations about *micro meaning* is quite a *good* thing to do. How do you (and they) want to be known when leaving a room? Even if you are fleeing from ISIS.

MACRO MEANING

Aside from independent "company of one" people like me, most people work for an organization. That organization could be in the public, not-for-profit, or private sector, or publicly traded. Whatever the case, a portion of your team will derive meaning from their workplace in addition to their role. *Macro meaning* stems from their desire to contribute to the big picture. It's supplemental to their *micro meaning* inputs. When team members feel they are influencing or impacting outcomes at an organization-wide level, they fulfill their aspiration for *macro meaning*. Note, though, that not all team members covet *macro meaning*, but certainly many will.

Think of a team member who is already performing at a high level in their role. They likely exhibit *micro meaning* already. That's the good news. However, because a person's overall sense of meaning ebbs and flows—never remaining at a uniform level—you should still engage in a dialogue about *macro meaning*. The high-performing individual may be looking to make additional contributions at a macro level. They might be seeking even more meaning from their work. Your job, as their leader, is to open the door to *macro meaning* and facilitate a discussion about it. Think of it as a retention strategy garden tool as well.

Some people are already there. They've long been a card-carrying member of the *macro meaning* club. *Micro meaning* is just not enough for them to feel fulfilled. These individuals need to be working on initiatives that progress the organization to new heights, projects or ideas that can be described as the proverbial "big rocks." I'm one of those types. I would have been miserable if I hadn't been involved in organization-wide initiatives that improved the employee or customer experience. I'd have been about as happy as a lost toddler at a crowded beach. Thankfully I had leaders who understood how I was wired and gave me a gigantic rope of leeway to make change happen across several roles and companies.

Whether your team member is established or you can sense they need something more in their role, you must be aware of both circumstances. *Macro meaning* is ultimately achieved when team members feel they are making a sizable contribution to the organization's future. They yearn to make an impact within their role and shift the organization in new ways. That shift might be related to strategy, product evolution, service enhancement, employee systems, or customer experience. You can consider a whole host of innovative and creative concepts. Whatever they are, they are the "big rocks" of your organization, and there will be a particular cadre of team members who want to move them so they can experience a sense of meaning in their work and lives.

MEGA MEANING

Carl Icahn, a famous activist investor worth billions, wrote an open letter in 2022 to W. Rodney McMullen, chairman of the board and chief executive officer of The Kroger Company. Kroger is a large grocery chain in the USA with annual revenues nearing US$150 billion. Icahn raised several concerns about the company's operations, namely animal welfare and McMullen's treatment of the firm's employees. One paragraph in particular from the open letter illustrates Icahn's ire:

> The Board of Kroger is also completely tone-deaf to other growing E.S.G. concerns, specifically that of providing a living wage to your

employees. You've helmed a company that certainly has the gravitas to steer change, yet instead have condoned cruelty towards those who are the most defenseless. What has happened at Kroger with the issues of animal welfare and employee wages is an affront to the basic fibers of our society—that of decency and dignity.[62]

What triggered Icahn's wrath about Kroger's treatment of its team members was an Economic Roundtable research paper published in early 2022. The non-profit group surveyed more than 10,000 Kroger workers in Washington, Colorado, and Southern California about their working conditions. The results were staggeringly awful.[63]

Roughly 75 percent of Kroger workers said they were food insecure, meaning they lacked consistent access to enough nutritious food to let them lead an active, healthy life. In addition, approximately 14 percent said they were unhoused or had been unhoused the previous year. And 63 percent indicated they did not earn enough money to pay their basic monthly expenses.

Icahn spoke directly to McMullen to air his concerns. He followed up the conversation by publishing the open letter. Icahn then went further—activating his anger to next-level furor—by announcing his desire to replace a few Kroger board members so that a change could be enacted at the company.

Your team members are unlikely to be billionaires or corporate activists. But Icahn's efforts do help us to define *mega meaning*.

Icahn's actions demonstrate how *mega* concerned he was for the wellbeing of Kroger employees and the company's treatment of animals. He may be an employee at Icahn Enterprises L. P., but Icahn was also motivated to "do good" in society by finding ways to fulfill his *mega meaning* quotient.

Icahn's actions call to mind a famous Peter Drucker line: "Efficiency is concerned with doing things right. Effectiveness is doing the right things."[64] *Mega meaning* points to people on your team who want to be effective by doing the right things inside and outside the organization. It's not about efficiency for them. The "right things" are about how they might make an effective difference in the lives of others outside the workplace.

Mega meaning refers to doing good in society. Sure, individuals come to work to perform in their roles and get paid, but for some that's not enough. They perceive a higher calling from their role and their employer, one that steers them to improve society overall.

If you are unaware of what makes these team members tick, you can be assured of dealing with either a demotivated personality or someone aiming to secure employment elsewhere. My best advice? Find out through a few open conversations if *mega meaning* is integral to your team members' work-life needs. If it is, make accommodations so they might fulfill some of these ambitions within their roles. If your organization has a community foundation, help them find a spot within that team.

The more you can do to help your team members meet their need to deliver *mega meaning* outside the workplace, the better your chances of leading someone who blooms.

Life-Factor No. 5: AGENCY

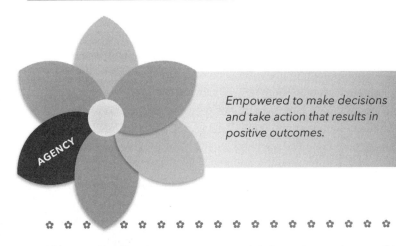

AGENCY

Empowered to make decisions and take action that results in positive outcomes.

✿ ✿ ✿   ✿

I bloom when I'm given agency, enough information to do something meaningful with it, enough oversight to get meaningful direction and then praise (if appropriate) if it goes well. That thread of consistency and authenticity makes all the difference.

DIRECTOR, ENTERTAINMENT/RECREATION, USA, 45-54 YEARS

✿ ✿

When Apple co-founder Steve Jobs said, "It doesn't make sense to hire smart people and tell them what to do; we hire smart people so they can tell us what to do,"[65] I like to think he was referring to—at least in part—fulfilling each Apple employee's level of agency. His views on hiring and Apple's culture, in general, bring to mind another powerful adage, this one via Greek philosopher Epicurus: "Freedom is the greatest fruit of self-sufficiency."[66]

While *agency* is deemed a life-factor in the Work-Life Bloom model, it also references the relationship between a person's decision-making ability at work and the capacity to impact others. How your team members feel capable of performing—which includes a sense of freedom to operate with relevance—is another telling component of agency.

Agency is vital to being in control of our lives. That point is somewhat irrefutable. But, unfortunately, it's also why life can feel so unpleasant for people who do not have the ability to influence a situation at work.

At home, you might flick a switch and the light comes on in a room. That's your free will at play. It's you enacting your freedom. You ponder the situation, own the decision, and then act. Think. Decide. Do. Presto! Light. What does it feel like for a team member if someone else constantly controls the lights at work, turning them on and off without input or consequence? It feels as good as missing that last bus you just sprinted for. So close, yet so far.

When team members feel they lack control and freedom over decision-making—that is, they have no real workplace agency or personal power—they can develop negative attitudes, decreased performance, and dips in well-being. But when the opposite is true, you will see a person who is blooming.

In 2019, Eldar Yusupov, a Tel Aviv-based copywriter at McCann Worldgroup, was working with one of the firm's biggest clients, IKEA. Yusupov, who has lived with cerebral palsy since birth, realized one day that life could be a bit better if only his home furniture were improved. The 33-year-old took stock of his situation: "I am surrounded by furniture that reminds me on a daily basis of my disability. I cannot open a regular closet, sit on a regular sofa, turn on a regular lamp — everyday activities that most people take for granted are very difficult for me."[67] Enter the life-factor called *agency*.

IKEA has an extraordinary purpose statement, crafted in 1976: "To create a better everyday life for the many people."[68] Yusupov recalled the company's declaration and surmised the following: "As a copywriter working on the IKEA account, it always bothered me that I couldn't buy IKEA's furniture like most Israelis I know. I was also familiar with IKEA's agenda to create a better life for many. But unfortunately for me, I wasn't the many." Chock full of freedom and verve to change IKEA's ways—not to mention his home life—Yusupov challenged the company to reinvent its thinking.

Yusupov's idea was to hack IKEA's furniture to make it more accessible to people with cerebral palsy and other disabilities. Several designers, engineers, and an assortment of people who lived with a variety of disabilities came together in this epic Allen wrench versus IKEA challenge. Over several days, the cohort of creatives successfully invented numerous furniture enhancements.

Sofas were outfitted with uniquely elevated legs. Distinct handles were added to the famous IKEA PAX closet. Other hacks and enhancements were suggested across myriad IKEA products. All of the furniture augmentations happened through the magic of 3D printing.

Yusupov poignantly captured the success of his initiative: "Next to my bed is an IKEA lamp with a big switch. Every night when I turn it off, I remind myself that anything is possible."

Eventually, news of Yusupov's creativity found its way to IKEA headquarters. The idea was branded ThisAbles, articulated as follows: "To allow people with special needs to enjoy the quality of life provided by IKEA products."[69] The company joined forces with two non-profit organizations based in Israel, Milbat and Access Israel. Together the firms finalized a line of products that addressed the gaps between existing IKEA furniture and the unique needs of people who live with a disability. Additional patents and recommendations have since been developed and are available worldwide. In addition, some of the product enhancements can be printed by the general public on independent 3D printers.

Were it not for Yusupov's agency, ThisAbles might never have been conceived, let alone gotten off the ground. Not only did he feel compelled to push his employer, McCann Worldgroup, in a new direction, Yusupov also simultaneously persuaded one of the company's most important clients, IKEA, to change its thinking. He possessed the courage, felt empowered, and thus decided to do something about his idea. In return, people all around the world who live with disabilities are benefiting from Yusupov's agency.

Agency is not simply about passive independence at work, though. Nor is it about leaving team members to function on their own without any form of guidance or leadership. It is not a free-for-all.

Agency arrives through autonomy when people are permitted to ideate and act, bolstered by their ability to make informed, uncoerced decisions. That's why I've made it a life-factor. If we can apply agency in our lives—as we should—how do we use those same constructs of agency at work? How might your team members feel more like Eldar Yusupov and less like a number in a spreadsheet? Before we look for answers to those questions, let's take our penultimate reading from the Farmer's Almanac and the Global Work-Life Assessment Survey results related explicitly to agency.

FARMER'S ALMANAC: **AGENCY**

Comments from directors from three different countries will lead us into our exploration of the Farmer's Almanac entry for agency. Their commentary is telling:

✿ ✿

Micromanagement by the CEO is terrible: they probably think they are "helping," however we have recently seen significant churn in senior roles due to this lack of empowerment or agency.

DIRECTOR, BUSINESS/PROFESSIONAL SERVICES, CANADA, 55-64 YEARS

Sometimes my decisions are stopped by the hierarchy without any explanation.

DIRECTOR, MANUFACTURING, FRANCE, 45-54 YEARS

Independent decision-making is not possible here. Each and every time, I have to get permission which hinders the pace of progress of a job.

DIRECTOR, MANUFACTURING, INDIA, 55-64 YEARS

✿ ✿

To ensure I am being crystal clear with you, here is my definition of the *agency* life-factor:

The ability to make decisions and take action that results in positive outcomes.

Given the comment from the director in India, however, there are at least a few workers globally who may not be experiencing agency at work. As a result, they will not feel supported and thus empowered to take such decisions and actions. Their level of autonomy is low.

It is difficult to establish one's self-worth—one's sense of meaning—without agency and autonomy. When we are encouraged to think for ourselves, make decisions, and then act on our decisions, not only does our self-esteem ooze from every pore, but we feel a sense of ownership too. And when humans feel as though they own their ideas, decisions, and actions, they are more likely to bloom.

According to the results from the survey, when it comes to agency, not all is lost. For instance, examine the breakdown of responses from frontline professionals, managers, directors, and senior executives to the statement "I feel I have the power to make my own decisions in life":

I feel I have the power to make my own decisions in life.

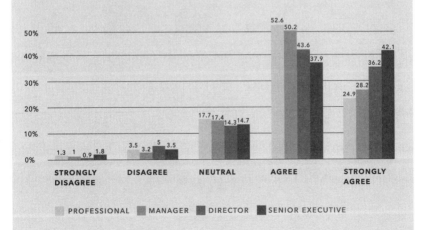

While there are fascinating differences between the "agree" and "strongly agree" responses when broken down by role, overall, people on all rungs of the corporate ladder overwhelmingly believe they have agency in their lives. Notably, there is only a two-percentage-point difference between professional frontline team members and senior executives.

Seventy-eight percent of frontline professionals agree or strongly agree they have agency in their lives, and 78 percent of managers and 80 percent of directors and senior executives feel the same. In general, fewer frontline professionals and managers than their directors and senior executive counterparts disagree or strongly disagree that they have agency in their lives. In sum, agency is prevalent in the lives of the majority of people who participated in the survey.

A more significant gap emerged between the four roles when I asked if agency was important or not to people in work and life.

How important is a sense of agency to you—your ability to make decisions in work and life?

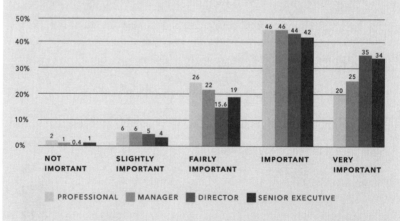

While there is a 10-percentage point difference between frontline professionals and senior executives, on the whole, more than two-thirds of all team members believe agency is an important or very important part of their work and life.

As with several other work- and life-factors from the Global Work-Life Assessment Survey, things took a rather dismal turn when I focused the lens on people's employers.

Does your current employer help you with your confidence in decision-making and thus your agency?

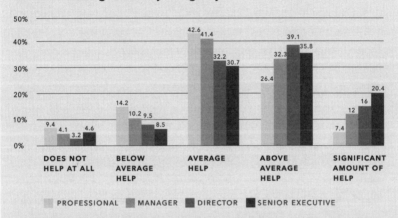

	DOES NOT HELP AT ALL	BELOW AVERAGE HELP	AVERAGE HELP	ABOVE AVERAGE HELP	SIGNIFICANT AMOUNT OF HELP
PROFESSIONAL	9.4	14.2	42.6	26.4	7.4
MANAGER	4.1	10.2	41.4	32.3	12
DIRECTOR	3.2	9.5	32.2	39.1	16
SENIOR EXECUTIVE	4.6	8.5	30.7	35.8	20.4

Only 56 percent of senior executives and 55 percent of directors feel their employer provides such support for the *agency* life-factor. The figures are even lower for managers (44 percent) and frontline professionals (34 percent). Averaged across all employees regardless of rank, only 44 percent of people believe their employer helps them exercise agency.

The data above should be enough to give you the garden box heebie-jeebies. We must attend to agency-eating insects should you wish to help your team members develop their ability to make confident decisions and to act on them.

The Garden Tools of Agency

In the spring of 2021, the world's top-ranked female tennis player pulled out of the French Open. Her reason? Anxiety around press conferences, and by extension the media. Japan's Naomi Osaka, who had experienced depression and anxiety since 2018, made a choice before the French Open: she would not talk to the media in the lead-up to the tournament or during the tournament. Osaka took stock of her mental health, made a decision, and then went further by reflecting on what more she could be doing to protect herself. She believed that any interactions with the press would be detrimental to her health.

Osaka told the tournament organizers about her decision when she arrived in Paris. The baffled officials fined her US$15,000. Shortly thereafter, French Open leaders threatened to expel her from the tournament if she continued to boycott the press conferences. Taking umbrage with their ultimatum and realizing her stance was becoming a distraction, Osaka withdrew from the tournament before it started, depriving her of a potential Grand Slam win and fans of the chance to see her in action. In a note posted to Twitter, Osaka expressed her rationale and next steps:

> I would never trivialize mental health or use the term lightly. I am not a natural public speaker and get huge waves of anxiety before I speak to the world's media. I get really nervous and find it stressful to always try to engage and give you the best answers I can. So here in Paris I was already feeling vulnerable and anxious so I thought it was better to exercise self-care and skip the press conferences. I'm gonna take some time away from the court now.[70]

Osaka's story illustrates how important agency is to people, both in their lives and at work. She would not allow a bunch of tennis bureaucrats to get in the way of her needs. Osaka was making decisions that helped her personally, but some of them also had an impact on her work as a professional tennis player. Her story also introduces the three key facets of agency: review, react, and reflect.

- **Review the options**: Assess the pros and cons of next steps.
- **React with aplomb**: Regulate decisions and actions.
- **Reflect on the results**: Institute self-efficacy around the outcomes.

For team members to feel empowered to make decisions and take action that produces a positive outcome, they need to believe their leaders will support them through the three facets of agency. Let's look more closely at the three facets.

REVIEW THE OPTIONS

Founded in 1895, Givaudan is a global leader in fragrance, beauty, and well-being products. Its headquarters are in Geneva, Switzerland, and it operates in 52 countries, employs over 12,000 people, and brings in annual revenues of over US$7 billion. The company's purpose is "Creating for happier, healthier lives with love for nature. Let's imagine together."[71] Frédéric Séguin is the firm's global head of Environment, Health & Safety. He believes that agency is critical to any team member's engagement.

"The pandemic has been a very good revelation on the significance of agency," he outlined to me in an interview.[72] "Indeed, at that time, I was head of operations managing 17 factories spread across the globe. Suddenly, we faced an unexpected and major crisis without any idea of how the story would end. As a team, we were used to managing social, technical, or supply chain crises, but this one was quite new. Our ways of working were well-proven, and fortunately, our trust was solid. But what really made the difference was the sense of ownership and the creativity of the local teams. Thanks to them, we were able to keep our people safe while continuing to produce and deliver for customers."

Séguin's teams were spread out across the world. Instead of hierarchically mandating what must happen during the lockdown months, he encouraged the teams to review and suggest what local options made the best practical sense for their region to keep operating. He empowered the teams to *review the options*, to invoke their agency.

"Most of the important failures I have witnessed in my professional life," added Séguin, "were because of micromanaging and overwhelming leaders. These kinds of bad practices have their limits mainly because they are exhausting and unsustainable."

Séguin believes that a person's autonomy triggers their engagement, which is a far more powerful tool than compliance. He reckons that agency and autonomy are compelling enablers of creativity. Across two years of the pandemic, prioritizing agency and autonomy was a crucial aspect of how his team handled the challenges of remaining operational at Givaudan. By trusting his team to review their options—and to make decisions based on local circumstances and requirements—Séguin demonstrated the effective application of a tactic that every leader should consider.

How can you allow your people to *review the options*? How might you empower team members to ideate and craft suggestions without your heavy-handed intrusion? Being their leader does not mean you have the best ideas or answers. When you are heavy-handed or viewed as the only one with the answers—when you do not establish a *review the options* mindset—you can be assured that team members will not feel confident in their agency. Whatever agency they have crafted in their lives outside of work will feel stunted by your inability to permit them the chance to *review the options*.

The most prominent subject matter expert on agency was arguably Albert Bandura, a Canadian psychologist who spent many years at Stanford University teaching and researching. (He's also one of my favourites, way ahead of Freud, and the prominent source of my agency thinking.) One element of his research related to *review the options* proposed that people desire forethought for achieving agency.

According to Bandura, people's behaviour is governed by "visualized goals and anticipated outcomes, rather than pulled by an unrealized future state."[73] Bandura felt that people yearn to ideate goals, yet they are also motivated to anticipate the likely outcome. This consistent combination of forethought over time "provides direction, coherence, and meaning to one's life."[74] Thus, without the opportunity to *review the options*, your team members may not feel a sense of direction, rationality, or even meaning in their life.

The best advice for making this happen is simple: find clever and meaningful ways to empower your team members so they can envisage ways that help move forward not only your unit's goals but also their personal development goals. It might be as basic as asking them for feedback on your team's annual objectives before finalizing them or as far-reaching as empowering them to make the decisions on how to successfully enact said goals for the year, but one thing is certain: it will benefit your team members and your organization.

REACT WITH APLOMB

In 1850, the U.S. government passed a far-reaching law called the *Fugitive Slaves Act*. This ruthless bill permitted enslavers to capture (or recapture) enslaved people anywhere in the USA—including those in the free North of the country, which had already outlawed slavery—and return them to the South.

Anyone harbouring an escaped enslaved person could be jailed for six months or fined US$1,000, equivalent to nearly US$40,000 today. Enslaved people who were captured and returned to their owners were often beaten and mutilated. The act was causing unimaginable harm to Black people in North America. Something had to be done to help them. Enter Harriet Tubman, the "Black Moses."

Tubman was herself a runaway enslaved person from Maryland. When the *Fugitive Slaves Act* became law, she was determined to do something to mitigate the harm it was causing. On a visit to Philadelphia, the City of Brotherly Love, Tubman came into contact with like-minded abolitionists and learned about the Underground Railroad, a secret network of safe houses via various routes into Canada that helped Black people escape slavery.

The second component of the *agency* life-factor is the ability to *react with aplomb*, to have the ability to self-regulate one's decisions and actions. Tubman was one determined human being. She was bold and selfless, helping many Black people to freedom. Despite the inherent risks to her, Tubman led over 300 fugitive enslaved men and women through 19 different Underground Railroad journeys into Canada.

Tubman even led her elderly parents and three brothers to St. Catharines, Ontario, where the entire family lived for many years. Tubman's personal agency and commitment to *react with aplomb* led enslavers in the South to post a US$40,000 (the equivalent of more than US$1.5 million today) reward for her capture, dead or alive. They never caught her. And Tubman never lost any of her passengers. Every single one of the people she helped over a 10-year period made it safely across the 49th parallel into Canada. The family lineages continue to this day.

When people *react with aplomb*, they feel empowered to not sit back and wait for things to happen; instead, they make them happen. These people possess the wherewithal to construct their paths to execution. They not only know what needs to get done but also develop plans to get it done, and then they go out and do it.

Tubman could have come up with a good plan in Philadelphia. She might have conjured up some cool ideas with fellow abolitionists. The playbook to help enslaved people might have been filled to overflowing to *review the options* and it could all have ended there. Instead, Tubman opted to *react with aplomb*. She took the next step to solidify her agency.

As a leader, you must not only inspire your people's ideas but also encourage and empower them to *react with aplomb*. Tubman's full human agency was on display by virtue of her willingness to both ideate *and* take action. That brings us to what you can do to empower your team members to *react with aplomb*.

You must *embolden* your team members to act. You ought to instill in them the audaciousness and courage to overcome misgivings or timidity and thus enable team members to deliver a positive result. To *embolden* is a necessary prerequisite to *react with aplomb*.

REFLECT ON THE RESULTS

✿ ✿

The best leaders provide their reports with latitude and trust to do what they do best and do it in a way that brings out their best.

VICE-PRESIDENT, MINING, CANADA, 35-44 YEARS

✿ ✿

This Canadian vice-president brings up a salient point if we bend their comment ever so slightly toward the *agency* life-factor. People are in a constant state of contemplation. We are endlessly reviewing our actions. You are, and so am I.

Did I almost hit that person on their bike? Why was I driving so erratically? Did I just slice my golf shot into the trees? Why didn't I take more time to think about the drive? Did I really yell at my child for spilling their cereal all over the floor? Why wasn't I calmer and more patient? Did I seriously just cancel my Disney+ subscription? But I love *Star Wars*. What was I thinking?

Back at work, if a leader does not trust their team members or give them the latitude to reflect on their actions, agency will diminish, if not disappear entirely. If we want people to *be their best* and to bloom—as the vice-president from Canada points out—we have to create safe spaces for thoughtful deliberation. You must establish an ethos that gives your team members the time and the means to *reflect on the results.*

When leaders cultivate the conditions for team members to institute self-efficacy in their outcomes, they create a culture in which people can believe in themselves. If there is no self-belief—if individuals do not have the confidence to evaluate their results through self-efficacy—they will likely struggle to cope if things go sideways.

Albert Bandura referred to this as "functional self-awareness." He wrote: "The metacognitive capability to reflect upon oneself and the adequacy of one's thoughts and actions is the most distinctly human core property of agency."[75] Without reflection, there is no agency.

While in my post as chief learning officer at TELUS, I occasionally facilitated workshops on Fair Process, a five-step collaboration model for all team members. Fair Process became systemic to the culture of TELUS, a critical component of the TELUS Leadership Philosophy. I didn't invent Fair Process. That honour belongs to Ludo Van der Heyden, the INSEAD chaired professor in Corporate Governance.

The fifth step of Fair Process is "evaluate." It's also the most forgotten and unheralded step. Once you have engaged with others, explored your options, explained the decision, and then executed the result of the decision, you are then asked to evaluate how things went. Did you hit the mark? Were there any learnings? What might you do differently next time? In other words, you are left to *reflect on the results.*

Van der Heyden describes the *evaluate* stage of Fair Process as follows:

> Seek critical feedback from relevant stakeholders on the decision, the plan and the process followed to get there, by collecting feedback and analyzing lessons learnt, based on evidence — this objectivity and involvement can improve the process for next time and change the decision, approach or organization as needed.[76]

You don't need to involve or set up a series of committees to reflect on your results. It's not mission critical to seek out feedback from all stakeholders. Instead, let's pay homage to Fair Process and in particular the *evaluate* stage. As your team's leader, you must point out the importance of self-evaluation, of making the time to cogitate.

As Bandura suggested, if team members are unaware of the importance of reflecting on the adequacy of their thoughts and actions, the chance for agency diminishes. Why not advise individuals to carve out reflection time on their calendars to review what worked and didn't work over the past week? Perhaps you could suggest that they document their evaluations using an online app or physical moleskin book to detail the learnings from past actions.

Team-based reflection moments are also subliminal opportunities to instill agency in individuals. Imagine a project that involved many people finally completes after several months. Holding one or several meetings where you perform an autopsy on the results of the initiative by allowing all team members to fully speak their minds—with no feedback held against or in favour of anyone—is itself not only an evaluation and reflection methodology but also a chance for people to invest in their autonomy and subsequently feel agency through the review.

Whatever methods are proposed for whatever situation, the key is to have that conversation on the importance of reflection with your team members. When you ignore the need to *reflect on the results*, you knowingly block team members' opportunity for agency.

Life-Factor No. 6: RESPECT

Appreciated and continuously treated with dignity; feeling admired for who you really are.

✿ ✿

I have an employer who clearly values my input and is prepared to consider ideas I might have. I feel respected by leadership.
PROFESSIONAL, GOVERNMENT, AUSTRALIA, 35–44 YEARS

✿ ✿

On October 26, 1967, roughly six months before his assassination, Dr.
Martin Luther King Jr. delivered a speech to a group of students at Bar-
ratt Junior High School in Philadelphia. He began by asking the students a
poignant question: "What is your life's blueprint?" What followed was a
remarkable exemplification of the final life-factor in the Work-Life Bloom
model and its direct alignment with respect and the concept of self-worth.

> Number one in your life's blueprint, should be a deep belief in your
> own dignity, your worth, and your own somebodiness. Don't allow
> anybody to make you feel that you're nobody. Always feel that you
> count. Always feel that you have worth, and always feel that your life
> has ultimate significance.[77]

Dignity is critical to establishing one's self-worth and living a fully
realized, blooming life. But what happens to people when the workplace
becomes rife with disrespect? How are individuals affected when abuse,
mismanagement, or other deleterious behaviours prevail? Leaders must
become both the initiators *and* defenders of respect under the auspices of
developing people's self-worth and dignity. If, as King suggests, people
are urged to prevent anyone from making them feel that they're a nobody,
they will need a willing partner to help them. That willing partner is *you.*

An entry from the Global Work-Life Assessment Survey proves my
point perfectly:

✿ ✿

Within my current role, my supervisor is completely invested in promoting my self-worth. The organization is inconsistent with this but the
positive supervision helps me to feel completely connected with the
role, colleagues, and my life.
MANAGER, GOVERNMENT, U.K., 25–34 YEARS

✿ ✿

A different manager from the U.K.—one who works in healthcare—shrewdly points out how easy it is for leaders to help shape an employee's journey to self-worth: "Our senior manager does actively listen to each member of the team without interrupting. This is more difficult than it sounds, but it makes me feel respected."

Back in Philadelphia, when MLK closed out his time with those high school students, he got them thinking ahead to their future selves. He ended with some remarkably prescient advice, particularly as it relates to the relationship between one's self-worth, dignity, and respect:

> If it falls your lot to be a street sweeper, sweep streets like Michelangelo painted pictures, sweep streets like Beethoven composed music, sweep streets like Leontyne Price sings before the Metropolitan Opera. Sweep streets like Shakespeare wrote poetry. Sweep streets so well that all the hosts of heaven and earth will have to pause and say: "Here lived a great street sweeper who swept his job well." If you can't be a pine at the top of the hill, be a shrub in the valley. Be the best little shrub on the side of the hill. Be a bush if you can't be a tree. If you can't be a highway, just be a trail. If you can't be a sun, be a star. For it isn't by size that you win or fail. Be the best of whatever you are.[78]

As I pointed out at the beginning of this book, there is no such thing as work-life balance. People are either blooming—or they're at least close to blooming—or they're not. Furthermore, you shouldn't ask team members to bring their best or most authentic selves to work. You should instead create an environment where, as MLK pointed out, people can simply *be the best* at whatever they are. Helping individuals *be their best* requires helping them feel consistently respected and appreciated. When your dignity is intact, your character will develop further. It should come as no surprise to learn that people desire self-worth. When we disrespect our team members—when the opposite of respect prevails—we deny them their worth.

As a leader, you must ensure all your team members feel respected for who they really are. Your responsibility is to enlarge their self-worth, which will complement their dignity and character. *Respect* may be the final life-factor in Work-Life Bloom, but it might be the most important one for you to enact.

FARMER'S ALMANAC: **RESPECT**

For the most part, results from the Global Work-Life Assessment Survey indicate that people feel respected in their lives but not at work. Unfortunately, most respondents do not believe that their employer provides enough support to help employees achieve respect in the workplace. Three comments from different corners of the world get us started in our final Farmer's Almanac report.

During the implementation of our cloud platforms and updating our legacy systems, I felt I could express myself fully with no worries. I gained respect and was honored for a job well done.
MANAGER, GOVERNMENT, USA, 55-64 YEARS

In my past role, I had a very old-school sexist director who actively and openly disrespected middle-aged women. Our VP was aware and chose not to act.
MANAGER, FINANCE/BANKING/INSURANCE, CANADA, 45-54 YEARS

I'm not respected enough and am seen more as a "human resource."
DIRECTOR, COMPUTERS, GERMANY, 25-34 YEARS

The term *respect* was found hundreds of times in the anecdotal comments of the survey. The remarks above highlight the essence of all feedback related to respect. Many people simply want to be respected at work. Statements like "I want respect" appear several times in the survey. Some respondents—like the Canadian manager and German director quoted above—provided concrete details about their adverse employment situations and why they do not feel respected. Not all is lost, however. As is evident from the U.S. employee, some individuals do experience respect.

When asked if they felt respected, 72 percent of male respondents and 74 percent of female respondents agreed or strongly agreed. Almost three-quarters of all global employees believe they are respected in life. However, when asked if their employer helped them to feel respected in the workplace, only 49 percent of men and 47 percent of women agreed.

From a generational perspective, Baby Boomers possess the largest cohort of people who feel respected, coming in at 77 percent. At the low end is Gen Z at 68 percent. Fifty-two percent of Gen Z respondents believe their employer helps them to feel respected in the workplace but only 44 percent of Gen X agree.

A Canadian frontline Millennial in the financial services sector summed up their workplace respect plight in stark detail: "My manager is a micro-manager, disrespectful, and vengeful. It's definitely not safe to speak up on the team." Judging from the breakdown of leaders versus non-leaders, when I asked if people's current employers helped them achieve respect in the workplace, I can easily surmise that many more people feel like this Canadian Millennial.

Does your current employer help you achieve respect in the workplace?

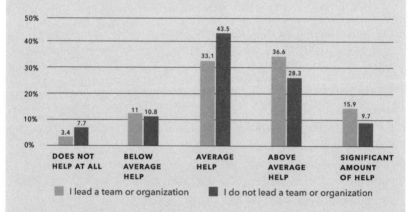

Reviewing the above results, you can see that only 53 percent of leaders believe that their employer assists them in feeling respected at work. You may think that figure is low, but it drops to a wretched 38 percent for non-leaders. When only one-third of your organization's non-leader team members deem their employer as one who advocates a workplace of respect, there is much to do. As we close out the *respect* life-factor details of the Farmer's Almanac, let us take a moment to read what a vice-president from Sweden has to say:

✿ ✿

I think every boss must respect their employees. They must also encourage the natural self of a person, not the fake one, which an employee has to do all the time.

VICE-PRESIDENT, HEALTHCARE, SWEDEN, 35–44 YEARS

✿ ✿

The Garden Tools of Respect

Drawing on research that she had conducted, Christine Porath wrote the following in the *Harvard Business Review* in 2014: "Being treated with respect was more important to employees than recognition and appreciation, communicating an inspiring vision, providing useful feedback — even opportunities for learning, growth, and development." [79]

The business case for respect that she discovered was quite compelling. When team members feel respected by their direct leader, they experience the following:

- 56 percent better health and well-being.
- 89 percent greater enjoyment and satisfaction in their jobs.
- 92 percent greater focus and prioritization.
- 1.72 times more trust and safety.
- 1.26 times more meaning and significance.
- 1.1 times more likely to stay with their organizations.

As part of my research for this book, I sat down with Porath to ask if anything had changed or evolved from her 2014 research. "It's still the leader's behaviour that matters most to people," [80] she said. "Leaders are now more aware of respect. What is at the heart of the leader should be care for people, and respect is an important seed for that to happen." Did I ever enjoy her garden metaphor! She did confess, however, that motivating leaders to prioritize respect remains a challenge.

It's a perfect segue, like a hoe to the soil. I recommend three seeds you can sow to prioritize respect and thus grow a prosperous and caring culture:

- Visible respect
- Invisible respect
- Marked respect

VISIBLE RESPECT

Visible respect is observable deference, respect directly delivered to team members.

"Show me some respect" is a line uttered daily by millions of parents to their teenagers around the world. It doesn't enter the conversation because of hate or happenstance. Instead, the teen has likely said or done something the parent deems stupid—as a parent of three teenagers, I speak from experience—and the respect contract between the parent and child has been temporarily broken. (You can thank the teenager's undeveloped prefrontal cortex—and subsequent amygdala-based reactions—for a majority of these situations.)

If we shift our attention back to the workplace, "show me some respect" may not be publicly uttered by people, but it certainly goes through their minds a lot. As far as I know, leaders do have fully formed prefrontal cortices, so they should be able to stop themselves from being insolent. But research—like Porath's, for example—suggests that disrespect continues to be an issue for many team members.

Your team members expect respect. You should therefore make sure you show it positively and clearly. When you use the *visible respect* gardening tool, you initiate verbal, written, or even physical respect in any encounters with team members. Your actions get backed by a high degree of emotional intelligence in every instance. You are civil, kind, and amiable, always mindful of what your team members may be dealing with at work or in life.

Think about expressing *visible respect* as delivering an endless round of applause. In other words, teach yourself to CLAP: care, listen, accept, and prevent.

- **Care**: Central to leadership is *how* you care about your team members. Not *if*, but *how*. In the specific context of *visible respect*, you are polite, empathetic, and patient, and your interactions with team members are bursting with care. You conduct yourself with civility, good manners, and unyielding kindness in all exchanges. You never demean or put people down publicly or privately. You are easygoing and mindful that mistakes happen, never reprimanding or belittling people. You are conscious of your physical, verbal, and written presence, willing not only to be vulnerable (and, ideally, self-deprecating) but also to encourage team members not to feel threatened by your title or hierarchical rank. To care is to demonstrate platonic affection and respect people as human beings. (I wrote an entire book on the concept, *Lead. Care. Win.*)

- **Listen**: First, let's tackle live interactions with team members. When you are visibly silent, you are actively listening. No interruptions. No midsentence top-ups. No "I'm sorry, but I must stop you there" intrusions. When you're engaged with a team member in a synchronous dialogue situation, you keenly encourage them to voice their opinions, ideas, and feedback. This is not a one-way street of communication from you as their leader. You command respect by asking them to contribute while being an active listener. A different yet similar approach can be employed for asynchronous (non-live) situations, like emails, texts, or DMs. The key is not to ghost your team member, particularly if they are expecting a response from you. ("Ghosting" refers to refusing to acknowledge someone's most recent query or communication such as from a text and instead leaving them waiting for a reply.) In this case, to listen is to invite a response from your team member. Once you've received it, your responsibility is to acknowledge it—either for the purposes of making a decision in the future or to confirm that the message has been received. "Thanks for this. I'll get back to you shortly" is a good example of a respectful reply.

- **Accept**: To accept is to be mindful of people's differences, idiosyncrasies, cultural backgrounds, current work-life circumstances, and societal milieux. As a respectful leader, you fully accept what makes people distinct. However, it's not enough to *accept* someone's variance. You should also *acknowledge* it through demonstrably positive conduct. For example, how do you recognize a team member who recently underwent sex reassignment surgery (SRS)? Do you ignore them, or do you visibly respect their decision by being fully inclusive in team-based or one-on-one interactions? Another team member admits to you that they have an addiction of some sort. Are you adopting a new attitude of face-to-face and offline shunning, or have you visibly respected them by offering whatever support you and the organization can provide and then following up to ensure that the support is proving effective? Or, maybe you notice that an individual on your team has begun regularly using your organization's prayer or meditation room for 30 minutes daily. You establish a pattern and realize they use the room just before lunch. Do you discuss this new ritual with your team member or ignore it? Do you avoid scheduling meetings at this time? Is there anything else you might be doing to accept, acknowledge, and thus respect them? There are myriad other examples, of course, but the point is clear: accept people's differences but don't do so without also acknowledging them through a positive exchange.

- **Prevent**: I might have called this tip *proactive*, but to *prevent* is to be pre-emptive about safeguarding your team members' well-being and personal brand. You respect them enough that you're willing to help avert a potential disaster of their doing. You smell a brewing calamity by virtue of your leadership acumen, but by virtue of your respect for the person, you ultimately provide advanced—yet discreet—guidance to help circumvent the fiasco. For instance, let's say you observe an email chain or a Slack or Teams thread in which your team member is clearly heading in the wrong direction on some matter. It's nowhere near the debacle stage, but you can envision where it might go. Ever so discreetly, you contact the individual and provide proactive leadership coaching to help them see the light. Because you respect them, you are protecting them from any real or permanent personal brand damage. A leader who respects their team members is always willing to prevent disasters caused by those team members from happening. While this may feel uncomfortable—after all, it's not as though you want to offend anyone—you must keep in mind how a team member's unfortunate conduct may be interpreted as disrespectful by their peers and the possible resulting consequences.

INVISIBLE RESPECT

Invisible respect is imperceptible admiration, respect indirectly delivered without the team member's realizing it.

Imagine the following scenario. You're a director attending the monthly team meeting with your vice-president and seven other peers. It's a face-to-face meeting for half a day in a standard, nondescript office. One of your peers starts talking about one of their team members during the mid-morning break. That team member—a manager—is nowhere in sight and is not expected to join the meeting.

According to your colleague, during a client review call the previous day, the team member's seven-year-old burst into their home office twice. Apparently, the child was caught on camera both times. As you are refilling your coffees, your colleague says they're going to buy the manager a door lock for their upcoming five-year anniversary at the company. "If she can't figure out work-from-home," your colleague says, "then I'm going to make things difficult. What a joke."

You dig a little into the comment, remembering something about the employee in question. "Doesn't she normally work here in the office?" you ask. "Maybe she had to work from home because her kid was sick or something."

Nonplussed, your peer says, "So you're in favour of embarrassing client meetings?"

Shaking your head in disagreement, you reply, "But you don't even know if the interruption was an issue for the client. Was it?"

Invisible power comes with the territory of being a leader. By virtue of your title, you have an invisible ability to shape people's beliefs. If you put down a team member when they're nowhere to be seen, the invisible power you hold over them has become noxious. Your perniciousness can influence others by not only changing their perception of the people you mock but also effectively giving them permission to mock them too.

Invisible respect is an offshoot of invisible power. You can shape or protect someone's character even when that person isn't in the room. The same applies online. The director who is planning to buy a door lock for the manager is wielding their invisible power. It's akin to invisible disrespect. The manager has no idea that the director is disparaging her and has no way to defend herself. Invisible disrespect is all too common in leadership circles.

As a leader, you have a responsibility to be respectful to others at all times, and especially when they're not present. You may even think about the legal principle "presumption of innocence," whereby people are considered innocent until proven guilty. Jumping to conclusions without evidence or facts to back them up is not only disrespectful to your team member but also an obvious rapport-building violation in the making. To practice *invisible respect* is to BEAR: believe, eavesdrop, abolish, and refer.

- **Believe:** Developing confidence in your team members is a necessary first step to practising invisible respect. If you don't believe in your team members, it will be hard to advocate for them when they're not around. When you demonstrate conviction in their abilities, you are promoting their current and future performance. Whether it's an email, project meeting, or elevator conversation, when you express belief in your team members, you are supporting them, even when they're not present.

- **Eavesdrop:** While I'm not trying to turn you into a corporate spy, I recommend that you pay attention to organizational chatter. It can tell you a lot. When you eavesdrop, don't ignore disrespectful online or in-person comments about team members. Don't turn a blind eye to microaggressions or blatant rumours. Instead, be cognizant of them, refuse to overlook the insult, and, when warranted, take a stand to support the team member in question. The least you can do is talk to the person who made the disrespectful remarks to set the record straight.

- **Abolish:** In the context of *invisible respect*, to abolish is to eliminate all impudent behaviour from your conduct. It's rather blunt yet unambiguous: you agree to fully disengage from any disrespectful commentary about others. Whether you're communicating face-to-face or online, you commit to discourse and interactions that are civil and considerate when you are discussing other team members. That means no snide remarks, sidebar jokes, or hurtful gags. All discourse about someone else—regardless of whether it's someone from your team or someone from outside of the organization—is conducted with the utmost courteous professionalism.

- **Refer**: There's a reason recruiters ask for references before they make a job offer. References from people who have first-hand experience of a candidate's habits and behaviours can give you valuable insight into the candidate's abilities. To employ *invisible respect*, consider using the same tactic. Whether you're face-to-face or online, when there is an appropriate opportunity to refer your team member to a new network connection, a project opportunity, or other prospects that will help them to prosper, just do it. It's a great chance to be respectful without them knowing, and you're again advocating for their abilities.

MARKED RESPECT

Marked respect is influence-derived reverence, a set of criteria that establish a leader-led respectful workplace culture.

Like it or not, team members under your direction often mimic your conduct in and out of the workplace. For example, if the boss is rude to someone in another part of the organization, team members probably think it's okay for them to be rude to others as well. If a manager is late to a meeting without apologizing, it's acceptable to be late going forward. If the leader constantly ignores or deletes emails, inbox zero, here we come!

Leaders hold the power. Leaders can also *be* the power. Therefore, leaders are capable of quickly influencing people's conduct. Behaviour often flows organization-wide, spilling directly from a leader's demeanour. In that case, a respectful workplace organizational culture can more easily take shape if you define and endorse a set of respect conditions—*marked respect* standards.

Your responsibility is to identify and endorse these *marked respect* standards. You can think of them as the accompanying definitions to your *visible* and *invisible respect* criteria. Perhaps you have different respect ideas or monikers than CLAP and BEAR. That's completely fine. I've provided these *visible* and *invisible respect* options simply as a starter kit. After that, you can come up with respect standards that are fit for purpose in your own workplace.

Building a collection of respect standards should be one of your top personal leadership priorities. If you haven't already established them, today is a good day to start. If the organization has not offered such a guideline via H.R. or People & Culture, yesterday has already passed. It's time to act.

You might consider involving your H.R. colleagues, or maybe not. Perhaps you will align yourself with a few other leaders to begin crafting the *marked respect* criteria list. Again, maybe not. Perhaps this will be a solo act. It's your call.

When your *marked respect* tenets get established, they become a de facto *visible* and *invisible respect* cheat sheet. It's how you turn the potential for respectful behaviour — the idea of being respectful as a leader — into consistently observable and unobservable actions. After all, your goal is to continuously appreciate your team members, treating them with dignity while continuing to admire them for who they really are. You are building a community of team members, respected for their efforts and way of being.

Respect can be broken down into visible and invisible conduct opportunities. Writing down these desired respect behaviours to define your *marked respect* approach is a prudent leadership action. We might even coin it a "mark of respect."

This all reminds me of the legendary management professor and thinker Henry Mintzberg's work. Mintzberg wrote something on the concept of respect in his book *Simply Managing* that resonates deeply with me. Perhaps it explains why you should immediately craft your *marked respect* guidelines: "What could be more natural than to treat our organizations, not as mystical hierarchies of authority, but as communities of engagement, where every member is respected and so returns that respect?"[81]

In the Greenhouse: LIFE-FACTORS

As with the six work-factors from Chapter III, there is much for you to unpack, consider, and apply when it comes to the six life-factors. I never once said that establishing and following the model in this book would be easy.

You may have caught on to the multiple times in which I presented in this chapter various life-factors and how they are impacted by workplace circumstances or situations. I detailed several scenarios in which you—a leader—affect team members' life-factors while on the job. "Why not coin them 'work-factors,' Dan?" you may have muttered.

Let's go back to Paulo Coehlo's *The Alchemist*, and his introduction of the "Personal Legend," which I discussed at the beginning of this chapter.

Remember what Coehlo wrote: "To realize one's Personal Legend is a person's only real obligation." And recall what I urged you to also consider: "Will you become a positive force and assist in your team members' life-journey?"

You are not responsible for someone's life but you most certainly can help them to potentially bloom in it. The six life-factors presented in this chapter are crucial to helping create that opportunity. For at least 40 hours a week, team members count on you for guidance, leadership, and mentoring. You can, without a shadow of a doubt, impact a team member's "Personal Legend" and thus by extension their life-journey.

As with the work-factors, team members will regularly scrutinize, interpret, and assess the life-factors, frequently questioning their role and responsibility in the context of each one. And, as with the work-factors again, regular conversations about the life-factors with your team members will not only serve you well but also aid in their quest to fulfill their "Personal Legend" and life-journey. Please consider the following questions to help you measure your success as a leader in the context of all six of the life factors and how you lead your team members:

❁ **Relationships**: Does the team member feel they have a strong network of connections that facilitate exchanges of assistance?

❁ **Skills**: Does the team member feel they have the skills and abilities to perform confidently at work and in life, now and into the future?

❀ **Well-being**: Does the team member feel healthy when it comes to their emotional, social, physical, and financial wellness?

❀ **Meaning**: Does the team member feel and exhibit self-worth daily?

❀ **Agency**: Does the team member feel empowered to make decisions and then take action that results in positive outcomes?

❀ **Respect**: Does the team member feel appreciated and continuously treated with dignity, and thus admired for who they really are?

To further assist you with the six life-factors, you may choose to use a dashboard to remain informed about your team members' opinions or perspectives across each of the six life-factors. Unlike with the six work-factors, though, you really don't need to track their sentiments across the four dimensions of team, organization, leader, and themselves. A current state versus desired state separation, however, is something to consider. Feel free to use something like the chart below or visit www.worklifebloom .com/extras to download a copy.

TEAM MEMBER:	CURRENT STATE	DESIRED STATE
	How does the team member currently view themselves in terms of enacting or living up to this life-factor?	How does the team member wish to view themselves in terms of enacting or living up to this life-factor? (1-2 years from now)
Relationships		
Skills		
Well-being		

Meaning		
Agency		
Respect		

THIS BOOK IS nearing a close. Next, we will explore two leadership tests—aptly called the "Soil and Water Tests"—where I encourage and provide you with the means to a) continually scan your team members' work-life factors status, and b) self-reflect on and test your own proficiency in understanding and applying the 12 work-life factors. It's a short chapter but an important one. You've come this far. Let's do everything possible so both you and your team members have every chance to bloom.

"When a flower doesn't bloom you fix the environment in which it grows, not the flower." [1]

DR. ALEXANDER DEN HEIJER

CHAPTER V

In Bloom

WE BEGAN THIS book with the story of Angie Kim. If you remember, Kim spent a decade at Loblaw Companies Limited, growing from an individual contributor to vice-president. She bloomed for many years, only to suddenly crash toward the renewal persona. She had to deal not only with the effects of a pandemic on team members in 56 stores and on store revenues but also with personal challenges. She put an immense amount of pressure on herself as a minority, female, and LGBTQ+ ally to be a positive role model living her values within the company. But she felt she was being constantly judged by other Loblaw leaders as a minority, female, LGBTQ+ ally leader and not simply as a leader. Her self-worth as a leader was put into question.

Realizing that she needed to prioritize her well-being and mental health, Kim resigned from her vice-president role at Loblaw in the summer of 2021. During her self-care recovery over the ensuing months, she and her husband, Matt, made an important decision. Ultimately it rebounded her to the blooming persona.

"What I learned is that not every single flower blooms at the same time or in the same way," Kim told me. "Every flower has a different petal composition, length, and width. What it takes for them to bloom is also different. I realized there are different ways that I personally wanted to bloom and that I don't have to be the picture-perfect flower. I don't want any misalignment with how I want to feel internally and how I need to portray myself externally."

Kim was now fully in charge of her garden box. She outlined the conversations she was having with her husband. He asked Kim to think back to when she was happiest and when she felt like she was blooming, being her best. They discussed times when Kim was back at home after a day on the job and still thinking about work, but not feeling stressed out about it, because the work-life relationship that existed was harmonious.

"'Work-life balance' is a bullshit term," she confessed, "because it automatically makes you feel like you're doing something wrong." Kim and her husband reflected deeply on that dreadful phrase before making the decision of a lifetime.

"I realized I wanted to focus on taking care of people and being connected to the front line. The entire journey to becoming a vice-president, and all that is celebrated with the role, was about inciting meaningful change in others. Matt and I came to the conclusion that it had to be retail, people-focused, and a noteworthy Canadian brand that's growing and has future potential."

Kim and her husband applied to become owners of a Canadian Tire franchise. Their store operates out of St. Marys, Ontario, population 7,613, barely twice the size of the team Kim used to lead at Loblaw, but exactly what she needed for a renewal. She got back to blooming.

"The freedom to truly cater to the community and team members of St. Marys by serving directly in the front line, walking the walk every day, has me blooming again," divulged Kim. "I mean, we fell in love with the idea of being able to—again, I'm not just trying to use the word because that's the title of your book—bloom. But that's exactly how it is. I can bloom along with the town. I can help an old lady fix her flat tires and help a little boy pick out his first bike. Every small moment has been so empowering. It gave me back a sense of purpose and meaning. Everything that I stand for means something here, and I can wake up and feel proud not only because I'm alive but because I know I will make a positive difference in someone's life every day. I choose to bloom in the way I want to, while feeling like it's my flower."

From blooming to renewal to blooming. It's a story so many of us can relate to either as a human being or as a leader inspiring people to do the same.

When a leader like Kim divulges that they're no longer blooming at work, we know that there has been a serious change in their work-life persona. It doesn't matter if their work-life persona is now budding, stunted, or in renewal. Something major is up. Kim recognized her situation and with some help made a very impactful change. But for every Kim who has made their way back to bloom, there are many more who are still trying to figure out their path back to a lush garden box.

Take, for example, Sharina, a senior level leader at a large multinational firm based in the USA. She asked me to use a pseudonym for her, and I've honoured that request. Sharina joined her company just over a decade ago as an individual manager reporting to a director. She quickly took on senior level responsibilities and projects. Five years later, she was offered a plum leadership role outside her original business unit to lead initiatives that helped team members perform in their account executive roles.

Sharina was now a director. Her work was improving the customer experience, which was important to her, and she was leading a good-sized team, which she enjoyed. Everything at work was going very well. For several years thereafter, the organization and business unit had an overall employee engagement score that oscillated between the high 70s and low 80s, meaning a large majority of its team members felt very good at work. Sharina was one of them. She took great pride in her accomplishments, and her contributions were noticed by many people within the organization.

By this time Sharina had added two children into her life mix. She bought and moved into a new house, established new hobbies, built tons of new relationships in and out of the company, and deftly revised her sense of meaning along the way. She developed new skills, in terms of both financial investment prowess and collaborative networking through a moms' group that she joined. She also set out to support two not-for-profit organizations to help people in need. Agency was in abundance. Sharina was, to all intents and purposes, in bloom.

In the fall of 2022, Sharina shared with me her annual employee engagement score: *moderately engaged.* For the first time since she was hired, her score was not *fully engaged.* The external firm that Sharina's company hires to annually measure employee engagement uses a four-level range. *Moderately engaged* is one level below *fully engaged* and one level above *moderately disengaged.* (The fourth and final level is *actively disengaged,* which I might cheekily call the "pants are on fire" category.)

"Dan, it's the first time I've ever been moderately engaged here. It's just a score, but I feel that something isn't right with me."[2]

Isn't right with her? That's a lot of pressure to bear. Sharina wasn't totally wrong. Something definitely wasn't right; that part was spot on. But it wasn't just with her. It wasn't merely her fault. The problem was twofold. First, her interpretation of the 12 work-life factors had evolved over the past year, with several dropping in stature. And second, the organization she worked for—including Sharina's direct leader—had made alterations that now negatively impacted several of her work-life factors.

Sharina's drop in employee engagement was the result of a one-two punch: things were adversely changing for her at work and how she saw the factors and experienced them in her life were evolving. Remember, we bring our work to life every day. However, our life is also entangled in our work. Therefore, Sharina falling out of the bloom persona was not her fault. Rather, her not feeling fully engaged at work was simply a repercussion of the messy confluence of life and work. Regardless, it made Sharina *feel* like it was all on her, and that is telling. Work and life cannot be balanced, and it is not solely within the power of an individual to choose to bloom. Work-life balance, be gone. It's a lie. We all need to think differently for the sake of our health.

After Sharina automatically received her score from the survey website, a graphic displayed several employee engagement descriptors. The image proposed that an employee's engagement score is a measure of their emotional and intellectual commitment to the organization. Sharina agreed. She felt as though she was less emotionally and intellectually committed by the end of 2022 and that that change was causing the drop in her score. Sharina also divulged to me that the deteriorating work situation was beginning to have a negative effect on her at home.

Our last conversation was about her options for the following year—that is, what she might do to re-establish her blooming state. We debated whether she might best achieve that goal by staying in her current role, or if she should seek a new one either within her current firm or with a different company. Did her boss of five years even have it within them to address Sharina's scenario? A potential leave of absence was also put on the table. I reminded Sharina during our discussions that the drop was perfectly normal, that it happens to almost everybody.

Sharina and Angie Kim are but two examples from an endless field of global garden box stories via people working in organizations. But each story also illustrates what can happen to any team member whom you lead. One year people are blooming; the next they're not. They might be on top of their gardening game for a decade—growing an unspoiled bounty of crops—and then suddenly, the driest of soil dominates. The garden box and its contents fall into decay. The gardener feels broken.

I have suggested repeatedly throughout this book that people are ultimately responsible for their own personal garden box. Leaders are not wholly accountable for their team members' overarching welfare. But you can most definitely create conditions that give someone the opportunity to bloom or not and to burn out or not. And while this book isn't about happiness, as their leader, you do hold *some* responsibility for the state of your team members' work-life persona. You can (and do) hold some of the power that causes people to dip in form. Or to bloom. And now you have a shed full of garden tools that can help them to bloom.

Angie Kim and Sharina were each operating in a blooming state for about a decade. And then things fell apart rather quickly. It took about a year for both of their garden boxes to ultimately become choked with weeds. Growth, let alone blooming, was now difficult. In the case of Sharina, her direct leader was clearly not helping the situation either. Business unit changes and leaders caused a host of issues that negatively impacted her. Kim took matters into her own hands and is now the co-owner of a Canadian Tire franchise. She has returned to the blooming state whereas Sharina continues to fight through the weeds.

Millions of people annually fall from bloom to another persona. Millions more cannot seem to move up—or back up—to the bloom state. Others are perfectly content to remain in the renewal, budding, or stunted personas. Thus, for team members to *be their best*, the summary question I want you to consider in this chapter is as follows:

How can I become a more intentional work-life leader?

An intentional work-life leader is not only purposeful with their leadership conduct but also fully present. They give their team members the space and time to cycle through the inevitable weather events, ensuring those people feel cared for and valued, so that, when they are ready, they have a better chance to bloom. Regardless of a team member's current work-life persona, an intentional leader wants to help people to *be their best* throughout their tenure on the team. They are active participants in the overarching wellness of their team members and the quest to bloom.

When you become an intentional work-life leader, you facilitate ways in which people can *be their best*. The 12 work-life factors that I detailed in the previous two chapters are essential to your intentionality as a leader. If you can't get the work-life factors right, there really isn't much hope that your team members will bloom.

However, I urge you to consider two additional tactics. In essence, they will help you become a more intentional work-life leader, one well-equipped to further assist your team members:

- **Conduct soil tests**: A soil test is a leader's continual scanning of their team members' current work-life factors.

- **Conduct water tests**: A water test is a leader's regular self-reflective test to see if they can both recognize and apply the work-life factors for their team and for themselves.

Conduct Soil Tests

"K=R=P is an equation I wrote because I was trained as an engineer. Kindness equals Repeat business equals Profit. But leadership itself is an intimate act. It is a genuine conversation. It is a real human interaction between the two of us, in which we're both interested in what we're doing."[3] — **TOM PETERS**

Tom Peters is a legendary management thinker and the co-author of *In Search of Excellence*, one of the seminal books on leadership. They just don't make them like Peters anymore. His quote above, which I've taken from my interview with him, bridges two important concepts that align nicely with the idea of the *soil test*.

To be intentional as a work-life leader requires you to be in a persistent interchange with each of your team members. Peters refers to that conversational and inquisitive skill as "MBWA: managing by wandering around." As you're wandering around and hopefully being kind—demonstrating what he calls "extreme humanism" while having fun in the process—you are relationship-building with your people to build up the work-life factors outlined in this book.

Someone who excels at MBWA knows the names of their team members' kids, how home renovations are going, and when a family vacation to Disney World is happening. They comment positively on a new haircut, tattoo, or garment and interact with joy because it is joyful to genuinely *connect* with people. As Peters said, "If you don't have fun while doing MBWA, do the world a favour, go home, and resign yourself as a leader."

In other words, you must be persistently intentional with your scanning. The *soil test* is just as it sounds—you are assessing and testing the soil of your team members' garden box to understand what's going well with them and what's not. You use the 12 work-life factors as a basis for the dialogue that forms the *soil test.*

I've created a set of questions for each of the 12 work-life factors that you can adapt to use in those work-life conversations with your team members. In addition, there are several work-life persona (bloom, budding, stunted, renewal) questions for you to weave in as you see fit.

The key word in the previous paragraph is "adapt." Do not ask all the questions exactly as they're written. Treat them as signposts. MBWA can't be scripted. It needs to be genuine. With that in mind, it is important that the content contained within these questions is raised over the course of your interactions with team members, be it during a formal one-on-one meeting or while you are practising your informal wandering. Don't ask all the questions in a single session.

If you go an entire year without covering the content of most, if not all, of the questions, you're not leading intentionally. These are evergreen questions. Repeat the process every year. The more aware you are of your team members' work-life situation, the more likely it is you will be able to help them to bloom and to *be their best.* (Visit www.worklifebloom.com /extras to download a copy of the various soil test questions.)

Work-Factors: Soil Test

SOIL TEST QUESTIONS: WORK-FACTORS

WORK-FACTOR	QUESTIONS TO ASK YOUR TEAM MEMBER
TRUST	**Do you feel safe to speak your mind at work?** ☒ If not, what's getting in the way? ☑ If yes, what can I do to make certain that it continues?
BELONGING	**How connected do you feel to others on the team around here?** ☒ If not, what can I do so you feel better understood, represented, and more connected? ☑ If yes, share with me what needs to happen so you always feel this way.
VALUED	**Do you feel valued in your role/at work?** ☒ If not, what will it take to turn that around? ☑ If yes, let me know what makes you feel valued.
PURPOSE	**Do you feel our organization operates with a high sense of purpose?** ☒ If not, what is it we should be doing differently to become purpose-driven? ☑ If yes, how does our purpose help you to succeed in your role and/or life?
STRATEGY	**Do you feel connected to our organization's strategy/do you know where we're heading?** ☒ If not, what can I do today to support you with our strategy? ☑ If yes, what suggestions do you have to complement our current strategic direction?
NORMS	**Is it easy to get work done around here?** ☒ If not, what suggestions do you have to improve our culture and operating practices? ☑ If yes, what more can we do to build upon our existing principles and processes?

Life-Factors: Soil Test

SOIL TEST QUESTIONS: LIFE-FACTORS

LIFE-FACTOR	QUESTIONS TO ASK YOUR TEAM MEMBER
RELATIONSHIPS	**Do you feel you have a strong, reliable network in and out of the organization?** ☒ If not, can I do anything to help you make a few more connections? ☑ If yes, what more do you need to further strengthen your network? Can I help?
SKILLS	**Do you feel confident about your current skills and abilities?** ☒ If not, how can I assist you to develop any current skills gaps that you might have? ☑ If yes, what other skills are you thinking to develop for your next role or gig? Can I assist with that?
WELL-BEING	**Do you consider yourself to be in a positive state of wellness right now?** ☒ If not, are there any facets of your emotional, social, physical, or financial well-being that I can assist with? ☑ If yes, is there anything with your wellness that you're worried might decline and that I can help with?
MEANING	**Do you feel a sense of meaning and self-worth?** ☒ If not, how can I help you establish confidence? ☑ If yes, what have you done to keep it up?
AGENCY	**Do you feel you can make decisions and take action on them?** ☒ If not, how can I help increase your levels of empowerment and self-action? ☑ If yes, what other aspects of autonomy and decision-making can be improved?
RESPECT	**Do you feel you are respected?** ☒ If not, what actions can I immediately take to help you gain greater respect? ☑ If yes, are there any aspects of respect that I can further assist you with?

Work-Life Personas: Soil Test

SOIL TEST QUESTIONS: WORK-LIFE PERSONAS

WORK-LIFE PERSONA	QUESTIONS TO ASK YOUR TEAM MEMBER
RENEWAL	• There are several roadblocks getting in the way of your performance: where do you need the most assistance in the short term? • Is there anything you'd like to discuss with me about your role, the organization, or anything outside of it that will help you "clear the air"? • If this role isn't the right fit, what can I do to help you with your next career move?
BUDDING	• You seem to be doing very well at work but there remain a few areas where you could use some self-development assistance. • Is there anything I can do to support you with your <relationship-building, skills development, well-being, meaning, decision-making/agency, or respect> self-development?
STUNTED	• You seem to be doing well outside of work and with your self-development, but there are a few areas where you could still use some help. • Is there anything I can do to assist you with your workplace <trust, belonging, value, purpose, strategy, or culture/norms> understanding and development?
BLOOMING	• Even though you are blooming at work and outside of it, is there anything that you are worried about that I can help you with? Short-term or long-term concerns? • Do you envision any significant changes in the near future that might alter your high-performing/blooming state?

Continual conversations with your team members are at the *root* of the soil test. These conversations can become the fertilizer you need to help grow blooming crops, also known as your team. Don't underestimate their contribution to the garden box. And don't forget, you can send your team members to take the free Work-Life Bloom personal assessment at www.worklifebloom.com/assessment. It will only take 5–8 minutes to complete the survey and it will reveal their work-life persona.

Conduct Water Tests

It doesn't take a Bachelor of Horticulture Science degree to appreciate the critical importance of water to a garden. Without water, no crop stands a chance. The 12 work-life factors presented in this book are positioned to you as garden tools, instruments from your garden shed to positively alter the conditions to give your team members a better chance to bloom. But gardens still need water to grow.

The *water test* pays homage to any garden's need for H2O. When you are self-reflective as a leader, think of it as watering the garden. You've got your hose, and while you're standing there spraying liquid gold over the crops, you've entered a contemplative state of self-assessment. Thus, the water test relates specifically to your ability to a) self-reflect on how well you are administering each of the 12 work-life factors, and b) self-assess why your team members are blooming or not. By metaphorically watering a team member's garden, you're specifically thinking about what you can do to improve your overall Work-Life Bloom leadership.

As with the *soil test*, you are not required to ask all questions presented below in one go with yourself. It is not compulsory to be in a constant state of self-reflection. Too much water can be as harmful as not enough. But it is important to weave the questions into your leadership calendar.

Use the following questions solely as a guide, one that you can use on a schedule that makes the most sense to you. (And again, visit www .worklifebloom.com/extras to download a copy of the table below if you like.)

WATER TEST QUESTIONS: LEADERSHIP QUESTIONS

CATEGORY	LEADERSHIP QUESTIONS TO ASK YOURSELF
WORK-LIFE PERSONAS	• On my team, do I know who is blooming and who is not? Who occupies a different persona? • Do I know why team members are blooming or why they are not? • Do I know if people are satisfied in their current persona? Do they even want to bloom or are they content in another persona? • If they are blooming, what might it take for them to drop? (Do I know their triggers?) • If they are content in their non-blooming persona (budding, stunted, renewal), how can I still support them? • Regardless of their work-life persona, what is needed from me for each team member to *be their best*? • Do I know my persona? Regardless, do I know what is needed for me to *be my best*?
WORK-FACTORS (trust, belonging, valued, purpose, strategy, and norms)	• Am I doing everything possible to positively enact the six work-factors for me? For my team? • Do I know where the team stands with my leadership on each of the work-factors? • How will I fix any of the six work-factors that might be viewed as deficient or negative?
LIFE-FACTORS (relationships, skills, well-being, meaning, agency, and respect)	• Am I doing everything possible to positively enact the six life-factors for me? For my team? • Do I know where each team member stands specific to the six life-factors? • How might I help team members develop any of the life-factors that are viewed as deficient or negative?

The ability to be self-reflective is the real *nutrient* of the *water test.* Your contemplative moments not only will help your Work-Life Bloom intentionality but also will become the method you use to continually reflect on your overall leadership abilities. As the novelist Edith Wharton once wrote, "There are two ways of spreading light: to be the candle or the mirror that reflects it."[4]

THERE IS ONE final chapter to this book, fancily titled the Coda. A coda is the ending part of a work of literature, separate from the earlier parts. The coda for *Work-Life Bloom* ties a bow on the book's central argument: our lives shape our work; nevertheless, our work shapes us. The work-life persona we hold today may not be what we held three years ago. It may not be how we feel in a year's time either.

And let me tell you, I can relate to that argument. After all, I'm going to turn the lens on myself to share a snippet of the journey I've navigated through work and life toward my "Personal Legend."

Coda

KNOW FROM MY direct experience what it feels like to get terminated from your role at work. My tears fell like an atmospheric river event when it happened. I'd rather have a monthly spinal fusion than go through another termination. Maybe that's why I'm now a company of one.

Over my career I've experienced trust breakdowns, questionable if not laughable so-called strategic organizational changes, and unhealthy eras. My life-factors have also failed me from time to time.

Of course, there have also been many periods when everything clicked and I was glowing like an omniscient sun. It was a magical feeling when the majority of my work-life factors were blooming. Everything I touched felt radiant, whether I was in the office or at home. I was Jesse Owens at the 1936 Summer Olympics, Serena Williams at the height of her tennis greatness. Unstoppable—even by *Deadpool*.

Have I always been able to *be my best* in work and life? Have I constantly bloomed? Have I needed to renew? Did I ever feel stunted or budding?

The answer is no to the first two questions and yes to the last two. I'm no different than anyone else.

For 20 years, I was a full-time team member working for a firm. I was employed by five different organizations in the education, high-tech, and telecom industries between 1998 and 2018. I was a leader with local, national, and/or global teams ranging in size from 10 to over 100 team members.

Let me share a small snapshot from those 20 years. When I was working at a global high-tech firm called Business Objects, it was an incredible period of blooming. Every facet of the workplace was positive, from its culture and purpose through to its strategy. I was trusted and valued, and I sincerely felt as though I belonged. My skills and relationships were growing, my well-being oozed with my young family of five, and I was highly respected, operating with deep meaning and exhibiting agency in and out of work. Blooming might have been an understatement.

However, I knew that the high-tech industry was always in acquisition mode and that it had a particular habit of sniffing around business intelligence companies like Business Objects. And then, one day in the fall of 2007, boom! (Not bloom!) Software giant SAP acquired Business Objects.

For the next several months, we worked on integrating the two companies. Who would go where, how operations would unfold, and which initiatives would be cut and which would survive were the only topics of endless conversations happening across multiple time zones and countries. I felt as though I had gone from bloom to renewal almost overnight. Life was stark and wretched for me for many months.

My direct leader lived and worked in Silicon Valley. He unexpectedly arrived in Vancouver one day in the spring of 2008 and met me for a beer.

"You're an invaluable asset to the organization, Dan," he said, "but I'd like to offer you a way out." He went on to discuss the fine print of a severance package. I wasn't being fired; it was my choice if I wanted to leave. But it sure felt like I was getting terminated—which is an odd way to feel when you're supposedly "invaluable."

During the integration, it was clear that what we had built at Business Objects was going to be dismantled by SAP. The team of over 100 people I led through a group known as the University of Business Intelligence (UBI) was to be parsed into three different units across the acquiring organization.

I felt torn. On one garden glove, I had failed to keep the team together yet I did manage to secure everyone a new role at SAP. On the other garden glove, I was handed a severance package to potentially leave the organization instead of being offered a new position that might have met most or all my work- and life-factors. It was all so surreal. Could I actually leave SAP and my colleagues of the previous five years? Would there be anything "better" outside of SAP? Would I be able to shoot back to a blooming state if I stayed at SAP after suffering from the renewal work-life persona for several months?

After several weeks of deliberation, I accepted the package and left. I knew that my life-factors were being seriously endangered, and I hypothesized that SAP was not going to offer me a positive set of work- or life-factors that would fill my emotional and professional buckets. I knew that if I remained at SAP, things could get even worse for me. I instinctively understood that my garden box was about to rot.

With nowhere to go in terms of a new role or company—but fortunately with enough financial security for a few months to allow me to contemplate my next steps—I was both relieved and devastated. I fell from feeling on top of the world—genuinely blooming—to the need for a complete work and life renewal in a matter of months.

I have learned during my time as a leader that no one should take anything for granted. Things change. Expect anything. People come. People go. Some leaders are fond of you; others are not. There are dot-com booms and busts. Bull markets. Bear markets. Fiscal cliffs. Pandemics. Inflation. Stagflation. Hiring freezes. Travel freezes. Budget freezes. Trends. Politics. Infighting. Benevolent giving. Malevolent mischief. Awards. Nepotism. Racism. Cliques. Promotions. Creativity. Fun. So many slide decks. Fancy titles. Furloughs. Firings. Good hires. Awful hires. Tears. Lies. Laughs. Love. You name it.

Upon reflection and in hindsight, I recognized that my story—like yours and that of the team members you lead—is littered with highs and lows. I can think of countless instances when I've felt like I've been at the top of a wave and then sucked in by the undertow, nearly drowning. In these moments, reflecting on my declaration of purpose has aided my judgment and actions, though it certainly has not been the silver bullet of ultimate joy or attempts at renewal.

I have lived by a purpose statement for many years. It guides me in the darkest of moments and helps me reach the highest of highs. Like magnetic north on a compass, it pinpoints my journey between work and life, helping me to bloom:

We're not here to see through each other; we're here to see each other through.

When I made the difficult decision to accept the severance package offer and depart SAP, I knew I was leaving behind something very special. But it had to be done. I was blooming again about a year later. Roughly five years after that, I received an email from one of my former team members at SAP. He didn't report to me but was—and still is—one of the nicest people you might ever meet.

T-Bone, as I affectionately call him, wanted me to know that another colleague of ours had written an essay that was posted on the global SAP intranet. The topic was leadership. He pasted the entire column into an email for me to read. I was by myself on a flight, sobbing into an Air Canada napkin when I read it.

Laura Jamieson (L. J.) reported to me for about six years during the Business Objects and SAP years. I still call her L. J. because she reminds me of the words "love" and "joy." The essence of her essay was pretty much that: love and joy.

She started her piece by mentioning my declaration of purpose (L. J. called it a "motto" in her article) that helped bond our global team, and the critical importance of mutual care. Without knowing it, L. J. captured the core of the Work-Life Bloom model years before I put it together in this book. Ultimately, she wrote about what it was like to bloom.

L. J. is now a senior leader and vice-president at SAP. With her permission, I have pasted part of her article below:

> I bet there isn't a single person from that organization who couldn't repeat that motto because we heard it over and over again. More importantly, we lived it every day. Our organization was about a hundred people strong located in sixteen different cities across five continents. This might have presented a lot of virtual working challenges, but it felt like a family.

We had regular meetings with everyone around the world, so even if you were the only person in Virginia, you felt connected. Our manager would share a lot of himself as a person – his happy and unhappy moments. It created a very human organization. One time I had a personal crisis, and I was trying hard to hold it all together. He pulled me aside, asked me what was going on, and sent me home. He was in tune with what was happening in people's lives and very supportive. He didn't just acknowledge people's efforts – he acknowledged them for being people.[1]

The research I conducted for this book made me rethink many things in my work *and* life. It made me evaluate my sense of self and my identity. It forced me to ask questions. For example, have I always felt agency? When, when not, and why? Is my network really my net worth? Have my non-family relationships actually been there for me in times of need? Why have my well-being and respect life-factors experienced such highs and awful lows?

While pondering these questions, I realized that my life lows eventually turned to highs. But I'm not naïve enough to think there will not be more lows ahead in my life. Troughs will come. The storms are inevitable. There will always be pests attacking my tomatoes.

There have been all sorts of scenarios in which I questioned or loved a particular organization's purpose, culture, norms, and strategy. The highs with people like L. J. and T-Bone were truly spectacular. Yet I've been both confident and insecure when it comes to feeling like I belong, I'm valued, and I'm trusted.

I have learned that any work- or life-factor can positively or negatively affect your performance at work *and* your demeanour in life. And your direct leader has a lot of influence over your work-life factors.

Throughout my years of working full-time in an organization, I remained a leader of people, a father of three, a husband of one, and so on. Work and life continued. I could not give up on myself, and in most of these situations, I had to continue leading others. I had to help others while simultaneously running the operations of me: Dan, the human being.

The Work-Life Bloom model is as much about analyzing and fixing yourself as it is about preparing you to lead others more thoughtfully. Of course, the workplace contains some very distinct factors that most probably need to be improved for you and your team to succeed. However, you must also pay attention to several aspects of a person's life—the traits that help define and enact one's identity and character—if you are to make any real headway. It's why the concept of work-life balance is a lie, a zero sum game. It's why the term itself is as useful as a comb for a bald man.

I felt compelled to end the book with a screenshot of the reality of my work and life. A few summary points come to the fore upon my self-reflection:

I have suffered in my career. Yet, I have experienced tremendous pride as well.

I have suffered in my life. Yet, I have experienced great joy as well.

At various stages, I have bloomed, felt stunted, been budding, yet I have also needed renewing.

So have you. So will you. And so have and will the people you lead.

Although his words refer to different circumstances entirely, we might heed the wisdom of Frederick Douglass:

> If there is no struggle, there is no progress. Those who profess to favour freedom, and yet depreciate agitation, are men who want crops without plowing up the ground. They want rain without thunder and lightning. They want the ocean without the awful roar of its many waters. This struggle may be a moral one; or it may be a physical one; or it may be both moral and physical; but it must be a struggle.[2]

When we work, we bring our lives into our jobs every day, and our work creeps into our lives every day as well. There is no escaping the relationship between work and life. The pandemic certainly proved that. There is no hiding from the fact you might be simultaneously feeling great with your life-factors while experiencing misery at work. The reverse is also true. We might be suffering with our life-factors while having to continue working at a high level and enjoying it.

Sometimes both work and life will feel like the doldrums, as if we need a complete overhaul. In another personal example, I once received a text, while recovering from an emergency cholecystectomy, about the shutdown of a work venture that I had founded several years earlier. For a few months, I fell into a mentally, physically, and emotionally draining low point in my work and life. I honestly was not in a good place.

My family felt it. Everyone in the house suffered. After all, *our lives shape our work; nevertheless, our work shapes us.* To this day, it is the darkest period of my career and life. Eventually, I bloomed again.

However, per Douglass, to progress in life and work, there must be a struggle. To bloom, we must endure and learn from the inclement weather events.

If people are lucky, most of the time, work and life will be in lockstep, a wonderful symbiosis that mirrors a garden of blooming flowers. But it takes effort, and you must expect there to be highs and lows. There will always be bad weather ahead. You never know when the pH balance of the soil might suddenly alter.

I urge you to rethink how you as a leader handle the work- and life-factors for yourself and analyze what you are doing to improve these factors for the team members you serve. And from this moment onward, stop using the terms "work-life balance" and "best selves"!

I may be the author of *Work-Life Bloom*, but you, the team members you lead, and I are all simply human beings wandering along the meandering garden path of life *and* work. The various factors may differ, but in the end, we're all just gardeners tending to our garden box, ideally getting some help along the way to grow a few delectable tomatoes.

The psychologist Carl R. Rogers wrote in his 1961 book, *On Becoming a Person: A Therapist's View of Psychotherapy*, "A person is a fluid process, not a fixed and static entity; a flowing river of change, not a block of solid material; a continually changing constellation of potentialities, not a fixed quantity of traits."[3]

You are not fixed, and neither are the team members you lead. To that end, I'd like you to metaphorically consider the following as you contemplate your next steps regarding work, life, and your leadership style:

I am a garden box full of potential.

To bloom, we must come to grips with something fundamental, a complete metanoia. There is work, and there is life. Between the two lies not only challenge but also seeds of hope, of leadership potential.

I do hope you find it in you to help your people to bloom, to *be their best.*

I also sincerely wish for you to bloom and to *be your best.*

Thank you for reading.

Nolite te bastardes carborundorum.

ACKNOWLEDGEMENTS

WORK-LIFE BLOOM IS my fifth book—and was the hardest to write. I felt it was "hard" primarily because I finally conducted global proprietary research resulting in primary quantitative and qualitative data that I had to sift through, analyze, and summarize. For that, I must thank Julia Kirby, a senior editor at Harvard University Press. "Dan," she said to me early in the project, "you should complement your opinion and storytelling with evidence." Her advice made the book writing process harder, but the final product is so much better—a massive tip of the hat to Julia for that sage counsel. I am indebted to you for your blooming advice.

The Global Work-Life Assessment Survey research conducted for the book was complemented by an array of stories, insights, and feedback gathered from people worldwide. Early readers were incredibly helpful in shaping the book. In no particular order, I am indebted to the following remarkable human beings for their direct—and even indirect—generosity and goodness during the development of *Work-Life Bloom*: Arianna Huffington, Alan Mulally, Angie Kim, Laura Gassner Otting, Adrian Fluevog, Stephen Fluevog, Maja Korica, Michael Bungay Stanier, Roger L. Martin, Nicole Forward, Terrence Woodson, Kiran Mohan, Dave McIntyre, Keven Fletcher, Jenn Fletcher, Laura Jamieson, Tomasz Zima, Adam Kreek, Ian Sohn, John Baldoni, Liane Davey, Tom Peters, Cathryn Barnard, Mitch Joel, Jennifer Riel, Marguerite Behringer, Conrad Cone, Bruce Daisley, Robert Waldinger, Des Dearlove, Stuart Crainer, Eric Termuende, Ranjay Gulati,

Alyson Kittler, Brian Scudamore, Nilofer Merchant, Paul Zak, Ron Carucci, Susie Lee, Daniel Kligerman, Amy C. Edmondson, Paul Bleier, Rebecca Kirstein Resch, Marie-Louise Collard, Stephanie Redivo, Jane McConnell, Joanna Denford, Bryan Wish, Rita Giacalone, Chuck Hamilton, Sarah McArthur, Danielle Campbell, Nick Hixson, Rose Kattackal, Brian Reid, Aaron Hurst, Phil Goddard, Josh Blair, Robert Pasin, Mondo Cozmo, Scott Stratten, Heather McGowan, Josh Bersin, Megan Smith, Christine Porath, Vipul Dave, Ruth Gotian, Terry VanQuickenborne, Lynda Gratton, Hilton Barbour, Jocelyn Bérard, Krystal Gabriel, Ehren Lee, Mark Komlenic, Tiffani Bova, John Lyons, Tanveer Naseer, Glain Roberts-McCabe, Vince Molinaro, Terence Mauri, Michael Griffiths, Henry Mintzberg, Dorie Clark, Ravin Jesuthasan, Simon Brown, Lee Chambers, Vlatka Hlupic, Céline Schillinger, Eloise Skinner, Muhammad Lila, Frédéric Séguin, and Ludo Van der Heyden. Shoutout to the Thinkers50 community as well as 100 Coaches. Don Loney was instrumental during the early days of my book sketching. Thank you, Don.

To the thousands of people who contributed to the Global Work-Life Assessment Survey, thank you. I felt like I was conversing with you for many months. May the bloom be with you, always.

To everyone I've worked with—whether as a full-time team member or a hired gun—I appreciate all that you've done to teach me to bloom. (Or, in some cases, the lesson of pain and renewal.)

To all of my guests on *Leadership NOW*, thank you. Your bounteousness is bodacious and beautiful. Thank you for offering a PhD in humanity every single time we get together.

A huge bouquet of thanks to the entire team at Figure 1 Publishing, specifically Chris Labonté, Steve Cameron, Naomi MacDougall, Heidi Waechtler, Mark Redmayne, Michael Leyne, Lesley Cameron, Michelle Young, Teresa Bubela, and Lara Smith. I wholeheartedly appreciate what you do to listen to the seed of an idea only to help nurture it into a blooming book that flourishes. (See what I did there!?!)

You may have noticed that I elected to use Standard Canadian English throughout *Work-Life Bloom*. My *colours* are red and white so I thought it was time to *honour* my heritage. Thanks to the team at Figure 1 for understanding and accommodating. Furthermore, this book is AI-free.

My eldest child, Claire, initially helped me by conducting preliminary secondary research on the concept of agency in the summer of 2021. Her findings and our discussions helped me, in part, to reshape the entire point of the book! *Work-Life Bloom* wouldn't be what it is today without you. Thank you, Claire. Love ya.

My youngest child, Cate, also played a crucial role. Cate's eye for design helped pin down the *Work-Life Bloom* book cover. With Naomi MacDougall of Figure 1 at the helm, my back-and-forth with Naomi to finalize the book cover was aided by Cate's artistic counsellor role to me. Thank you, Cate. Love ya.

My middle child, Cole, is central in my life, and not just because he is my only son. Cole unknowingly gave me the strength to keep writing through the entire *Work-Life Bloom* project. Each day over almost two years, I watched his palpable tenacity, which compelled *me* to dig deep. Thank you, Cole. Love ya.

My infinitely better half, Denise, did not witness my best side over good portions of this book. It's a long story (err, stories!) for another day. From the bottom of my heart, Denise, please know that I appreciated your patience and compassion. Thank you for being my best friend and bloom partner, whatever the weather brings. Love ya. xxx

NOTES

CHAPTER I: GARDEN BOX

1. Christy Ann Martine, *She'll Find the Sky: A Collection of Poems* (Independently Published, 2021).
2. Alain de Botton, *Essays in Love* (McClelland & Stewart, 2008).
3. Arlie Russell Hochschild, *The Managed Heart: Commercialization of Human Feeling* (University of California Press, 1983).
4. Dan Pontefract, "The Issues of Leadership with Dr. Maja Korica," audio podcast episode, *Leadership NOW with Dan Pontefract*, Apple Podcasts, https://podcasts.apple.com/us/podcast/the-issues-of-leadership-with-dr-maja-korica/id1449213490?i=1000553765476
5. Jennifer Williams, *Morning Affirmations: 200 Phrases for an Intentional and Openhearted Start to Your Day* (Adams Media Corporation, 2019).
6. Siva Raja and Sharon L. Stein, "Work-Life Balance: History, Costs, and Budgeting for Balance," *Clinics in Colon and Rectal Surgery*, no. 2 (June 27, 2014): 71–74.
7. "Burn-Out an 'Occupational Phenomenon,'" World Health Organization (2019), accessed September 29, 2022, https://www.who.int/news/item/28-05-2019-burn-out-an-occupational-phenomenon-international-classification-of-diseases
8. Winston Churchill, speaking at United Kingdom House of Commons, "House of Commons Rebuilding," Hansard, HC Deb 28, volume 393, cc403-73, accessed June 26, 2022, https://api.parliament.uk/historic-hansard/commons/1943/oct/28/house-of-commons-rebuilding
9. Arianna Huffington, *Thrive: The Third Metric to Redefining Success and Creating a Life of Well-Being, Wisdom, and Wonder* (Harmony, 2014).
10. Haruki Murakami, *After Dark*, trans. Jay Rubin (Alfred A. Knopf, 2007).

CHAPTER II: BLOOM OR BUST

1. Gianpiero Petriglieri, "Humanizing Leadership: Principles, Practices, and People" (annotated remarks for the Evidence-Based Leadership Development symposium 2022 Academy of Management Annual Meeting, August 8, 2022), accessed August 9, 2022, https://gpetriglieri.com/aom2022/
2. *State of the Global Workforce Report*, Gallup (2022), accessed June 27, 2022, https://www.gallup.com/workplace/349484/state-of-the-global-workplace-2022-report.aspx?thank-you-report-form=1
3. Alex Bryson and George MacKerron, "Are You Happy While You Work?," *Economic Journal* 127, no. 599 (2017): 106–25.
4. George Ward, "Workplace Happiness and Job Search Behavior: Evidence from a Field Experiment," MIT Sloan School of Management Working Paper 6607-22 (2022), 39, https://mitsloan.mit.edu/shared/ods/documents?PublicationDocumentID=8153
5. "Your Guide to Winning @Work: Decoding the Sunday Scaries," LinkedIn Official Blog, accessed July 9, 2022, https://blog.linkedin.com/2018/september/28/your-guide-to-winning-work-decoding-the-sunday-scaries

6. Laura Silver et al., "What Makes Life Meaningful? Views from 17 Advanced Economies," Pew Research Center's Global Attitudes Project, accessed June 27, 2022, https://www.pewresearch.org/global/2021/11/18/what-makes-life-meaningful-views-from-17-advanced-economies/

7. *State of the Manager Report 2022*, Humu (January 31, 2022), accessed July 11, 2022, https://www.humu.com/state-of-the-manager-report-2022

8. Dan Pontefract, "The Joy of Work with Bruce Daisley," audio podcast episode, *Leadership NOW with Dan Pontefract*, Apple Podcasts (February 8, 2022), https://podcasts.apple.com/us/podcast/the-joy-of-work-with-bruce-daisley/id1449213490?i=1000550862845

9. "A Chapter of Definitions," *Daily Crescent* (June 23, 1848), *Chronicling America*, accessed April 24, 2023, https://chroniclingamerica.loc.gov/lccn/sn82015378/1848-06-23/ed-1/seq-2/

10. Thomas G. West, *Plato's Apology of Socrates: An Interpretation, with a New Translation* (Cornell University Press, 1979), 38a.

11. OECD, "Life Satisfaction," OECD Better Life Index, accessed July 10, 2022, https://www.oecdbetterlifeindex.org/topics/life-satisfaction/

12. John F. Helliwell et al., eds., *World Happiness Report 2022* (Sustainable Development Solutions Network, 2022).

13. Julie Ray, "World Unhappier, More Stressed Out Than Ever," Gallup (June 28, 2022), accessed July 10, 2022, https://news.gallup.com/poll/394025/world-unhappier-stressed-ever.aspx

14. "Global Report: 45 Percent of People Have Not Felt True Happiness for More Than Two Years," Oracle (June 15, 2022), accessed July 10, 2022, https://www.oracle.com/news/announcement/oracle-cx-happiness-research-study-2022-06-15/

15. Michael Miller, "Want a Good Life? 3 Lessons from Harvard Grant Study," Six Seconds (April 26, 2021), accessed July 10, 2022, https://www.6seconds.org/2021/04/19/harvard-grant-study/

16. "2nd Generation," *Harvard Second Generation Study* (2022), accessed July 10, 2022, https://www.adultdevelopmentstudy.org/2nd-generation-study

17. Zameena Mejia, "Harvard's Longest Study of Adult Life Reveals How You Can Be Happier and More Successful," CNBC (March 20, 2018), accessed July 10, 2022, https://www.cnbc.com/2018/03/20/this-harvard-study-reveals-how-you-can-be-happier-and-more-successful.html

18. Robert Waldinger, "Marshall Goldsmith 100 Coaches [Coaching Conversation]," MG100, Zoom Meeting, January 30, 2023.

19. Robert Waldinger, "What Makes a Good Life? Lessons from the Longest Study on Happiness," TED Talk, accessed July 9, 2022, https://www.ted.com/talks/robert_waldinger_what_makes_a_good_life_lessons_from_the_longest_study_on_happiness/transcript?language=en

20. Annie Dillard, *The Writing Life* (Harper Perennial, 2013).

21. Forrester Consulting on behalf of Indeed, *Indeed Workplace Happiness Report* (Indeed, 2021).

22. Jackie Wiles, "Employees Increasingly Seek Value and Purpose at Work," Gartner (January 13, 2022), accessed August 9, 2022, https://www.gartner.com/en/articles/employees-seek-personal-value-and-purpose-at-work-be-prepared-to-deliver

23. Paul Davidson, "'I Let Money Get in the Way': Most Recent Job Quitters Have Regrets or Don't Plan to Stay in New Role," *USA Today* (March 30, 2022), accessed July 12, 2022, https://www.usatoday.com/story/money/2022/03/28/great-resignation-regret-workers-quit-jobs-not-content/7163041001/

24. Alex Tanzi, "Millions Regret Quitting Their Jobs during the Great Resignation," *Financial Post* (July 12, 2022), accessed July 13, 2022, https://financialpost.com/fp-work/millions-regret-quitting-great-resignation

25. Tineke Roegiers et al., "How Big or Warm or Old Are the Stars?," ESA-European Space Agency (June 13, 2022), accessed August 16, 2022, from https://www.cosmos.esa.int/web/gaia/dr3-how-big-or-warm-or-old-are-the-stars

26. Ranjay Gulati, "The Great Resignation or the Great Rethink?," *Harvard Business Review* (March 25, 2022), accessed August 8, 2022, https://hbr.org/2022/03/the-great-resignation-or-the-great-rethink

27. Dan Pontefract, "Understanding Deep Purpose with Harvard's Dr. Ranjay Gulati," audio podcast episode, *Leadership NOW with Dan Pontefract*, Apple Podcasts (June 11, 2022), https://podcasts.apple.com/us/podcast/understanding-deep-purpose-with-harvards-dr-ranjay-gulati/id1449213490?i=1000566098899

28. Robert Kavcic and Douglas Porter, *Workers Wanted: Demand, Demographics and Disruption*, BMO (August 5, 2022), accessed August 10, 2022, https://economics.bmo.com/en/publications/detail/da5fa646-e606-4873-902d-992aa7dd87d9/

29. "Q2 2022 United States Job Market Report," Joblist (July 11, 2022), accessed July 21, 2022, https://www.joblist.com/jobs-reports/q2-2022-united-states-job-market-report

30. "Resign, Resigned, or Re-Sign?," UKG (January 2022), accessed August 4, 2022, https://www.ukg.com/resources/article/resign-resigned-or-re-sign

31. r/antiwork, reddit, accessed July 12, 2022, https://www.reddit.com/r/antiwork/

32. "Abolish WFH? Enjoy Mass Resignation," r/antiwork, reddit, accessed July 12, 2022, https://www.reddit.com/r/antiwork/comments/vwwod5/abolish_wfh_enjoy_mass_resignation/

33. *KellyOCG Global Workforce Report 2022—Re:work Calibrating to Power the Life-Work Shift*, KellyOCG (May 10, 2022), accessed July 11, 2022, https://kellyocg.turtl.co/story/rework-report-2022/

34. *State of the Manager Report 2022*, Humu (January 31, 2022), accessed July 11, 2022, https://www.humu.com/state-of-the-manager-report-2022

35. Kathy Woods, "Well-Being and Resilience of Senior Leaders," Deloitte Canada (August 4, 2021), accessed August 3, 2022, https://www2.deloitte.com/content/dam/Deloitte/ca/Documents/consulting/ca-senior-leader-well-being-resilience-report-2021-en-aoda.pdf

36. James Baldwin, "As Much Truth as One Can Bear," *New York Times* Book Review (January 14, 1962), BR1, BR38, column 5, ProQuest.

37. Pico della Mirandola, "The Oration on the Dignity of Man," in eds. Francesco Borghesi, Michael Papio, and Massimo Riva, *Oration on the Dignity of Man: A New Translation and Commentary* (Cambridge: Cambridge University Press, 1486/2016).

38. "Inclusion & Diversity," About Netflix, Netflix, accessed July 22, 2022, https://about.netflix.com/en/inclusion

39. Dominic Patten, "Dave Chappelle's Latest Netflix Special Doesn't Cross 'The Line on Hate,' Ted Sarandos Says Despite Controversy: Staffer Who Criticized Trans Remarks in 'The Closer' Suspended," Deadline (October 30, 2021), accessed July 22, 2022, https://deadline.com/2021/10/dave-chappelle-trans-controversy-netflix-reaction-ted-sarandos-staffer-suspended-the-closer-trans-remarks-1234853974/

40. Matt Donnelly, "Ted Sarandos Doubles Down on Dave Chappelle Defense: 'Content Doesn't Directly Translate to Real-World Harm' (Exclusive)," *Variety* (October 14, 2021), accessed October 24, 2022, https://variety.com/2021/film/news/ted-sarandos-dave-chappelle-defense-1235088647/

41. Matt Donnelly, "'I Screwed Up': Netflix's Ted Sarandos Addresses Dave Chappelle Fallout," *Variety* (October 20, 2021), accessed July 22, 2022, https://variety.com/2021/film/news/dave-chappelle-netflix-ted-sarandos-i-screwed-up-1235093098/

42. Matthew Weaver et al., "Google Walkout: Global Protests after Sexual Misconduct Allegations," *Guardian* (November 1, 2018), accessed July 22, 2022, https://www.theguardian.com/technology/2018/nov/01/google-walkout-global-protests-employees-sexual-harassment-scandals

43. Zoe Schiffer, "Apple Just Fired a Leader of the #AppleToo Movement," The Verge (October 15, 2021), accessed July 22, 2022, https://www.theverge.com/2021/10/15/22727123/apple-fires-leader-apple-too-movement

44. Shannon Liao, "Activision Blizzard Staff Walk Out, Protesting Loss of Abortion Rights," *Washington Post* (July 21, 2022), accessed July 22, 2022, https://www.washingtonpost.com /video-games/2022/07/21/activision-blizzard-roe-walkout/

45. Associated Press, "Disney Workers Walk Out to Protest Company's 'Don't Say Gay' Bill Response," Global News (March 23, 2022), accessed July 22, 2022, https://globalnews.ca /news/8703175/disney-workers-dont-say-gay-walk-out-protest/

46. Edward Segal, "Amazon's Next Crisis-Global Protests and Strikes on Black Friday," *Forbes* (December 10, 2021), accessed July 22, 2022, https://www.forbes.com/sites /edwardsegal/2021/11/25/amazon-prepares-for-next-crisis---a-global-strike-by -workers-on-black-friday/?sh=cbad2b0498a8

47. Jonny Diamond, "Simon & Schuster Workers Are Protesting Their Employer's Publishing Decisions," Literary Hub (April 20, 2021), accessed February 9, 2023, https://lithub.com /simon-schuster-workers-are-protesting-their-employers-publishing-decisions/

48. Dan Pontefract, "Former Ford and Boeing CEO Alan Mulally and the Importance of 'Working Together,'" audio podcast episode, *Leadership NOW with Dan Pontefract*, Apple Podcasts (July 14, 2022), https://podcasts.apple.com/us/podcast/former-ford -and-boeing-ceo-alan-mulally-and/id1449213490?i=1000569569104

CHAPTER III: WORK-FACTORS

1. Russell L. Ackoff, "A Lifetime of Systems Thinking," The Systems Thinker (November 19, 2015), accessed August 15, 2022, https://thesystemsthinker.com/a-lifetime-of-systems-thinking/

2. Scott Davis, "Burberry's Blurred Lines: The Integrated Customer Experience," *Forbes* (July 17, 2014), accessed August 23, 2022, https://www.forbes.com/sites/scottdavis/2014/03/27 /burberrys-blurred-lines-the-integrated-customer-experience/?sh=5d3015103cc6

3. PLOS, "An Engaging Leadership Style May Boost Employee Engagement: Engaging Leaders Also Appear to Enhance Workplace Effectiveness at the Level of Entire Teams," ScienceDaily (June 29, 2022), accessed August 25, 2022, www.sciencedaily.com /releases/2022/06/220629150254.htm

4. "About Us," O2E Brands, accessed August 24, 2022, https://www.o2ebrands.com/about-us

5. Nancy Hass, "Earning Her Stripes," *Wall Street Journal Magazine* (September 9, 2010), O2E Brands, accessed August 24, 2022, http://magazine.wsj.com/features/the-big-interview /earning-her-strips/

6. William Shakespeare, *All's Well That Ends Well* (Penguin, 1970).

7. "Anger over Shocking Covid Bonus Stunt at West Midlands Trains," TSSA (May 10, 2021), accessed August 27, 2022, https://www.tssa.org.uk/news-and-events/tssa-news /anger-over-shocking-covid-bonus-stunt-at-west-midlands-trains

8. Sally Murrer, "Shocking Stunt by Train Bosses Left Workers Angry and Disappointed in Milton Keynes," *Milton Keynes Citizen* (May 10, 2021), accessed August 27, 2022, https://www .miltonkeynes.co.uk/news/people/shocking-stunt-by-train-bosses-left-workers-angry-and -disappointed-in-milton-keynes-3231192

9. "Anger over Shocking Covid Bonus Stunt."

10. Gerald J. Holton and Yehuda Elkana, *Albert Einstein, Historical and Cultural Perspectives: The Centennial Symposium in Jerusalem* (Princeton University Press, 2016).

11. Nilofer Merchant, *The Power of Onlyness: Make Your Wild Ideas Mighty Enough to Dent the World* (Viking, 2017).

12. Paul Zak, "The Neuroscience of Trust," *Harvard Business Review* (January-February 2017), accessed August 28, 2022, https://hbr.org/2017/01/the-neuroscience-of-trust

13. Dan Pontefract, "Ron Carucci-Are We Really Honest at Work?," audio podcast episode, *Leadership NOW with Dan Pontefract*, Apple Podcasts (September 24, 2022), https://podcasts.apple.com/us/podcast/ron-carucci-are-we-really-honest-at

14. Albert Camus, *Notebooks, 1942–1951*, trans. Justin O'Brien (Ivan R Dee, 2010).

15. Aleesha Khaliq, "New Zealand Minister Demoted after Trip to the Beach during Lockdown," CNN (April 7, 2020), accessed September 15, 2022, https://www.cnn.com/2020/04/07 /world/new-zealand-minister-lockdown-intl-scli/index.html

16. Danica Kirka, "One Scandal Too Many: British PM Boris Johnson Resigns," AP NEWS (July 7, 2022), accessed September 15, 2022, https://apnews.com/article /boris-johnson-resignation-60da3c4b29a4e9c93c7db9f53034ad0e

17. Anonymous, "Workplace Loneliness Is a Real Problem. For 45 Hours a Week I Feel Isolated," *Guardian* (February 1, 2016), accessed September 10, 2022, https://www.theguardian.com /commentisfree/2016/feb/01/loneliness-at-work-introvert-sadness-bereft-in-bustling-office

18. Evan W. Carr, Andrew Reece, Gabriella Rosen Kellerman, and Alexi Robichaux, "The Value of Belonging at Work," *Harvard Business Review* (December 21, 2021), accessed February 13, 2023, https://hbr.org/2019/12/the-value-of-belonging-at-work#:~:text=Annotate -,Social%20belonging%20is%20a%20fundamental%20human%20need%2C%20 hardwired%20into%20our,lower%20organizational%20commitment%20and%20 engagement

19. "Loneliness and Its Impact on the American Workplace," *Cigna* (2020), accessed October 10, 2022, https://www.cigna.com/static/www-cigna-com/docs/about-us/newsroom/studies -and-reports/combatting-loneliness/loneliness-and-its-impact-on-the-american-workplace .pdf

20. "Focusing on What Works for Workplace Diversity," McKinsey & Company (November 21, 2019), accessed October 10, 2022, https://www.mckinsey.com/featured-insights /gender-equality/focusing-on-what-works-for-workplace-diversity

21. Aaron De Smet et al., "'Great Attrition' or 'Great Attraction'? The Choice Is Yours," McKinsey & Company (March 28, 2022), accessed October 10, 2022, https://www.mckinsey.com/capabilities/people-and-organizational-performance /our-insights/great-attrition-or-great-attraction-the-choice-is-yours

22. Liz Mineo, "Over Nearly 80 Years, Harvard Study Has Been Showing How to Live a Healthy and Happy Life," *Harvard Gazette* (November 26, 2018), accessed October 10, 2022, https://news.harvard.edu/gazette/story/2017/04/over-nearly-80-years-harvard-study-has -been-showing-how-to-live-a-healthy-and-happy-life/

23. Angela Theisen, "Is a Sense of Belonging Important?," Speaking of Health, Mayo Clinic Health System (August 25, 2022), accessed February 13, 2023, https://www.mayoclinichealthsystem .org/hometown-health/speaking-of-health/is-having-a-sense-of-belonging -important#:~:text=Depression%2C%20anxiety%20and%20suicide%20are,weakens%20 a%20sense%20of%20belonging

24. Susie Lee, "Why Belonging Is Key to Building the New Workforce," *MIT Sloan Management Review* (June 13, 2022), accessed September 10, 2022, https://sloanreview.mit.edu/article /why-belonging-is-key-to-building-the-new-workforce/

25. Colleen Bordeaux, Betsy Grace, and Naina Sabherwal, "Elevating the Workforce Experience: The Belonging Relationship; Why Does Belonging Matter in the Workplace?," Deloitte United States (November 23, 2021), accessed October 10, 2022, https://www2.deloitte.com/us/en/blog /human-capital-blog/2021/what-is-belonging-in-the-workplace.html

26. Daniel Coyle, *The Culture Code: The Secrets of Highly Successful Groups* (Bantam Books, 2018).

27. G. M. Walton et al., "Two Brief Interventions to Mitigate a 'Chilly Climate' Transform Women's Experience, Relationships, and Achievement in Engineering," *Journal of Educational Psychology* 107, no. 2 (2015): 468–85, https://doi.org/10.1037/a0037461

28. Amy Edmondson, "Psychological Safety and Learning Behavior in Work Teams," *Administrative Science Quarterly* 44, no. 2 (1999): 350, https://doi.org/10.2307/2666999

29. Amy Edmondson, "Psychological Safety and Learning Behavior."

30. Amy C. Edmondson, *The Fearless Organization: Creating Psychological Safety in the Workplace for Learning, Innovation, and Growth* (Wiley, 2018).

31. "Michelle Obama's Speech at the Democratic National Convention (Full Text)," *Washington Post* (September 4, 2012), accessed September 12, 2022,

https://www.washingtonpost.com/news/post-politics/wp/2012/09/04/dnc-2012-michelle
-obamas-speech-at-the-democratic-national-convention-full-text/

32. D. Fricke, "Jeff Tweedy: The Strange Birth of Wilco's 'Yankee Hotel Foxtrot,'" *Rolling Stone*
(June 25, 2018), accessed April 8, 2023, https://www.rollingstone.com/music/music-news
/jeff-tweedy-the-strange-birth-of-wilcos-yankee-hotel-foxtrot-244927/

33. Molly Fogarty, "Innovating for a Better World," Nestlé USA (August 2022),
accessed October 10, 2022, https://www.nestleusa.com/stories/fast-company
-best-workplaces-sustainability-innovation

34. Molly Fogarty, "Innovating for a Better World."

35. *Work and Well-Being 2021 Survey Report: The American Workforce Faces Compounding
Pressure—APA's 2021 Work and Well-Being Survey Results*, American Psychological
Association, accessed September 10, 2022, https://www.apa.org/pubs/reports
/work-well-being/compounding-pressure-2021

36. "Stress in America," American Psychological Association, accessed October 1, 2022,
https://www.apa.org/news/press/releases/stress

37. "Performance: Accelerated. A New Benchmark for Initiating Employee Engagement, Retention
and Results," O. C. Tanner, accessed June 29, 2022, https://www.octanner.com/content/dam
/oc-tanner/documents/global-research/White_Paper_Performance_Accelerated.pdf

38. David Sturt et al., *Appreciate: Celebrating People Inspiring Greatness* (O. C. Tanner Institute
Publishing, 2017).

39. *Fair Pay Impact Report*, Payscale (July 21, 2021), accessed October 1, 2022,
https://www.payscale.com/research-and-insights/fair-pay-impact/

40. William Damon, *The Path to Purpose: How Young People Find Their Calling in Life* (Free
Press, 2010).

41. "Hot Chicken Takeover is Restoring Promise," *Columbus CEO* (July 10, 2016), accessed
October 11, 2022, https://www.columbusceo.com/story/business/briefs/2016/07/01
/hot-chicken-takeover-is-restoring/22767172007/

42. Lacey Crisp, "Hot Chicken Takeover Thrives during Pandemic," 10tv.com (April 29, 2022),
accessed October 11, 2022, https://www.10tv.com/article/news/local
/hot-chicken-takeover-pandemic/530-1776a91f-3ae1-4cea-90bd-b8b2e2b057de

43. "Our Story: Nashville Hot Chicken," Hot Chicken Takeover (August 15, 2021), accessed
October 11, 2022, https://hotchickentakeover.com/our-story/

44. Katlin Smith, "How We Created Our Company Culture and Why It's Working," Inc.com
(March 30, 2017), accessed July 11, 2022, https://www.inc.com/katlin-smith/how-we
-created-our-company-culture-and-it-doesnt-include-foosball-tables.html

45. "Mission," Simple Mills, accessed October 11, 2022, https://www.simplemills.com/Learn
/Mission.aspx

46. Nate Dvorak and Bryant Ott, "A Company's Purpose Has to Be a Lot More Than Words," Gallup
(July 28, 2015), accessed September 26, 2022, https://www.gallup.com/workplace/236573
/company-purpose-lot-words.aspx

47. "Putting Purpose into Practice: 2022 Alight International Workforce and Wellbeing Mindset
Study," Alight (September 2022), accessed October 11, 2022, https://www.alight.com
/thought-leadership/alight-international-mindset-study-2022

48. "Employees Increasingly Seek Value and Purpose at Work," Gartner (January 13, 2022),
accessed October 11, 2022, https://www.gartner.com/en/articles
/employees-seek-personal-value-and-purpose-at-work-be-prepared-to-deliver

49. *Making the Case for the Long Term*, FCLTGlobal (2017), accessed October 11, 2022,
https://www.fcltglobal.org/wp-content/uploads/FCLT_Compass_Report_2021_digital.pdf

50. *Walking the Talk: Valuing a Multi-Stakeholder Strategy*, FCLTGlobal (February 8, 2022),
accessed October 11, 2022, https://www.fcltglobal.org/resource/stakeholder-capitalism/

51. Karsten Strauss, "How Volkswagen Rallied Its Employees after Its Emissions Scandal
(At Least for Now)," *Forbes* (July 26, 2017), accessed October 11, 2022,
https://www.forbes.com/sites/karstenstrauss/2017/07/26/how-volkswagen
-rallied-its-employees-after-its-emissions-scandal-at-least-for-now/?sh=6be80351181b

52. Bethany McLean, "How Wells Fargo's Cutthroat Corporate Culture Allegedly Drove Bankers to Fraud," *Vanity Fair* (May 31, 2017), accessed October 11, 2022, https://www.vanityfair.com/news/2017/05/wells-fargo-corporate-culture-fraud

53. "Boeing Charged with 737 Max Fraud Conspiracy and Agrees to Pay over $2.5 Billion," United States Department of Justice (January 7, 2021), accessed October 11, 2022, https://www.justice.gov/opa/pr/boeing-charged-737-max-fraud-conspiracy-and-agrees-pay-over-25-billion#:~:text=Burns%20of%20the%20Justice%20Department%27s,to%20cover%20up%20their%20deception

54. Dan Pontefract, *The Purpose Effect: Building Meaning in Yourself, Your Role, and Your Organization* (Figure 1 Publishing, 2018).

55. Dan Pontefract, "Understanding Deep Purpose with Harvard's Dr. Ranjay Gulati," audio podcast episode, *Leadership NOW with Dan Pontefract*, Apple Podcasts (June 11, 2022), https://podcasts.apple.com/us/podcast/understanding-deep-purpose-with-harvards-dr-ranjay-gulati/id1449213490?i=1000566098899

56. Matt Bishop, "Writing a Declaration of Purpose," BVT (May 9, 2021), accessed September 25, 2022, https://bvtengineering.com/news-resources/writing-declaration-of-purpose

57. "BVT Declaration of Purpose," BVT, accessed September 19, 2022, https://static1.squarespace.com/static/5d118d5d95293c0001945358/t/5fa085540e88b773779a4fde/1604355413141/Declaration+of+Purpose+2020.pdf

58. "A Stronger Canada Delivered," Canada Post, accessed October 3, 2022, https://infopost.ca/blog/a-stronger-canada-delivered/

59. Doug Ettinger, "President's Message," Canada Post, accessed October 3, 2022, https://www.canadapost-postescanada.ca/cpc/en/our-company/transform/presidents-message.page

60. "Ben & Jerry's Values," Ben & Jerry's, accessed February 14, 2023, https://www.benjerry.com/values

61. "Ben & Jerry's Corporate Social Responsibility," Ben & Jerry's, accessed February 14, 2023, https://www.benjerry.com/whats-new/2014/corporate-social-responsibility-history

62. Jeff Fromm, "The Purpose Series: Ben & Jerry's Authentic Purpose," *Forbes* (June 4, 2019), accessed February 14, 2023, https://www.forbes.com/sites/jefffromm/2019/06/04/the-purpose-series-ben-jerrys-authentic-purpose/?sh=1b9868d55bad

63. Bertha Coombs, "CVS Kicks the Habit, Dropping Tobacco Products," CNBC (February 5, 2014), accessed September 3, 2022, https://www.cnbc.com/2014/02/05/ale-of-cigarettes-tobacco-at-its-stores.html

64. Graham MacKenzie, "Pop Withdrawal from a Pharmacy and the New WHO Sugar Recommendations," Stone's Pharmasave (March 5, 2015), accessed July 3, 2022, https://stonespharmasave.com/blog/?p=715

65. *Mahindra & Mahindra Limited Annual Report 2021–2022*, Mahindra & Mahindra (May 28, 2022), accessed April 8, 2023, https://www.mahindra.com/sites/default/files/2023-01/MM-Annual-Report-2021-22.pdf

66. E. O. Wilson, *Consilience: The Unity of Knowledge* (Knopf, 1998), 85.

67. "Immersion." In *Canadian Oxford Dictionary*, second edition, ed. Katherine Barber (Oxford University Press, 2004).

68. "Our Culture Code," Autodesk, accessed June 5, 2023, https://www.autodesk.com/company/culture

69. Dan Pontefract, "Behind the Scenes of Autodesk's Culture Code," *Forbes* (October 25, 2021), accessed February 15, 2023, https://www.forbes.com/sites/danpontefract/2021/10/23/behind-the-scenes-of-autodesks-culture-code/?sh=2edec3524ac5

70. J. G. Hart, "Exploring Tribal Leadership: Understanding and Working with Tribal People," *Journal of Extension* 44, no. 4 (August 1, 2006), retrieved April 8, 2023, from https://tigerprints.clemson.edu/joe/vol44/iss4/5/

71. Dan Pontefract, "World Renown Thinker Roger L. Martin and a New Way to Think," audio podcast episode, *Leadership NOW with Dan Pontefract*, Apple Podcasts (September 8, 2022), https://podcasts.apple.com/us/podcast/world-renown-thinker-roger-l-martin-and-a-new-way-to-think/id1449213490?i=1000578785282

72. Ljubica Cvetkovska, "Shark Attack Statistics: Why, When, and Where They Attack," Petpedia (September 20, 2022), accessed October 9, 2022, https://petpedia.co/shark-attack-statistics/

CHAPTER IV: LIFE-FACTORS

1. Isabelle Allende. See, for example, "Isabel Allende: Quotes; Quotable Quote," Goodreads, accessed June 6, 2023, https://www.goodreads.com/quotes/348638-you-are-the-storyteller-of-your-own-life-and-you

2. Paulo Coelho, *The Alchemist: 25th Anniversary Edition*, trans. A. R. Clarke (HarperOne, 2014), 23-24.

3. Coelho, *The Alchemist*, 132.

4. Dan Pontefract, "Royal Mail Letter Carrier Phil Goddard," audio podcast episode, *Leadership NOW with Dan Pontefract*, Apple Podcasts (March 23, 2022), https://podcasts.apple.com/us/podcast/royal-mail-letter-carrier-phil-goddard/id1449213490?i=1000555042092

5. Brené Brown, *Rising Strong: How the Ability to Reset Transforms the Way We Live, Love, Parent, and Lead* (Random House, 2017).

6. Kathleen Winter, *Annabel* (House of Anansi Press, 2010).

7. Daniel Kahneman and Angus Deaton, "High Income Improves Evaluation of Life but Not Emotional Well-Being," *PNAS* 107, no. 38 (2010): 16489-93.

8. William Harms, "AAAS 2014: Loneliness Is a Major Health Risk for Older Adults," *University of Chicago News* (February 16, 2014), accessed October 21, 2022, https://news.uchicago.edu/story/aaas-2014-loneliness-major-health-risk-older-adults

9. Y. S. Jung, H. S. Jung, and H. H. Yoon, "The Effects of Workplace Loneliness on the Psychological Detachment and Emotional Exhaustion of Hotel Employees," *International Journal of Environmental Research and Public Health* 19, no. 9 (2022): 5228, doi: 10.3390/ijerph19095228

10. M. Mohapatra, P. Madan, and S. Srivastava, "Loneliness at Work: Its Consequences and Role of Moderators," *Global Business Review* 10 (2020): 1-18, doi: 10.1177/0972150919892714

11. Ryan Jenkins and Steven Van Cohen, *Connectable* (McGraw-Hill Education, 2022).

12. Juliet Michaelson, Karen Jeffrey, and Saamah Abdallah, "The Cost of Loneliness to UK Employers," New Economics Foundation (February 20, 2017), accessed October 21, 2022, https://neweconomics.org/2017/02/cost-loneliness-uk-employers

13. "The Business Case for Addressing Loneliness in the Workforce," Cigna (2020), accessed October 22, 2022, https://newsroom.cigna.com/business-case-addressing-loneliness-workforce

14. Donna Lu, "Ill Health Due to Loneliness Costs Australia $2.7bn Each Year, Report Suggests," *Guardian* (November 18, 2021), accessed October 22, 2022, https://www.theguardian.com/society/2021/nov/19/ill-health-due-to-loneliness-costs-australia-27bn-each-year-report-suggests

15. "Government's Work on Tackling Loneliness," GOV.UK, accessed October 21, 2022, https://www.gov.uk/guidance/governments-work-on-tackling-loneliness

16. "The Peer Coaching Platform," Imperative, accessed August 24, 2022, https://www.imperative.com/about

17. Dan Pontefract, "If You Want Purpose, Relationships Are Key—Best-Selling Author Aaron Hurst," audio podcast episode, *Leadership NOW with Dan Pontefract*, Apple Podcasts (October 12, 2022), https://podcasts.apple.com/us/podcast/if-you-want-purpose-relationships-are-key-best-selling/id1449213490?i=1000582445442

18. Scott Stratten, personal communication, October 23, 2022.

19. Jeffrey M. Jones, "U.S. Church Membership Down Sharply in Past Two Decades," Gallup (November 20, 2021), accessed October 23, 2022, https://news.gallup.com/poll/248837/church-membership-down-sharply-past-two-decades.aspx

20. H. Sherwood, "Attendance at Church of England's Sunday Services Falls Again," *Guardian* (November 14, 2018), accessed April 15, 2023, https://www.theguardian.com/world/2018/nov/14/attendance-church-of-england-sunday-services-falls-again

21. Sebastian Buck and Brian Hardwick, "A Sense of Belonging Drives Well-Being—and It's Disappearing," *Fast Company* (August 18, 2021), accessed October 23, 2022, https://www.fastcompany.com/90666944/a-sense-of-belonging-is-what-drives-wellbeing-and-its-disappearing

22. Erin Karter, "As Newspapers Close, Struggling Communities Are Hit Hardest by the Decline in Local Journalism," Northwestern Now (June 29, 2022), accessed October 23, 2022, https://news.northwestern.edu/stories/2022/06/newspapers-close-decline-in-local-journalism/

23. "Local News Map Data Reports," Local News Research Project (October 13, 2022), accessed October 23, 2022, https://localnewsresearchproject.ca/2022/10/13/local-news-map-data-reports/

24. Robert D. Putnam, *Bowling Alone: Revised and Updated; The Collapse and Revival of American Community* (Simon & Schuster, 2020).

25. John Hagel III, John Seely Brown, and Lang Davison, "Leadership Ecosystem," *Leadership Excellence* 27, no. 7 (July 2010): 12–13.

26. Dan Pontefract, "How Mastering Community Moves Us from Surviving to Thriving," *Forbes* (March 9, 2022), accessed October 23, 2022, https://www.forbes.com/sites/danpontefract/2022/03/08/how-mastering-community-moves-us-from-surviving-to-thriving/?sh=35544d07e5da

27. Harvey Schachter, "Mintzberg: Real Leaders Don't Take Bonuses," *Globe and Mail* (September 8, 2011), accessed October 23, 2022, https://www.theglobeandmail.com/report-on-business/careers/careers-leadership/mintzberg-real-leaders-dont-take-bonuses/article556910/

28. Dan Pontefract, "Wall Street Journal Best-Selling Author Dorie Clark Discusses 'The Long Game,'" audio podcast episode, *Leadership NOW with Dan Pontefract*, Apple Podcasts (October 17, 2021), https://podcasts.apple.com/us/podcast/wall-street-journal-best-selling-author-dorie-clark/id1449213490?i=1000548048318. clark/id1449213490?i=1000548048318

29. Heather E. McGowan and Chris Shipley, *The Empathy Advantage: Leading the Empowered Workforce* (Wiley, 2023).

30. Dan Pontefract, "Author Ravin Jesuthasan: Are We Entering the Era of Work without Jobs?," audio podcast episode, *Leadership NOW with Dan Pontefract*, Apple Podcasts (October 2, 2022), https://podcasts.apple.com/us/podcast/author-ravin-jesuthasan-are-we-entering-the-era-of/id1449213490?i=1000581317092

31. Simon Brown, personal communication, December 2022.

32. Dan Pontefract, "The Shift to a Skills-Based Organization with Deloitte's Michael Griffiths," audio podcast episode, audio podcast episode, *Leadership NOW with Dan Pontefract*, Apple Podcasts (October 7, 2022), https://podcasts.apple.com/us/podcast/the-shift-to-a-skills-based-organization/id1449213490?i=1000581955845

33. Sue Cantrell et al., "The Skills-Based Organization: A New Operating Model for Work and the Workforce," Deloitte Insights (September 22, 2022), accessed October 12, 2022, https://www2.deloitte.com/us/en/insights/topics/talent/organizational-skill-based-hiring.html/#endnote-5

34. E. E. Ghiselli, "Some Perspectives for Industrial Psychology," *American Psychologist* 29, no. 2 (1974): 80–87, https://doi.org/10.1037/h0036077

35. Roger L. Martin, *The Opposable Mind: Winning through Integrative Thinking* (Harvard Business School Press, 2007).

36. Cantrell et al., "The Skills-Based Organization."
37. Reid Hoffman, Ben Casnocha, and Chris Yeh, "Tours of Duty: The New Employer-Employee Compact," *Harvard Business Review* (June 13, 2013), accessed March 7, 2023, https://hbr.org/2013/06/tours-of-duty-the-new-employer-employee-compact
38. Aman Kidwai, "Inside Unilever's Program That Allows Employees to Try Out New Jobs and Gig Working Opportunities at the Company," *Business Insider* (May 5, 2021), accessed September 29, 2022, https://www.businessinsider.in/careers/news/inside-unilevers-program-that-allows-employees-to-try-out-new-jobs-and-gig-working-opportunities-at-the-company/articleshow/82418411.cms
39. *State of the Global Workplace Report 2022*, Gallup (September 23, 2022), accessed September 29, 2022, https://www.gallup.com/workplace/349484/state-of-the-global-workplace-2022-report.aspx
40. Kelly Greenwood and Julia Anas, "It's a New Era for Mental Health at Work," *Harvard Business Review* (November 15, 2021), accessed August 31, 2022, https://hbr.org/2021/10/its-a-new-era-for-mental-health-at-work
41. Steve Hatfield, Jen Fisher, and Paul H. Silverglate, "The C-Suite's Role in Well-Being," Deloitte Insights (June 22, 2022), accessed July 31, 2022, https://www2.deloitte.com/us/en/insights/topics/leadership/employee-wellness-in-the-corporate-workplace.html
42. Dan Pontefract, "Arianna Huffington Is the Empathy Leader You Ought to Be," audio podcast episode, *Leadership NOW with Dan Pontefract*, Apple Podcasts (June 24, 2022), https://podcasts.apple.com/us/podcast/arianna-huffington-is-the-empathy-leader-you-ought-to-be/id1449213490?i=1000567597806
43. *Workplace Mental Health & Well-Being,* Current Priorities of the U.S. Surgeon General (October 2022), accessed November 1, 2022, https://www.hhs.gov/surgeongeneral/priorities/workplace-well-being/index.html
44. Dan Pontefract, "Well-Being Psychologist Lee Chambers and the State of Our Organizations," audio podcast episode, *Leadership NOW with Dan Pontefract*, Apple Podcasts (March 2022), https://podcasts.apple.com/us/podcast/well-being-psychologist-lee-chambers-and-the-state/id1449213490?i=1000554883842
45. "World Mental Health Day 2021," IPSOS (October 8, 2021), accessed October 2, 2022, https://www.ipsos.com/en-ca/news-polls/world-mental-health-day-2022
46. GCHworkplaces, "Enhancing Physical and Psychosocial Wellbeing in the New Working World Webinar with GCHW, GSK & HSBC," video, YouTube (May 3, 2021), accessed October 2, 2022, https://www.youtube.com/watch?v=cIfy5SEeLH8
47. "GSK Reviews," Glassdoor, accessed December 3, 2022, https://www.glassdoor.com/Reviews/GSK-Reviews-E3477.htm
48. GCHworkplaces, "Enhancing Physical and Psychosocial Wellbeing."
49. G. Nimalan, "HSBC—Delivering Employee Wellbeing on a Global Scale," Shine Workplace Wellbeing (November 20, 2021), accessed September 2, 2022, https://www.shineworkplacewellbeing.com/hsbc-delivering-employee-wellbeing-on-a-global-scale/
50. GCHworkplaces, "Making Health & Wellbeing a Global Priority Webinar Hosted by GCHW and Optum," video, YouTube (October 13, 2022), accessed November 2, 2022, https://www.youtube.com/watch?v=b00PKj0EBzM&t=644s
51. GCHworkplaces, "Making Health & Wellbeing a Global Priority."
52. GCHworkplaces, "Making Health & Wellbeing a Global Priority."
53. Dan Pontefract, *Lead. Care. Win.: How to Become a Leader Who Matters* (Figure 1 Publishing, 2020).
54. Dan Pontefract, "From Law To Purpose—Why Eloise Skinner Shifted Her Career Entirely and What She Has Learned," audio podcast episode, *Leadership NOW with Dan Pontefract*, Apple Podcasts (June 3, 2022), https://podcasts.apple.com/us/podcast/from-law-to-purpose-why-eloise-skinner-shifted-her/id1449213490?i=1000565155617
55. Gary T. Reker, Edward J. Peacock, and Paul T. P. Wong, "Meaning and Purpose in Life and Well-Being: A Life-Span Perspective," *Journal of Gerontology* 42, no. 1 (January 1987): 44–49, https://doi.org/10.1093/geronj/42.1.44

56. Blake A. Allan, Ryan D. Duffy, and Richard Douglass, "Meaning in Life and Work: A Developmental Perspective," *Journal of Positive Psychology* 10, no. 4 (2015): 323–31, https://doi.org/10.1080/17439760.2014.950180

57. Dave Roos, "Viktor Frankl's 'Search for Meaning' in 5 Enduring Quotes," HowStuffWorks (April 28, 2022), accessed November 8, 2022, https://history.howstuffworks.com/historical-figures/viktor-frankl.htm

58. Victor E. Frankl, *Man's Search for Meaning* (Beacon Press, 2006).

59. "Sense of Meaning and Purpose in Canada, October to December 2021," Government of Canada (March 30, 2022), accessed October 8, 2022, https://www150.statcan.gc.ca/n1/daily-quotidien/220330/dq220330b-eng.htm

60. Dan Pontefract, "Muhammad Lila, Founder and CEO of Goodable," audio podcast episode, *Leadership NOW with Dan Pontefract*, Apple Podcasts (November 6, 2021), https://podcasts.apple.com/us/podcast/muhammad-lila-founder-and-ceo-of-goodable/id1449213490?i=1000548841733

61. "Goodable Announces Expansion into Classrooms; Educational Resources to Be Made Available to Teachers–For Free," Goodable (October 2022), accessed November 1, 2022, https://goodable.co/news/

62. Carl Icahn, "Letter to Chairman and CEO Kroger," CarlIcahn.com (March 29, 2022), accessed November 2, 2022, https://carlicahn.com/letter-to-chairman-and-ceo-kroger/

63. D. Fleming et al., "Hungry at the Table—White Paper on Grocery Workers at the Kroger Company," Economic Roundtable (January 11, 2022), accessed November 11, 2022, https://economicrt.org/publication/hungry-at-the-table/

64. Peter Drucker, *Management: Tasks, Responsibilities, Practises* (Harper Business, 1985).

65. Victor Lipman, "The Best Sentence I Ever Read about Managing Talent," *Forbes* (September 27, 2018), accessed November 12, 2022, https://www.forbes.com/sites/victorlipman/2018/09/25/the-best-sentence-i-ever-read-about-managing-talent/?sh=1c5b95cdcdfb

66. Epicurus, *Letters, Principal Doctrines, and Vatican Sayings*, trans. R. M. Geer (Macmillan, 1985).

67. Eldar Yusupov, "How My Cerebral Palsy Helped IKEA Democratise Design," LBBonline (August 2, 2019), accessed November 12, 2022, https://www.lbbonline.com/news/how-my-cerebral-palsy-helped-ikea-democratise-design

68. "The IKEA Vision, Values and Business Idea," IKEA, accessed November 12, 2022, https://www.ikea.com/gb/en/this-is-ikea/about-us/the-ikea-vision-and-values-pub9aa779d0#:~:text=%E2%80%9CTo%20create%20a%20better%20everyday,more%20sustainable%20life%20at%20home

69. "About the Project," IKEA ThisAbles (May 22, 2022), accessed November 12, 2022, https://thisables.com/en/how-did-it-all-begin/

70. Naomi Osaka, tweet (May 31, 2021, 10:48 AM), Twitter, accessed October 19, 2022, https://twitter.com/naomiosaka/status/1399422304854188037/photo/2

71. "Our Purpose Is at the Heart of Everything We Do," Givaudan (2021), accessed November 19, 2022, https://www.givaudan.com/our-company/about-givaudan/our-purpose

72. Frédéric Séguin, personal communication, October 2021.

73. Albert Bandura, "Toward a Psychology of Human Agency," *Perspectives on Psychological Science* 1, no. 2 (2006): 164–80, https://doi.org/10.1111/j.1745-6916.2006.00011.x

74. Albert Bandura, "Toward a Psychology of Human Agency."

75. Albert Bandura, "Toward a Psychology of Human Agency."

76. Ian Woodward, Elizabeth More, and Ludo van der Heyden, "'Involve': The Foundation for Fair Process Leadership Communication," INSEAD Working Paper No. 2016/17/OBH/TOM/EFE (February 2016), accessed November 3, 2022, https://ssrn.com/abstract=2747990 or http://dx.doi.org/10.2139/ssrn.2747990

77. Martin Luther King Jr., "What Is Your Life's Blueprint?," *Seattle Times* (January 15, 2017), accessed November 20, 2022, https://projects.seattletimes.com/mlk/words-blueprint.html

78. Martin Luther King Jr., "What Is Your Life's Blueprint?"

79. Christine Porath, "Half of Employees Don't Feel Respected by Their Bosses," *Harvard Business Review* (November 19, 2014), accessed November 1, 2022, https://hbr.org/2014/11/half-of-employees-dont-feel-respected-by-their-bosses

80. Dan Pontefract, "Mastering Community with Christine Porath," audio podcast episode, *Leadership NOW with Dan Pontefract*, Apple Podcasts (March 8, 2022), https://podcasts.apple.com/us/podcast/mastering-community-with-christine-porath/id1449213490?i=1000553243622

81. Henry Mintzberg, *Simply Managing: What Managers Do and Can Do Better* (Berrett-Koehler Publishers, 2013).

CHAPTER V: IN BLOOM

1. Alexander den Heijer, "Quotes," accessed April 16, 2023, https://www.alexanderdenheijer.com/quotes

2. "Sharina," personal communication, October 2022.

3. Dan Pontefract, "Management Guru Tom Peters and Extreme Humanism," audio podcast episode, *Leadership NOW with Dan Pontefract*, Apple Podcasts (December 11, 2022), https://podcasts.apple.com/us/podcast/management-guru-tom-peters-and-extreme-humanism/id1449213490?i=1000590507947

4. Edith Wharton, "Vesalius in Zante (1564)," *North American Review* 175, no. 552 (1902): 625-31, http://www.jstor.org/stable/25119328

CODA

1. SAP Global Intranet (September 2013).

2. Frederick Douglass, *Frederick Douglass: Selected Speeches and Writings*, eds. Philip S. Foner and Yuval Taylor (Lawrence Hill Books, 2000).

3. Carl Rogers, *On Becoming a Person: A Therapist's View of Psychotherapy* (Houghton Mifflin, 1961).

OTHER BLOOMING BOOKS

A s YOU THINK about applying the concepts from *Work-Life Bloom*, here is a short list of additional books curated by me and broken down by work- and life-factors, should you wish to expand your thinking further:

WORK-FACTOR: TRUST

Benkler, Yochai. *The Penguin and the Leviathan: The Triumph of Cooperation Over Self-Interest*. Random House Digital, 2011.

Edmondson, Amy C. *The Fearless Organization: Creating Psychological Safety in the Workplace for Learning, Innovation, and Growth*. John Wiley & Sons, 2018.

Stickel, Darryl. *Building Trust: Exceptional Leadership in an Uncertain World*. Simon & Schuster, 2022.

Zak, Paul. *Trust Factor: The Science of Creating High-Performance Companies*. AMACOM, 2017.

WORK-FACTOR: BELONGING

Brown, Jennifer. *How to Be an Inclusive Leader: Your Role in Creating Cultures of Belonging Where Everyone Can Thrive*. Berrett-Koehler Publishers, 2019.

Liswood, Laura A. *The Loudest Duck: Moving beyond Diversity While Embracing Differences to Achieve Success at Work*. John Wiley & Sons, 2009.

Meyer, Erin. *The Culture Map: Breaking through the Invisible Boundaries of Global Business*. PublicAffairs, 2014.

Rutherford, Adam. *How to Argue with a Racist: What Our Genes Do (and Don't) Say about Human Difference*. The Experiment, 2021.

WORK-FACTOR: VALUED

Chapman, Gary, and Paul E. White. *The 5 Languages of Appreciation in the Workplace: Empowering Organizations by Encouraging People.* Moody Publishers, 2011.

Gostick, Adrian, and Chester Elton. *The Carrot Principle: How the Best Managers Use Recognition to Engage Their People, Retain Talent, and Accelerate Performance* [Updated & Revised]. Simon & Schuster, 2009.

Pirsig, Robert M. *Zen and the Art of Motorcycle Maintenance: An Inquiry into Values.* Turtleback Books, 1978.

Sturt, David, Todd Nordstrom, Kevin Ames, and Gary Beckstrand. *Appreciate: Celebrating People.* Inspiring Greatness, 2017.

WORK-FACTOR: PURPOSE

Gulati, Ranjay. *Deep Purpose: The Heart and Soul of High-Performance Companies.* HarperCollins, 2022.

Hurst, Aaron. *The Purpose Economy: How Your Desire for Impact, Personal Growth and Community Is Changing the World.* Elevate Publishing, 2014.

Izzo, John, and Jeff Vanderwielen. *The Purpose Revolution: How Leaders Create Engagement and Competitive Advantage in an Age of Social Good.* Berrett-Koehler Publishers, 2018.

Mackey, John, and Raj Sisodia. *Conscious Capitalism, with a New Preface by the Authors: Liberating the Heroic Spirit of Business.* Harvard Business Review Press, 2014.

WORK-FACTOR: STRATEGY

Kim, W. Chan, and Renée Mauborgne. *Blue Ocean Strategy, Expanded Edition: How to Create Uncontested Market Space and Make the Competition Irrelevant.* Harvard Business Review Press, 2015.

Lafley, A. G., and Roger L. Martin. *Playing to Win: How Strategy Really Works.* Harvard Business Review Press, 2013.

McGrath, Rita. *Seeing around Corners: How to Spot Inflection Points in Business before They Happen.* Houghton Mifflin, 2019.

Osterwalder, Alexander, Yves Pigneur, Alan Smith, and Frederic Etiemble. *The Invincible Company: How to Constantly Reinvent Your Organization with Inspiration from the World's Best Business Models.* John Wiley & Sons, 2020.

WORK-FACTOR: NORMS

Coyle, Daniel. *The Culture Code: The Secrets of Highly Successful Groups.* Bantam, 2018.

Hamel, Gary, and Michele Zanini. *Humanocracy: Creating Organizations as Amazing as the People Inside Them*. Harvard Business Review Press, 2020.

McCord, Patty. *Powerful: Building a Culture of Freedom and Responsibility*. Silicon Guild, 2018.

McHale, Siobhan. *The Insider's Guide to Culture Change: Creating a Workplace That Delivers, Grows, and Adapts*. Thomas Nelson, 2020.

LIFE-FACTOR: RELATIONSHIPS

Grant, Adam. *Give and Take: Why Helping Others Drives Our Success*. Penguin, 2014.

Parker, Priya. *The Art of Gathering: Create Transformative Meetings, Events and Experiences*. Penguin UK, 2018.

Waldinger, Robert, and Marc Schulz. *The Good Life: Lessons from the World's Longest Scientific Study of Happiness*. Simon and Schuster, 2023.

Wickre, Karen. *Taking the Work out of Networking: An Introvert's Guide to Making Connections That Count*. Simon and Schuster, 2018.

LIFE-FACTOR: SKILLS

Bersin, Josh. *Irresistible: The Seven Secrets of the World's Most Enduring, Employee-Focused Organizations*. Ideapress Publishing, 2022.

Dweck, Carol S. *Mindset: The New Psychology of Success*. Ballantine Books, 2007.

Ellis, Sarah. *The Squiggly Line Career: How Changing Professions Can Advance a Career in Unexpected Ways*. Penguin Life, 2020.

Epstein, David. *Range: How Generalists Triumph in a Specialized World*. Pan Macmillan, 2019.

LIFE-FACTOR: WELL-BEING

Allen, Jennie. *Get Out of Your Head: Stopping the Spiral of Toxic Thoughts*. WaterBrook, 2020.

Birsel, Ayse. *Design the Long Life You Love: A Step-by-Step Guide to Love, Purpose, Well-Being, and Friendship*. Hachette UK, 2022.

David, Susan. *Emotional Agility: Get Unstuck, Embrace Change and Thrive in Work and Life*. Penguin UK, 2016.

Huffington, Arianna. *Thrive: The Third Metric to Redefining Success and Creating a Happier Life*. Random House, 2014.

LIFE-FACTOR: MEANING

Frankl, Viktor E. *Man's Search for Meaning: An Introduction to Logotherapy*. Beacon Press, 1992.

Kalanithi, Paul. *When Breath Becomes Air*. Random House, 2016.

Pausch, Randy. *The Last Lecture*. Hachette Books, 2008.

Pink, Daniel H. *The Power of Regret: How Looking Backward Moves Us Forward*. Penguin, 2022.

LIFE-FACTOR: AGENCY

Clark, Dorie. *The Long Game: How to Be a Long-Term Thinker in a Short-Term World*. Harvard Business Review Press, 2021.

Coelho, Paulo. *The Alchemist: 25th Anniversary Edition*. HarperOne, 2014.

Merchant, Nilofer. *The Power of Onlyness: Make Your Wild Ideas Mighty Enough to Dent the World*. Penguin, 2017.

Stanier, Michael Bungay. *The Coaching Habit: Say Less, Ask More & Change the Way You Lead Forever*. Box of Crayons Press, 2016.

LIFE-FACTOR: RESPECT

Angelou, Maya. *Letter to My Daughter*. Random House, 2008.

Porath, Christine. *Mastering Civility: A Manifesto for the Workplace*. Hachette UK, 2016.

Schein, Edgar H. *Helping: How to Offer, Give, and Receive Help*. Berrett-Koehler Publishers, 2011.

Schillinger, Céline. *Dare to Un-Lead: The Art of Relational Leadership in a Fragmented World*. Figure 1 Publishing, 2022.

INDEX

emperor penguins, 61–62
employees: activism, 44–45; benefits,
96; engagement, 14, 25, 88, 129,
163, 211–12, 235–36; financial
compensation, 90, 94–98; wellness
program, 96–97; work-life
reflections spurred by COVID-19
pandemic, 17–18, 31–35, 100
Enron, 108
Enso Group, 152
Environmental, Social, and Governance
(ESG), 105
Epicurus, 204
Ettinger, Doug, 107–8
external events, 157, 159
external (outside) networking, 156–57
extra effort nod, 90, 92–94

Fairmont, 94
Fair Process, 129, 215
FCLTGlobal, 100–101
feedback, 84, 120, 215–16
financial compensation, 90, 94–98
flexible mind, 188–91
Flexible Work Styles, 129
Fluevog, Adrian, 11–13
Fogarty, Molly, 87
forthright, 184–87
Forward, Nicole, 23–25, 28
Foulkes, Helena, 109
France, 29, 103, 196, 197
Frankl, Viktor E., 195
Free Agents program (Canada), 171
French Open, 209–10
fundamental attribution errors, 88–89

Gallup, 14, 25, 29, 31, 100, 178
garden box metaphor, 6
Gartner, 100
Gen Alpha, 76
gender: meaning and, 195–96, 197;
persona assessments by, 42, 42;
relationships and, 150; respect and,
219–20; well-being and, 182, 183;
working moms, 189–91
Gen X: on belonging, 75, 75; on meaning,
197; on relationships, 150; on respect,
220; on strategy, 114, 115, 115; on
trust, 65; on well-being, 182, 182,
183
Gen Y. See Millennials
Gen Z: on belonging, 75, 75–76; on
meaning, 196, 197; on relationships,

150; on respect, 220; on strategy, 114,
115, 115; on trust, 65; on well-being,
182, 183; workplace needs, 18
Germany, 103, 196, 197
Ghiselli, Edwin E., 169
ghosting, 223–24
Giacalone, Rita, 122–23
gift cards, 94
gig economy, internal, 170
Givaudan, 211–12
Global Work-Life Assessment Survey:
about, 18–19; on advocacy, 70; on
agency, 203, 206–9, 207, 208, 209;
on belonging, 47–48, 70, 75, 75–77,
76, 77, 77–78; on extra effort nod, 93;
on financial compensation, 95; on
flexible mind, 189, 190; on gratitude
attitude, 91; on meaning, 192, 195–
97, 197; on norms, 122, 125–28, 126,
127, 128; on online networking, 158;
persona self-assessments, 40–42, 41,
42; on portfolio investing approach
to skills, 175; on psychological safety,
45–46, 83; on purpose, 98, 102–4,
103; on reflecting on results, 214; on
relationships, 145–46, 150, 150–52,
151; on respect, 217, 219–21, 220;
on skills, 160, 161, 165–68, 166; on
strategy, 111, 113–14, 114, 114–16,
115, 116; on team member resource
groups (TMRGs), 155; on trust, 59,
63, 63–65, 64; on valued, 84, 88–90,
89; on well-being, 177, 179–80, 181,
181–83, 182, 183; on work-factors,
135; on work-life plight, 21, 36–37.
See also Work-Life Bloom
Goddard, Phil, 141–42, 143
Goodable, 198–99, 200
Google, 45
Grant and Glueck study (Harvard Study
on Adult Development), 29–30, 152
"The Grasshopper and the Ants" (Aesop),
112, 113
gratitude attitude, 90, 91–92
Great Resignation, 31–35
Griffiths, Michael, 164–65
GSK (formerly GlaxoSmithKline), 185
Gulati, Ranjay, 33, 105; Deep Purpose,
105

Hagel, John, III, 153
happiness, 25–28, 30–31, 72
The Harris Poll, 31

flexible mind and, 188–91; and forthrightness and openness, 184–87; Global Work-Life Assessment on, 177, 179–80, *181*, 181–83, *182*, *183*; self-reflection for supporting, 230; soil test questions for, 241

Wells Fargo, 101

West Midlands Trains, 60–61

Wilco, 86–87

Wilkie, Sharon, 185

Williams, Brian, 67

Wilson, E. O., 112–13

Wilson, Joseph, 155

Winnebago Tribe, 124–25

Winter, Kathleen, 145

wolves, 72–73

women. *See* gender

Wong, Melissa, 46, 47

Wong, Paul, 193

Woodson, Terrence, 23, 24–25, 28

work-factors: about, 13, 53–55, 56–58; belonging, 57, 71–84, 135, 240; dashboard for, 136, *136*; norms, 57, 121–34, 136, 240; pillars underpinning employees and, 55–56, 135; purpose, 57, 98–111, 135, 240; self-reflection questions for supporting, 135–36; soil test questions for, 240; strategy, 57, 111–21, 136, 240; supporting others in, 134; trust, 57, 59–71, 135, 240; valued, 57, 84–98, 135, 240; water test questions for, 244. *See also* life-factors; *individual factors*

"working together" model, 49–51

work-life balance, 4–5, 8–9, 27, 137, 218, 234, 252, 253

Work-Life Bloom: about, 7–8, 16–17, 20–21, 38–40, *39*, 251–52, 253–54; author's experience, 247–51, 252–53; author's research, 18–19, 32–33; vs. best self, 9–10, 253; falling out of bloom, 234–37; Global Work-Life Assessment on, 19, *19*, 40–42, *41*, *42*; helping others be their best, 9–11, 13–16, 19–20, 43, 218, 237–38; kind of blooming at work, 25–28; kind of blooming in life, 28–30; Mulally's "working together" model and, 49–51; personas, *39*; reflections by leaders, 35–37; reflections spurred by COVID-19 pandemic, 17–18, 31–35, 100; regaining bloom, 233–34;

relationship between work and life, 5–6, 10, 23; self-assessment, 40; soil tests and, 238–43; water tests and, 243–45; vs. work-life balance, 8–9, 218, 234, 252, 253. *See also* Global Work-Life Assessment Survey; life-factors; personas; work-factors

work-life factors, 6–7, 13–14. *See also* life-factors; work-factors

World Health Organization, 9

worth, self-, 217. *See also* respect

wrong, being, 84

Xerox, 155

Yammer, 159

Yusupov, Eldar, 204–5

Zak, Paul, 65–66

Zipline, 46–47

MIGHT YOU REVIEW THE BOOK?

NOW THAT YOU'VE finished reading *Work-Life Bloom*, would you mind publishing a short online review? Rating the book would also be very helpful. Book reviews and ratings go a very long way to helping authors gain new readers.

The most popular method is to leave a review and rating on Amazon.com. Of course, there are other book review sites, including but not limited to Goodreads. However, Amazon is by far the most prevalent. Scanning the QR code above with your phone or tablet will take you directly to Amazon, where you can craft your magic sentence or two and leave a (hopefully) five-star rating! Thank you so much in advance.

DAN
PONTEFRACT

HIRE DAN PONTEFRACT

L ET'S BE HONEST. Hiring an outsider is a leap of faith. So when you bring Dan Pontefract to the table, rest assured that the leap will not be the least bit frightening. In fact, it will be downright exhilarating.

With more than 25 years of experience conducting strategic planning sessions, organizational assessments, leadership modelling, and various consulting assignments, Dan knows precisely how to help you achieve your desired outcomes.

Are you seeking an engaging keynote or a facilitated workshop for your team members and stakeholders? Maybe based on *Work-Life Bloom*? Dan works with you directly to sculpt and curate a session (or sessions) that ensures attendees leave with positive behavioural changes applicable to their roles and situations.

Whether through a retainer contract, consultative projects, assessments, strategic planning, facilitated workshops, or keynotes and talks, rest assured that he can tailor an offering specific to your needs and goals.

Visit www.danpontefract.com or send an introductory email to speak@danpontefract.com.

OTHER BOOKS BY DAN PONTEFRACT

Lead. Care. Win.
How to Become a Leader Who Matters

Lead. Care. Win. is the product of relentless focus, observations, and research that have led Dan Pontefract to define nine insightful yet super-practical leadership lessons. His thinking will help you become a more caring and engaging leader, one who will fully (and completely) understand the critical importance of crafting meaningful, respectful relationships among all your stakeholders.

Every human interaction is crucial. Every exchange can be mutually beneficial.

These nine leadership lessons centre on your willingness to improve how you treat people, a call for meaningful change:

- Be relatable and empathetic.
- Act not out of ego but out of purpose.
- Share knowledge to build a wise organization.
- Stay present and attentive to the needs of others.
- Embrace change and the opportunity for growth it offers.
- Stay curious and adopt lifelong learning.
- Think and act with clarity.
- Commit to balance and inclusivity in all your dealings.
- Act with humility and thoughtfulness.

The bottom line is that when you care enough to champion others, the workplace becomes more engaged and the organization benefits in more ways than one.

It's time to care. Full potential is possible.

Winner of the 2022 Nautilus Book Awards Silver Medal in Leadership/Management

Open to Think
Slow Down, Think Creatively, and Make Better Decisions

While it may not occur to us on a daily basis, there is a widespread cultural tendency toward quick decisions and quick action. This pattern has resulted in many of our society's greatest successes but even more of its failures. Though the root cause is by no means malicious, we have begun to reward speed over quality, and the adverse effects suffered in both our personal and professional lives are potentially catastrophic.

Best-selling author Dan Pontefract offers the solution to this predicament with what he coins "Open Thinking," a cyclical process in which creativity is encouraged, critiquing leads to better decisions, and thoughtful action delivers positive, sustainable results. He proposes a return to balance between the three components of productive thought: dreaming, deciding, and doing.

Based on organizational and societal data, academic research, historical studies, and a wide range of interviews, *Open to Think* is an appeal for a world of better thinking. Pontefract introduces tangible, actionable strategies to improve the way we think as organizations and individuals.

Winner of the 2019 getAbstract International Book of the Year and the 2019 Axiom Business Book Award Silver Medal in the Leadership Category

The Purpose Effect
Building Meaning in Yourself, Your Role, and Your Organization

Best-selling author Dan Pontefract combines years of experience and research on employee engagement, behaviour, and culture to create a work about the three crucial areas of purpose: personal, organizational, and workplace role. If all three can come to fruition—if there is a positive interconnection between the three distinct definitions of "purpose"—the benefits should be felt by employees, teams, the organization, customers, and perhaps most importantly, society as a whole. We can refer to this balanced state as the "sweet spot." When one area is lacking or ignored, the results include disengagement, apathy, lack of growth, and even bankruptcy.

The Purpose Effect is aimed at leaders and employees who wish to achieve a purpose mindset on a personal level for the organization where they are employed and in their role at work.

A business leader who is committed to purpose will create purpose for the organization. A team member who feels their personal sense of purpose is being fulfilled at work will be an invaluable asset to productivity and success. An organization centred on purpose will benefit every stakeholder, from employees to society in general. This "sweet spot" of purpose creates a reciprocal relationship between all three areas and sits at the centre of Pontefract's work.

Flat Army
Creating a Connected and Engaged Organization

Your people are your most valuable asset. If you want them to excel (and your profits to soar), you must abandon your traditional command-and-control management style and adopt a collaborative, open leadership approach that engages and empowers your people.

While this isn't a particularly new idea, many leaders, while they may pay lip service to it, don't really understand what it means. And most of those who do get it lack the skills to put it into practice.

In *Flat Army*, you'll find powerful leadership models and tools that will help you challenge yourself and overcome your personal obstacles to change while pushing the boundaries of organizational change to create a culture of collaboration.

- Develops an integrated framework incorporating collaboration, open leadership, technologies, and connected learning.

- Shows you how to flatten the organizational pyramid and engage with your people more collaboratively and productively—without undermining your authority.

- Explains how to deploy a Connected Leader Mindset, a Participative Leader Framework, and a Collaborative Leader Action Model.

- Arms you with powerful tools for becoming a more visible leader who demonstrates the qualities and capabilities needed to become an agent of positive change.

ABOUT THE AUTHOR

DAN PONTEFRACT is a renowned leadership strategist, culture change expert, author, and keynote speaker with over two decades of experience in senior executive roles at companies such as SAP, TELUS, and Business Objects. Since then, he has worked with organizations worldwide, including Salesforce, Amgen, the State of Tennessee, Nestlé, Canada Post, Autodesk, BMO, Government of Canada, Manulife, Nutrien, and the City of Toronto, among many others.

An award-winning and best-selling author, Dan has written five books: *Work-Life Bloom, Lead. Care. Win., Open to Think, The Purpose Effect*, and *Flat Army*. Both *Lead. Care. Win.* and *Open to Think* won several book awards, including the coveted getAbstract International Book of the Year. Dan also writes for *Forbes, Harvard Business Review*, and additional outlets.

Dan is a renowned keynote speaker who has presented at four TED events and has delivered more than 600 keynotes over his career. He is an adjunct professor at the University of Victoria's Gustavson School of Business.

Dan's career is interwoven with corporate and academic experience, coupled with an MBA and B.Ed. He has received over 25 industry, individual, and book awards. Notably, Dan is listed on the Thinkers50 Radar, *HR Weekly*'s 100 Most Influential People in HR, PeopleHum's Top 200 Thought Leaders to Follow, and *Inc.* Magazine's Top 100 Leadership Speakers.

Join his popular community, Bloom Friday, by visiting www.danpontefract.com/sign-up/ or by scanning the QR code below.